REA ACPL ITEM
DISCARDED

Between East and West

My Life with Olivia

Volume One – In and Out of China

By

William S. C. Hwang

PublishAmerica
Baltimore

JAN 2 5 2006

© 2005 by William S.C. Hwang.
All rights reserved. No part of this book may be reproduced, stored in a retrieval system or transmitted in any form or by any means without the prior written permission of the publishers, except by a reviewer who may quote brief passages in a review to be printed in a newspaper, magazine or journal.

First printing

ISBN: 1-4137-5797-9
PUBLISHED BY PUBLISHAMERICA, LLLP
www.publishamerica.com
Baltimore

Printed in the United States of America

Volume One

In and Out of China

Dedication

My Father, Hwang Tzean
My Mother, Liu Wenshi
and
My Father-in-Law, Quek Shin
My Mother-in-Law, Pan Yuying

Between East and West
My Life with Olivia

Volume One
In and Out of China

1	Nostalgia in Turbulence — 9	
2	First Glimpse of Communist China — 17	
3	The School of Thought Reform — 26	
4	Reassigned to the Cultural Ministry — 36	
5	Parenthood in Uncertainty — 47	
6	The Literature Publishing House — 59	
7	Reunion with Grandparents — 71	
8	Happiness Under Hardship — 83	
9	The False Thaw — 94	
10	"Ming Fang" and "Anti-Rightist" — 117	
11	The "Great Leap Forward" into Starvation — 128	
12	The Complicated Overseas Ties — 140	
13	Surprises in Shenzhen — 152	
14	Anxieties in Different Cities — 163	
15	Refugee Life in Motion — 175	
16	Scratching Out a Living on a Scribe — 186	
17	An Impromptu Trip to Singapore — 197	
18	Hong Kong and the United States — 206	
	Postscript — 218	

1

Nostalgia in Turbulence

The Norwegian freight, *Reinholt*, was churning in the Pacific near the Philippine Seas. The captain was a middle-aged man, firm but gentle, likely a genuine descendant of the Vikings. There was a Scandinavian crew on the freight and two girls, one from Denmark and one from Sweden, working while touring the world.

On the voyage, eight Chinese passengers were sailing for Qingdao, a famous seaport in northeastern China. Among them, there was a newlywed couple, Olivia and I. We had come from the East Coast of the United States, taken the Santa Fe Rail, and embarked the ship at Los Angeles.

The story of my life with Olivia is a long one, starting from January the 31, 1950, in New York City. In 1949 and 1950, like overseas Chinese elsewhere, many Chinese students in New York City were agitated. The Chinese Communist Takeover that had occurred in October 1949 had inspired bookworms to become political activists in no time, and various Chinese student organizations mushroomed overnight.

There was the CSCA (The Chinese Students Christian Association), organizing weekly gatherings and summer camps. There was a monograph newsletter called the *Journal of Chinese Students in America*, which reported the changing situations in China and abroad. There was an organization called the Association of New Cultural Studies. There was a reading club named the Group Learning Society. Even more active than all of these was the Chinese Artists' Union to which Olivia and I belonged.

At the time, I had just written a play entitled *Nostalgia in Turbulence*. The Chinese Artists' Union and I were looking for a person to perform the heroine of my play. A friend recommended Olivia. She had just graduated from the Manhattanville College of the Sacred Heart in uptown New York.

January 31, 1950, was the day I went to visit her. She impressed me as a pretty and quiet young girl, somewhat reserved and withdrawn. To my surprise, however, she seemed a changed person the next day when she showed up at the meeting of the Chinese Artists' Union. She became active, enthusiastic, and very much at home with the others in preparing the show.

Nostalgia in Turbulence was a play describing the lives of Chinese students in the United States in the late 1940s. It portrayed their hardships and anguish caused by the turmoil back in Mainland China. When staged in the auditorium of the Teachers College of Columbia University in February 1950, Olivia performed the role of the heroine.

The Union nourished many of us in art, music and drama. Zhong Rixin, a close friend of ours, was then studying drama at Yale University. He directed *Nostalgia in Turbulence* and put it on stage. After returning to China, he taught at Zhongshan University in Guangzhou and maintained contact with us. Unfortunately, he passed away in the 1980s barely reaching the age of sixty.

In courtesy, I invited Olivia to lunch when I met her the second time and found her intriguing. After working together for several weeks, our mutual understanding and attachment grew deeper and stronger. It quickly turned into a passionate love. We both seemed to have found ourselves for the first time in our lives. A month and a half later, we were engaged and married.

Where did the bond come from that tied us so fast and taut? Was it love at first sight? Definitely, it was! We barely knew each other when we first met, yet we were mutually attracted instantly. On our first date, I took her to the Tavern on the Green in Central Park, a famous and prestigious place. While others were immersed in dancing, we ecstatically enjoyed our togetherness on the dancing floor. We were both Ingrid Berman's fans, but quickly forgot the scenes we had just watched after we went to see one of her movies together. That illustrated how passionately and deeply we fell in love, our true love in life.

But we were not dissolute young adults. There must have been a lot of ingredients that drew us together. We would not have been able to stick together for so long if we did not share common characters, values and aspirations. These attributes glued us together and sealed our bond after we told ourselves, "We finally found each other!"

Now, our bond has blessed us for more than half a century. It has forged us together strong enough to weather through numerous natural and manmade storms. It has empowered us to live more meaningfully in different times and places. We are now both in our late seventies. After scribbling down our past, we hope that our bond will continue to weather through storms and to flower in various cultures.

From 1949 to early 1950, I was working towards my Ph.D. in international relations at Columbia University with a scholarship. As my enthusiasm to see a new China grew, I joined all the above-mentioned student organizations and became the coordinator of certain activities. For instance, I was the chief editor of the *Journal of Chinese Students in America*, the group leader of the Group Learning Society, and the drama coordinator of the Chinese Artists' Union.

Unavoidably, these unusual extracurricular activities had taken a heavy toll on my graduate work. Very soon, it seemed that I had to decide whether I should continue my graduate studies or give it up along with my scholarship at Columbia.

It was early April of 1950, half a month after our marriage. The People's Republic of China had come into being half a year ago and the protracted Korean War had not yet started. The U.S. relationship with Communist China was in an ambiguous, delicate, but historically critical stage.

Olivia and I shared the enthusiasm of meeting a new China. We had been hoping that China would rid herself of her internal strife and sorrowful backwardness. But a piece of worrisome news unexpectedly reached me at that very juncture. I learned that my father had been arrested by the Communists in Chongqing. And I believed that my mother was probably alone in despair. I was their only son. Olivia and I decided to go back to Mainland China right away.

Our journey on the *Reinholt* served as our honeymoon voyage. On board, the Pacific Ocean appeared to be as peaceful as its name indicated. It was so smooth that it seemed like a huge mirror. Only a few flying fishes darting across the crystal waters would briefly break its tranquility. Other than the murmuring of the wind and the tide, everything was quiet.

But not so far away, on the horizon, there loomed a volcano. It was in hibernation at the moment, but its menacing presence seemed to augur that it might erupt again. Did the smoking volcano alarm us on our voyage? Even if it did, we were wrapped in the euphoria of our honeymoon. In front of us, the sky seemed to stretch to infinity. The mirage conjured up by the sea and sky fed us even more imaginations.

On our honeymoon journey on the *Reinholt*, we received a golden opportunity to learn more about each other. Indeed, we had many stories to tell and share. I learned that Olivia's given Chinese name was Kailan and her family name was Quek. "Quek" was a transliteration from the Hainanese dialect of the Chinese surname "Guo."

My family name was ordinarily transliterated as "Huang" in English. But we had been using the transliteration of "Hwang" for generations. The Hwangs claim that their family history runs back almost three thousand years. They are proud to be able to trace their ancestry directly to Huang Di, the legendary first emperor of China. Olivia joked when she heard the claim, saying that she did not marry me for legendary nobility, but she was still fascinated by many of the Hwang stories.

Olivia knew by Chinese tradition that the middle character "Shing" in my given name "Shingchi" was shared by all male members of the same generation in our extended family. She also learned that my father had bestowed "William" as my English name when I was very young. The transliteration of "William" in Chinese was "Weiliang." Therefore, my father gave "Weiliang" to me as my designated name in Chinese at the same time.

To our surprise, Olivia and I found the two of us were born in the same year of 1925, only forty days apart. I knew that she was from Singapore, but I knew little about her background. She told me that she had been very active in elementary and middle schools. Piano and violin were her favorite musical instruments. In sports, she enjoyed track and women's softball.

As Olivia recalled when the Sino-Japanese War erupted in 1937, Chinese patriotism in Southeast Asia was running high. It influenced many of the overseas Chinese and their children. A theatrical troupe, led by then famous Chinese movie stars Jin Shan and Wang Ying, came to Singapore from Mainland China. They were seeking support for China's war efforts.

Olivia's father, one of the influential overseas Chinese leaders in Singapore, hosted the troupe in his guesthouse. Thereby, Olivia became a young friend to some of the troupe's members. She joined them on stage and helped them in many other ways. With the same effort to support the Chinese resistance, she had participated in the popular street show entitled, *Put Away Your Whip, Please!* In school, she had once played on stage the role of a male general, the Chinese folk hero Yue Fei.

The Japanese invaded Singapore in 1940. Olivia remembered that her father put her and her older sister on one of the last flights to Mainland China. With the help of Professor Chen Xujing, she was enrolled into Nankai High School in Chongqing. Olivia told me that she had always been a student who studied hard and received high marks in schools. During those days in wartime Chongqing, she concentrated even more on schoolwork.

After graduating from Nankai High, Olivia was admitted to Jiaotong University in Chongqing in 1945. I knew that Jiaotong University was somewhat the equivalent to MIT in the United States. Olivia told me that she followed Jiaotong University to return to its original campus in Shanghai when the war ended. After another semester over there, her father sent her and younger sister Flora to the United States to continue college education.

While in Jiaotong University in China, Park College in Missouri, and Brown University in Rhode Island, Olivia had been majoring in mathematics and sciences. But a sudden change of interest took place in her senior year at Brown. Thus, when she transferred to Manhattanville College of the Sacred Heart in New York City, she changed her major to English literature.

"It was not easy to shift my major near the end of my college education," Olivia told me. For the entire year at Manhattanville, she did nothing but read all the necessary English classics to make up the requirements and to finish her thesis so she could get her B.A. degree in English literature. It was also hard for her to push all the physics, calculus, and chemistry out of her mind.

I had no experience in changing majors in college, so I listened attentively to Olivia. She confided in me that after her graduation, she felt somewhat lost. She was not sure what to do next.

"What?" I cut in with a joke. "Are you telling me that you are a 'lost and found' item?" Olivia did not take my joke. Her eyes were beaming with tears and I knew she was telling me something from the bottom of her heart.

"Why worry after we've already found each other?" I held her tightly in my arms. "We've just survived the Sino-Japanese War, and we still have a long way to go. Please don't ever feel that way again." A broad grin finally came across Olivia's lips. She started to ask about my childhood and college experiences.

I began to tell Olivia that I had similar experiences in my adolescent years, but I had started student activities earlier than she did. There were local militias in North China resisting the Japanese incursion a year before the Japanese launched their full-scale invasion. A general named Ma Zhansan was the leader of the resistance. Students in my middle school viewed him as their hero in 1936. We marched around to support him and his militias after school.

I remembered that I was then a seventh grader in Nanjing. One evening, a bunch of us marched into a resort area. A festival banquet was being held in one of the nicely decorated, high-class restaurants. A dozen returned overseas Chinese businessmen were celebrating something around a gigantic table. They listened to our solicitation of support to resist the Japanese aggression. Then, one after the other, they laid down their chopsticks. After discussing for a little while, they signaled the waiters to clear the table.

All of a sudden, two men stood up with big smiles. They came over and grabbed a girl classmate from Peru and me. After lifting us up onto the cleared dinner table, they urged us to speak more. While we stammered through our presentation, they responded with hearty laughter. After our childish but bold solicitation, we received generous hugs and bountiful donations. All the boys and girls in our group were also treated to fabulous food in the restaurant.

I told Olivia that that was my first encounter with returned overseas Chinese. The experience had been lingering in my memory. Years after that, in 1941, when I was a senior high school student near Chongqing, I carried on the student activities with the same enthusiasm. There was a drama group called The Windy Sky. I was its first and last president. In that year, we staged several plays, including the *Wild Rose* by playwright Chen Quan.

The most important thing for me in The Windy Sky was that I had written my first play, entitled *Swans from the South*. It was in three acts, honoring specifically some of the returned overseas Chinese. I told Olivia that it was no accident that I met and loved her because I had always cherished a strong sentiment for the overseas Chinese. Olivia listened to me with a mischievous smile.

My enthusiasm in literary activities, I told Olivia, did not stop in high school. It stretched all the way through my years in Wuhan University from 1942 to 1946. There was a society named The Contemporary Critics, organized by social science majors, which published a postal paper magazine. I was its president in my junior and senior years.

In addition, I helped organize a literary club called On the Ming River. We met regularly and had a good time together while exchanging our creative works in poetry, drama and essays. Under the wartime difficulty, we even bravely arranged weekend tours to nearby towns. It was unusual to see young men and women traveling together in conservative places. The elderly in the hinterland might have raised their eyebrows when they saw us.

On the *Reinholt*, Olivia and I often reviewed our wedding albums. In the middle of the Twentieth Century, photography was still an expensive hobby. But our dear friend, Chen Dieyun, was exceedingly generous. He took more than two dozen pictures on our wedding ceremony and sent them to us as gifts. The quality of his photographic technique was superb. Many of those photos have not faded away to this day.

Our wedding ceremony was held at the *China Institute*, a renowned Chinese institution in New York City. It was a fanfare for two young students still in school. More than a hundred of our elders, professors, friends and relatives came to share our happiness. Without their presence and help, it was inconceivable that we could have had such a beautiful wedding. Beyond that, many of our guests treated us as their kin, rendering us various kinds of assistance in Mainland China, Hong Kong and the United States in the years that followed. That was definitely another blessing God had bestowed upon us.

After Olivia and I fell in love, she introduced me to her younger sister Flora, who had also played a role in *Nostalgia in Turbulence*. Before our marriage, Olivia brought me to meet her elder sister Helen in Chicago and brother Kaichong in Indiana.

Later on, when we were preparing to return to Mainland China, Kaichong came to New York City to see us off. He insisted to buy us a gift. Olivia told him that we had already shipped our luggage to the *Reinholt* in Los Angeles. Kaichong murmured something in reply. But we could not make out what he said above the clamors before bidding him goodbye.

The Queks were a big family. It was fascinating to hear the stories of Olivia's father and uncle and their families. For the first time, I learned that my father-in-law was one of the prominent entrepreneurs in Singapore. Olivia's grandfather was a pioneer who left Hainan Island for Southeast Asia. But her father and his elder brother Quek Juchuan were the ones who laid down the family foundations in Malaya and Singapore. The two brothers first worked jointly. Their families also lived together for some years. Olivia, Flora, Helen and their brother Kaichong all had the same mother, who tragically passed away when they were very young.

There were about a dozen girls and boys in Olivia's generation living in "The Three Row Houses" and "The Jiadong Bungalow." They grew, played and studied together until World War II broke out. Now, they are all grownups and scattered around the world.

Olivia wanted to know more about the Hwang family too. I told Olivia that, as far as I could remember, my family belonged to the literati class in China, not poor but definitely not rich. There was a sense of pride among our family members. For generations, the emphasis in the family was more on education than on wealth.

I also told Olivia that I felt extraordinarily fortunate to be the son and grandson of my father and grandfather. To me, they were ordinary people with outstanding values who held quite an advanced outlook toward the world.

Both my father and grandfather were, in many ways, living ahead of their times. They held onto many traditional Chinese values, but realized that

China needed to reach out to the world. They believed that without mingling with other cultures, it would be hard for China to find its anchor in the modern world. Therefore, they both strongly encouraged their descendants to embrace the world's cultures while preserving the valuable parts of the Chinese tradition.

I told Olivia that my grandfather, Hwang Shaocheng, was born during the Qing Dynasty. Exceptionally smart, he got his "Xiu Cai" and "Ju Ren" degrees under the traditional examination system when he was very young. As soon as the Qing Government abolished its examination system in the early 1900s, he was sent by the Government to Japan to study railway engineering. However, the 1912 Chinese Revolution soon broke out. After that, regime changes in China finally compelled him to return home.

The widespread civil wars brought hard times to our family. My grandfather became the major bread earner. Caught in endless political and social upheavals, he was forced to teach Chinese classics to support the family. During the Sino-Japanese War, he was tragically murdered by a group of gangsters near Nanjing in 1938.

I had bragged to Olivia about my father ever since we first met. Olivia knew that my father Hwang Tzean had taught in the Nationalist Military Academy in the 1930s. During World War II, he served as military attaché under the Nationalist Government. He was my hero! All my friends envied me for having such a great father.

Now my father was in prison and my mother was alone in Chongqing. Although we did not and could not know their real situation, we believed that they must need us desperately, so we were on our way to take up our duty.

2

First Glimpse of Communist China

"Qingdao is in sight!" someone called out repeatedly from the deck of the *Reinholt*.

For all the Chinese passengers on board, Qingdao was the destination of their voyage. We rushed to the rails with excitement. By now, we had become more familiarized with one another.

Among the group, there was a female graduate student in chemistry going back to Mainland China to work. Her parents were in Manila, and her father was the manager of the China Bank in the Philippines.

Three days before, when the cargo ship stopped overnight at Manila, her father came on board to bring her home for the night. He had also invited all the Chinese passengers to a restaurant for dinner. Afterwards, he even brought us to his elegantly furnished bungalow. We spent almost a night there, playing bridge and enjoying different local delicacies. That was a memorable treat during our voyage across the Pacific Ocean.

The next day, another fellow passenger, a male graduate student majoring in international trade, announced that his family was in Qingdao and suggested that we all spend some time there. But most of the Chinese passengers already had their own schedules and plans.

There was an old Chinese saying that people who happened to be on the same ferry in life must have been pre-destined by fate. Were we, the eight Chinese passengers pre-destined by fate to be on the same ocean ferry? That might have been true. But after reaching Communist China, it seemed that we were also pre-destined by fate not to see one another again.

Suddenly, the engine of the freight was shut off. We were all perplexed. "What's going on?" someone asked. Looking around, we found the captain standing right behind us.

"Before entering the port, the freight has to stop for inspection," the captain explained. Noticing that the queries in our eyes were still there, he added, "This has been a routine since October 1949. Just wait, the Port authority will soon send inspectors up."

Indeed, a few minutes later, a small boat arrived and tied itself alongside the freight. Two middle-aged men in casual uniforms climbed on board. They gathered all the Chinese passengers in a cabin and asked to see our passports and traveling papers. While examining our documents, they also took detailed notes.

After reviewing our yellow immunization books, one of the two inspectors stood up and looked casually at Olivia. "You have a small rash underneath your chin," he remarked. A faint smile came across his face. "Are you allergic to something? It's not a big deal." He pulled out a notebook, and wrote down a prescription. "Here is something for the rash. You can get it from the counter of any drug store."

How friendly the inspector was! Was he a doctor? He seemed to act differently from many of the old Chinese government inspectors. Surely he did not look like a Communist from the countryside. Maybe this China was really a "new China."

Qingdao was once a German colony and its beautiful beaches and architecture had a touch of western appearance. But after stepping on shore, the first sight that came into view was the Liberation Army soldiers. So many of them! All in yellowish-blue uniforms! Some stood in front of the buildings and some sauntered around the port streets. We had never seen women soldiers in men's uniforms before. Their angled caps covered their heads and hairstyles. It was a captivating sight. Our luggage was brought ashore and we were told to go to the customs office.

When we entered the spacious customs building, we found a row of small windows. Passengers from the *Reinholt* were asked to line up in front of two of them. When our turn came, Olivia and I went up and saw a clerk sitting in front of a desk. Behind him, there was an officer in military uniform.

The clerk was dressed in a greenish tunic. From the way he collected customs duties, he appeared to be an experienced hand in customs services. He might have been working in the same office before the Communist takeover.

After paying customs duties, we got our luggage and were ready to leave. But the officer behind the clerk suddenly stepped forward. "Wait. You have one more item." He stopped us. "Is this your radio?" he asked, holding up a big box in his hands.

"What radio?" I was taken aback.

"This big one!" He showed me a cardboard box with slight annoyance. "The radio was mailed to the ship for you in this big box!"

"I don't have a radio." I looked at the rectangular radio in the mailing box and shook my head. "It's not mine."

"It was mailed to the ship for you." The officer held up the mailbox even higher. "See. Here is your name."

I was confused. How could anybody send anything to the ship? I could not believe it, so I turned to Olivia.

Olivia went closer to the customs window and carefully examined the writing on the box. After contemplating for a while, she whispered into my ear, "Bill, I think it must have been from brother Kaichong….Remember he wanted to give us a present when he saw us off in New York City. We declined, telling him that our luggage had already been shipped to the *Reinholt*."

I could not make out what Olivia was saying. While I stood there in perplexity, she continued, "Besides, I told him that because he was still in school, he should keep the money for himself. Brother Kaichong did mention something before leaving, but we did not make out what it was. For goodness' sake, I never thought he would really send it directly to our ship!"

In my awkward silence, the old customs clerk joined in with staggering words, "It's a Halicrafter! One of the best in the U.S. war surplus! Hot items in the flea markets!"

The officer gave the old clerk a dirty look. Apparently, the customs clerk was evaluating the radio as merchandise to be charged for customs duty alone instead of considering its other values. However, Olivia and I had learned accidentally for the first time that the brand name of that radio was Halicrafter.

The officer turned to me. "Are you still sure that this is not your radio?"

I could say nothing, so I kept quiet.

Then, he announced, "You know this is a short wave radio used by the military. You are not allowed to own or use it. Maybe you can sell it to the government later, but we have to keep it here for the time being."

We suddenly found ourselves in a panicky situation. The radio had held us up so long at the customs window and all our fellow Chinese passengers had already gone.

After the unexpected standoff, we had lost our interest in staying or even touring Qingdao. We decided to go straight to Beijing. Rushing to the railway station to catch the train, we even forgot to ask for a receipt for the radio.

On the train, we found only two fellow passengers from *Reinholt*. They were an old couple. The man looked like a politician, probably coming back to take a position in the new Communist government. His wife told us that they were very happy because they would soon see their daughter.

In courtesy, they inquired about our itinerary. Were we coming back to our family? Where would we go to work? And, who would come to meet us in Beijing?

Olivia and I were embarrassed because we did not have answers to any of their questions. In fact, we did not even know where to stay in Beijing yet. It was not easy to admit our ignorance. We were just absentminded and totally unprepared for the uncertainty at the time.

Due to the scarcity of telephones, ordinary people in those days could only rely on postal service to communicate in China. A piece of mail might take days, if not weeks, to travel back and forth. Therefore, we did not contact any of our relatives or friends in Mainland China before leaving the United States. We did not expect anyone to meet us at the railway station in Beijing. The last but not the least absurd thing was that we did not even book a hotel to stay in for the night.

It was quite late in the evening when we arrived in Beijing. Under the dim lights, there was no cement floor to meet our eyes when the train pulled into the station. On the platform, we could only see vaguely innumerable human heads.

The old couple descended first, gingerly picking their way through the throng. We followed them slowly, trying to get to the waiting room to claim our luggage. All of a sudden, a girl ran up and embraced the old couple.

From a short distance, we could see a young girl wearing a standard blue cadre uniform. She had tilted her angled cap in a cute way. She clapped her hands, jumped and hugged her mother again and again.

Beside her, there stood a young man. She introduced him to her parents and us as her boyfriend. The way she talked and moved around seemed to indicate that she might have also returned from the United States. She just kept on chatting merrily with her parents nonstop.

Finally, no more than five minutes later, her boyfriend edged up and tapped her on the shoulder. "It's time to return to our unit. We're late," he reminded her that discipline was important in revolutionary ranks. The girl quickly waved goodbye to her parents and disappeared with her boyfriend.

The old couple turned to us after their daughter's departure and meant to bid us farewell. But before the husband could utter a word, a man came forward and asked Olivia and me politely, "Are you the two returned students from the United States?"

It was a total surprise. We were speechless and nodded in reply.

The man introduced himself as a representative of a guesthouse, saying that he was dispatched to welcome us and bring us over there.

How could anyone know that we were students returning from overseas? Who told him that we were on this train and would arrive at this hour? We felt like we had returned to an unbelievably well-organized society. Since we had not made any reservations in any hotel, we thought we might as well follow him.

When we got to the guesthouse, we found it was actually a compound that consisted of a number of traditional Chinese courtyard dwellings. It was too dark to look around, but the size of the complex indicated that it might have been the property of some high-class people during the Qing Dynasty.

Embarrassingly, there was no room available for us. After checking the occupancy record, the night shift cadre in charge quickly made a decision. With an apologetic smile, he assigned us to a room that was already occupied by another couple and promised to give us a room the next day.

From the decisive manner of the cadre, we got a hint that this was a common practice. The guests had no pick. If there was no room available, two married couples have to share one room.

It was too late to move our luggage again, and we had not booked a hotel beforehand. So with extreme reluctance, we accepted the cadre's offer. The queer thing was that the other couple seemed to take no notice when we entered the room. During the entire night, there was no exchange of words.

The next morning, in a large room for breakfast, we found out that the so-called guesthouse was actually a dormitory packed with students who had returned from abroad. Because of the free lodging, many were there with family and children. Some might have been there for more than half a year, still waiting for job assignments. The scene was depressing. No one bothered to introduce oneself or to welcome any newcomers.

Olivia and I decided to ignore the dormitory. On that very day, we left our belongings at the dorm and went to Tangshan to see my third sister, Qiaoyu, and family. Tangshan was an industrialized city near Tianjin. My brother-in-law, Wang Dezhang, was the chief engineer of a power plant over there. We would have liked to make sure they were there and to inform them beforehand, but there was no way to contact them, so we just had to get set and go.

We had brought along with us a new radio-phonograph as a gift to Sister Qiaoyu and her husband. Because the customs office in Qingdao had not held up the item, we figured no more gadgets would cause us trouble. But believe it or not, another challenge popped up at the Tangshan railway station. This time, it was not caused by the radio-phonograph, but by an old alarm clock I had had for several years.

At the railway station, an army inspector in uniform insisted that I should open it for inspection. Since there was no screwdriver around, my fingernail became the only tool available. But the screw on the old alarm clock was rusty and would not yield to my fingernail. The standoff at the checkpoint lasted almost an hour. When all failed, the soldier could do nothing but let us go scornfully. Unavoidably, the episode turned our overview of Communist China from a well-organized society into a police state.

Married in 1947, Sister Qiaoyu now had two children, a boy of two and a baby girl of a few months. Our visit was a total surprise for her. After all the excitement, a swirl of memories came back to her when she calmed down. She began to tell us what had happened in the last few years, often dissolving into tears as she recalled her traumatic experiences.

It turned out that during the civil war at the end of 1948, the Communist Army had advanced rapidly from the North. Concerned with Sister Qiaoyu and the baby boy's safety, Brother-in-law Dezhang had sent them to Lanzhou to stay with his family members in the further northwest part of the country.

At that time, Sister Qiaoyu was expecting her second baby. Life in Northwest China was hard. After the baby girl was born, she could hardly take care of both of them. Therefore, as soon as she learned that our parents had returned to Chongqing from Hong Kong, she immediately flew to the Southwest to join them.

My father had been working as a military attaché abroad during World War II. He was in Hong Kong when the civil war was at its final stage in 1949. Instead of retreating with the Nationalists to Taiwan, he decided to become a private citizen and return to his native Sichuan Province. But the Communists would not let him go free. They arrested him in Chongqing, and put him in a prison called Baigongguan. It was such a dreadful place that people believed that whoever went in would rarely come out.

After Father's imprisonment, Mother was afraid that something might happen to herself and her daughter. She immediately dispatched one of my father's loyal menials to escort Sister Qiaoyu and her two little kids back to her husband in Tangshan.

What we had heard vaguely in New York City was true! Father was indeed in grave danger in an ill-named Communist prison. After listening to Sister Qiaoyu's narration, our eyes were beaming with tears. It became clear that I had two tasks at hand. While looking for a job, I got to find a way to rescue Father as quickly as possible.

Sister Qaioyu and I learned that one of my father's former superiors, a Nationalist general named Liu Fei, was then in Beijing. Liu Fei had been the Chief of Military Operations in the Nationalist Government when my father had served as the Division Chief of military attaché. He had then been a member of the Nationalist Delegation to negotiate with the communists, but decided to stay in Beijing instead of going back to Nanjing. Since he had known my father well, we thought he might render Father some help.

But, how could we locate Liu Fei? No one knew his whereabouts. After intensive discussions, Brother-in-law Wang Dezhang came up with an idea. His brother-in-law Ding Yizhong had been a high-ranking officer in the National regional government. He suggested that I should consult Ding Yizhong about Liu Fei's whereabouts.

When we returned to Beijing, Olivia and I found that there was indeed a separate room reserved for us in the guesthouse. It was in the big compound alongside a corridor, small but comparatively clean. We were glad to gain back our privacy.

While trying to locate Liu Fei through Ding Yizhong, I also started to look for a teaching post. The first person I visited was Professor Zeng Bingjun, my advisor in Wuhan University where I had written my B.A. thesis entitled *A Comparative Study of the Theories on Sovereignty by Clubb and Laski*. Now he was teaching at Qinghua University in Beijing.

Surprised by my unannounced visit, Professor Zeng Bingjun goggled at me and asked why I had returned from the United States so soon. I told him that I had given up my studies at Columbia and was now looking for a job.

Professor Zeng Bingjun had received his Ph.D. from Columbia University. After asking me about Columbia's current situation, he smiled sadly and confided to me that he himself was uncertain where to work at the moment. He informed me that the higher educational institutions in Mainland China were then undergoing an overall reorganization.

To help me understand the uncertain situation, he told me that Qinghua University, where he worked, would soon become a university solely concerned with natural sciences. Therefore, he advised me not to harbor hopes of getting a teaching post there. In a subdued tone, he further pointed out that henceforth, the social sciences we had studied and taught would not exist in Mainland China anymore.

I was stunned by his remarks, but I had noticed from the newspapers that, at the moment, the buzzword of "study" had spread over all educational and cultural institutions. There was a magazine called exactly *study*, directing and teaching people how to learn and follow Marxism-Leninism. Conventional social sciences had become the targets for criticism in academic circles. A long-lasting campaign of "Thought Reform" for intellectuals had been launched nationwide.

Before the People's Republic of China came into being, Mao Zedong had decided to tilt China's foreign policy one-sidedly towards the Soviet Union. In 1950, "Following the USSR" had become an official policy for the Chinese Communist Government. Now "Soviet Union's today will be China's tomorrow" was a widely used slogan.

Since Stalin was the leader of USSR and the whole socialist camp, pretty soon his pronouncements were also honored as the final words on every subject. Therefore, books with titles such as *Stalin on "This"* or *Stalin on "That"* instantly became best sellers in Beijing.

One day in a Beijing bookstore, I ran into Professor Jiang Sidao, a renowned law professor at Wuhan University. Several months ago, he had been overseeing my wedding with Olivia in New York City. Now he was also in Beijing looking for a book written by Vishingsky, the official jurist of the Soviet Union. He told me that he now had to learn the Soviet legal system to be qualified to teach.

In addition to Professor Zeng Bingjun, I also went to see a friend named He Ji, an instructor in world history at Qinghua University. He and I both belonged to the Association of New Cultural Studies in New York City. To my surprise, he was already a grandfather in his family. More pessimistic than Professor Zeng Bingjun, he told me that he was waiting to be transferred but still did not know his next job.

Olivia did not try to look for work immediately, but she was anxious to get in touch with Professor Chen Xujing in Guangzhou. Professor Chen Xujing had been a close friend of her stepbrother Kaitee. He was more or less her guardian in wartime Chongqing. Only years later did we learn that Professor Chen Xujing was under house arrest briefly at that juncture. No wonder Olivia tried to contact him but had received no reply.

So for the time being, it seemed like there was no prospective job for me in Beijing. Should I worry as Professor Zeng Bingjun and He Ji were?

Curiously, I did not. My youthful exuberance might have given me a kind of naive confidence. I seemed to be sure there would be something for me sooner or later. Therefore, instead of looking for jobs continuously, I put more energy on locating General Liu Fei by visiting Ding Yizhong, the brother-in-law of my brother-in-law Wang Dezhang. Ding Yizhong was a nice gentleman. He promised to locate Liu Fei for us right away.

In the interim of waiting for Ding Yizhong's message, Olivia and I spent more time at the returned students' guesthouse. It was quite boring to stay there, because there were no movies, games or other entertainments in the compound. The only diversion was to listen to the revolutionary stories told by the director of the guesthouse.

A veteran from the Red Army, the director had been a soldier in the "25,000 Li Long March" in the mid 1930s. That was an honorary resume in the Chinese Communist ranks. His gaunt face indicated that he had fought many battles. Now in his fifties, he served only as the figurehead of the guesthouse. His staff took care of all administrative chores.

Like most of the Communist old guards, the director of the guesthouse never wore his uniform in the regular way. He always threw his jacket over his shoulders without wearing it. Whenever sitting on a chair, he would put a foot on the chair's edge. As for his heroic revolutionary stories, it was interesting to listen for the first time. But the repeating episodes might easily put people into sleep.

One evening in mid May, while Olivia and I were sitting outdoors to listen to another round of the director's stories, the cadre in charge unexpectedly came to invite us to his office. After serving us tea and cookies, he congratulated us for being accepted by the Graduate School of the North China Revolutionary University.

Olivia and I knew nothing about the North China Revolutionary University. We did not apply for schools or jobs through the guesthouse. The offer came as a total surprise.

"You know, that's a newly formed higher learning center for revolutionary cadres." The cadre in charge smiled broadly. "Many people have applied, but you two are extremely lucky to be recommended and accepted."

Olivia and I looked at each other perplexedly. We did not know what to say for a while. We had not prepared for school, so the offer did not sound attractive. But without a definite plan at the moment, we could not find a reason to decline his offer either. In the end, we smiled to each other to signal our acceptance.

3

The School of Thought Reform

Built on a sweep of unused farmland in the western suburb of Beijing, the North China Revolutionary University was set up by the Chinese Communists to train cadres in 1950. Attached to it was a graduate school for political studies, specifically created to reform old intellectuals. Unlike the nearby campuses of the prestigious Beijing and Qinghua Universities, it consisted only of clusters of makeshift buildings and temporary houses. There was no library or bounded yard.

I had been in graduate studies for quite some time, first at the University of Maryland, then at Columbia University. Now, here I was at the graduate school of the North China Revolutionary University. When I went with Olivia for registration, I could not help kidding myself: *Will I ever be able to finish my graduate studies?*

It was almost at the end of May 1950. As soon as we moved into the dormitories, we found that this was not a regular school, but a place for thought reform. The names of "Revolutionary University" and "Graduate School for Political Studies" were only facets for political indoctrination and evaluation. The student body primarily consisted of middle-aged and older people the Communists had selected to be reformed. Most of them were established writers, professors and administrators in different cultural and professional fields. Olivia and I were among the youngest ones.

The Chinese Communists had been running revolutionary schools since their Yanan days. Those schools were outstanding for their military style and discipline. In order to accommodate the newly recruited older intellectuals, the Graduate School had apparently somewhat softened its discipline. Nonetheless, regimentation was still the bottom line of its organization and operation. Thus, the graduate students were organized into ten companies. Each company consisted of ten groups and every group had approximately twenty people. All together, there were probably two thousand people in the school compound, including the teaching and administrative staff.

Olivia and I were assigned to two different companies, the Sixth Group of the Eighth Company and the Fourth Group of the Fifth Company. To our surprise, some of our previous teachers had now become our classmates. For instance, one of Olivia's teachers at Nankai Middle School was in my group. And one of my own professors at Wuhan University was staying with me in the same room.

The two-story buildings that housed us were small. Each could only accommodate two groups, with two general rooms for washing and showering separated for male and female students. There were toilets, but no splashing equipment. The cafeteria was located in another building. Because it was shared by a number of companies, all graduate students were supposed to go there at designated hours.

The curriculum of the Graduate School was basically composed of two parts. The first part was group reading and discussion. The second part was lectures given by the teaching staff, or "Big Reports" delivered by high-ranking Communist Party leaders. There was one supervisor stationed in each group to guide the studies, discussions and activities. Each student was given a small stool to sit on while they listened to the lectures or "Big Reports" indoors or outdoors.

In the Graduate School, listening to a "Big Report" was a big event. One typical example was a four-hour talk given by Premier Zhou Enlai. Every student was reminded beforehand that it was an honor to attend the premier's lecture. Security was tight. Each listener was assigned to a specific place in the audience. When and how to form the line, who was supposed to sit beside whom, and how to conduct during intermissions were all important procedures to be memorized and rehearsed beforehand. No questions were allowed during the "Big Reports."

The supervisor of my group, the Fourth Group in the Fifth Company, was a woman cadre named Liu Tau. Probably in her early thirties, she had always been tacit and firm. A typical female Communist, she appeared to be softer than many others. She was not particularly pretty, but she had a kind of genuine dignity in continence.

At the time, one of the Graduate School's young lecturers named Li Xue was dating Liu Tau and often came to our group to see her. In Communist terminology, boyfriends, girlfriends, husbands and wives were all referred to as "lovers." Not knowing whether Li Xue was Liu Tau's husband or boyfriend, we were curious about how the revolutionary cadres expressed their affection, so it was fun for many of us to watch them whenever they got together.

One day, Li Xue was on the outside makeshift platform, lecturing on something related to Chinese modern history. He quoted some remarks from a famous modern Chinese scholar Wang Guowei in the 1920s, but attributed it as the words from Wang Wei, one of the prominent Chinese poets in the Tang Dynasty in the 900s. The names of Wang Guowei and Wang Wei differed by only one character. Obviously, Li Xue had mixed up the two by overlooking the character "Guo."

When his lecture was discussed in the group, a classmate pointed out his careless mistake. Liu Tau was sitting among us. We all expected her to say something, but throughout the discussion, she held her dignity by making no comment.

In the early 1950s, Mao Zedong's doctrines had not yet been officially formulated. On the Chinese Communist official reading list, there were only seven books prescribed as required readings for cadres. Chief among them was the *History of the Communist Party of the Soviet Union*, a basic tenet of Marxism-Leninism and Communist operational code sanctioned by Stalin.

However, while nominally following the Soviet tenet, Mao Zedong had been putting special emphasis on "thought reform" since the 1940s. In one campaign after another, he demanded that the Party cadres dig out their class roots and transform themselves into proletarian vanguards. For intellectuals whose class origins were landowners or bourgeois, Mao Zedong postulated that they had to betray their original classes, "cut off their class tails," and remold themselves into proletarians.

How could the intellectuals "cut off their original class tails"? That was the million-dollar question in the Chinese Communist revolution. Heaps of books had been written on the subject. In practice, the only acceptable way was for the intellectuals to expose their lives, bare their thoughts, betray their original classes, and surrender themselves to the workers, peasants and red soldiers as represented by the Party.

All the above tenets, however, were easier said than done. First of all, it was hard to tell whether an intellectual had truly remolded himself. No one except the Communist Party had self-appointed itself to be the judge in "thought reform." But the Party had gone through so many ruthless power struggles that only the surviving winners of the Party leaders seemed to have the final say.

In the beginning, there was not much tension in the Graduate School, because studies were centered on doctrines, but when the Korean War broke out in late June of 1950, the atmosphere began to change. At first, the North Korean army advanced quickly to the south and the Chinese Communists applauded. But the tide of the war soon reversed itself. After the U.S. army pushed back the North Korean invading forces, the Graduate School interrupted its regular program and discussions were suddenly shifted to the need of Chinese intervention on behalf of North Korea.

The ferocious civil war in Mainland China had not yet entirely ended. No sober mind would think that becoming involved in the Korean War would be in the interest of China. Yet the pitch of official propaganda was high. Each of us in the Graduate School was required to answer lots of questions, such as: "What do you think about fighting side by side with the North Koreans?" "Are you afraid of the American military might?" "What would you personally do to defeat the U. S. aggression?" A nation-wide mobilization was underway while the Chinese Communists prepared to send their so-called "volunteers" to Korea.

Decades later, when historical documents became available, it was found out that the Korean War was masterminded by Stalin. China had been used as a chip in the Communist international struggles. Mao Zedong had his ambitions, but it turned out to be a bloody and costly adventure for the Chinese Communists. In addition to millions of casualties and astronomical economic losses, Taiwan had also drifted away from the Chinese Communist grip because of the Korean War.

During the hysterical discussion of intervention in Korea, I remember one evening I met Olivia at a crossroad in the Graduate School. I told her that the war in Korea could affect our immediate future and that we might be separated for a while. I was not sure where I might be sent. In low voice, I confided to her that if I was sent far away, I wished her to pay a visit to my mother in Chongqing before taking up a job.

That was a sad private talk. Olivia responded only in silent nods. She too was at a loss of what we should do if we were sent to different places. I remember that she ventured to come to see me the next evening. After a brief chat, she handed me a note and ran away hastily. The note said: "Enough of the Marxist and Leninist doctrines! Give me back my husband!" It was a sweet note, but dangerous to keep. I read it with deep emotion and destroyed it with grave pain.

At that juncture, my thoughts also went to my father. The Chinese Communist Government officially sent their "volunteer" army into Korea on

October 25, 1950. Father's fate in Communist prison became more worrisome. Coincidentally, during that weekend, I received a message from Ding Yizhong, who informed me that he had finally found out that General Liu Fei was in Hankou. Now, Liu Fei had been appointed the Water Resources Minister of the Communist Central-South Regional Government.

I quickly got a leave permit and rushed to Hankou the next Saturday. Since I did not have Liu Fei's home address, I went directly to the Ministry of Water Resources. It happened that office was about to close in the late afternoon. A male receptionist told me flatly that Minister Liu Fei had left hours ago.

"You know, this is Saturday." He gave me a lecture with a stare. "How can you come so late and expect to see the minister?"

I pleaded with him to give me the minister's home address, but he flatly refused. Since I did not want to leave, he became annoyed, peppering me with a series of questions such as: "Where did you come from?" "What is the business you want to discuss with the minister?" No matter how I explained and argued, he simply told me that the office would be closed soon and I had to leave.

Hence, a day was wasted and lost. But I took it only as a minor setback. The next day was Sunday. A different receptionist was on duty at the ministry. But when I tried to get Liu Fei's home address from him, he put many of the same questions to me as the other receptionist did the day before.

In desperation, I finally showed my I.D. card to him, saying that I was going to return to Beijing that evening. Thank God! The word "Beijing" seemed to have a magic weight. It made the receptionist think more than twice. After checking my I.D. several times, he finally allowed me to copy down the home address of Minister Liu Fei.

With the feeling of winning a lottery, I rushed to Liu Fei's residence. It was far away, but eventually I got to his two-story house around the lunch hour. When I entered his house, one of his menials informed me that they had just finished their lunch. Since the general was upstairs for a nap, I had to wait downstairs.

Perhaps our voices in the conversation were too loud. Before I could settle down on a sofa, I saw a tall and hefty figure descending the stairway. He had a prominent nose and square jaw. Walking slowly in firm steps, his continence seemed to demonstrate that he was a commanding officer in the army even if not in military uniform.

I jumped up to greet him, and I introduced myself when he came close.

The general extended his hand and signaled me to take my seat. "I know who you are. Your father mentioned you to me many times."

I began to inform the general about my father's dangerous situation, imploring him to rescue Father from the prison.

"Your father never fought against the Communists!" General Liu Fei remarked after a brief contemplation. "He and I worked in the general staff departments. He knew little about the civil war because he had been serving as military attaché abroad."

From what I learned thereafter, what General Liu Fei said was true. He and my father had not fought in the civil wars. For years, General Liu Fei had been the chief of staff under Bai Chongxi, a famous and popular warlord in the Yunnan Province. During the Sino-Japanese War, Bai Chongxi became the Defense Minister in the Nationalist Government. Thus, General Liu Fei was appointed the Deputy Secretary for Military Operations of the Nationalist Government in the 1940s.

I informed the general that I was deeply worried about my father. I felt that the Chinese Communist involvement in the Korean War might complicate my father's safety.

General Liu Fei mused for a while and then assured me in a low voice: "Don't worry. The war won't be long. Maybe three months or, at most, half a year." After a pause, he added: "In the meantime, I will try to find out more about your father's situation."

Years later, when Father came to live with us, I told him about my visit to General Liu Fei. Father listened with interest, and suddenly commented aloud: "No wonder that happened!" Falling into reflection, he continued. "One day near the end of 1950, we were suddenly ordered to come out of our cells. When we went to the prison yard, the warden shouted: 'Some of you want to get early release. How dare you attempt to pull strings from outside! Wake up from your dreams and fantasies! Don't forget! You are now in our revolutionary iron fists!"

Most likely, General Liu Fei did try his hand at rescuing Father from the prison. Like many military experts, though, he might have underestimated the Communist resilience in the Korean War.

Soon, it was November 1950. Students at the Graduate School entered a state of panic. Marxism-Leninism and Mao Zedong's thoughts were doctrines meant for Communist cadres to follow in their lives. Approaching the final stage of "thought reform," however, students at the Graduate School were asked to temporarily put aside the books. Now, it was time for each of us to examine our lives. We had to submit an autobiography before school ended.

That was a shock to many students. Most of them started to worry about their work assignments after the "thought reform." Would they be allowed to return to their previous career after the school ended? Would there be a choice in their assignment to a new job? In the meantime, a delicate but forceful campaign was launched to indoctrinate everyone to "obey the Party's assignments!" Now each one's obedience to the Party was put on the test.

In Olivia's group, there was a talented musician named Mo Guixin. He was not a Party member, but strongly supported the Communist policies. Following the Party's call, he composed a song, pledging that "Wherever the People want us, we shall go! Whatever work the People give us, we shall do!" His pitch might have been very high. Few classmates in the Graduate School could afford to join the chorus.

In the revolutionary frenzy, Mo Guixin had incarnated the "People" as God. He wanted to follow the Communist Party line religiously. But seven years later, he was branded a Rightist and was exiled by the Communists to a labor camp in Beidahuang. He died at the tip of the Northeast during the Great Starvation. His wife, Zhang Quan, was a famous soprano. Persuaded by her husband to return to Mainland China from the United States, she was also branded a Rightist in 1957.

While Mo Guixin was promoting his song, most classmates at the Graduate School were laboring on their autobiographies. A hush seemed to have fallen over all the buildings. Some talkative people became tacit. Others sat with blank stares. Many skipped their meals without knowing it. Seldom had the usually crowded cafeteria had so many empty chairs.

"Self-criticism" in "thought reform" was a double-edged blade. Nobody would voluntarily inflict pain upon himself. However, according to Communist doctrines, class origin determined everyone's "class status" in society. People with non-proletarian class origins would carry with them various non-proletarian "class bags." In order to change their class status, they had to get rid of those "class bags" through self inflicted pains. Some of them might have to break their own backs to transform themselves.

In writing our autobiographies, Olivia and I seemed to be more at ease. It was not that we had no "class bags" to unload. We finished our autobiographies earlier simply because we were young and had less working experience. Paradoxically, we could not relax ourselves. There was too much tension hanging over the Graduate School.

One day in our building, I saw an old classmate walking back and forth alone in the washing room. He was in deep contemplation and seemed to pay no attention to anything or anybody. I was curious but dared not disturb him. A few hours later, I happened to walk into the room again and found that he was still there by himself. This time, he was standing in front of the only mirror there. To my alarm, when I passed by and looked into the mirror, I noticed a big scar under his chin.

The man lived in our building but belonged to another group. I did not know his name. I told my strange encounter to an old classmate, Meng Shouzeng, whom I considered a friend.

"You still don't know who that is?" he answered, sitting idly in his chair with a pen in his hand. "That's Shen Congwen, the famous novelist!"

Meng Shouzeng was an open-minded person with enormous experiences. He was at least fifteen years older, but he often chatted with me. Seeing that I was still thinking about my encounter, he continued with a feigned smile: "Don't you know that writers like to be left alone? As far as I know, Shen Congwen doesn't talk too much in school. Maybe the washing room provides him with the privacy and tranquility he wants."

Shen Congwen was a renowned and talented writer. I admired him and had read many of his short stories. I felt regret that I did not know he was living in our building. But Meng Shouzeng's description of him discouraged me to get to know him.

Years later, through reports, Shen Congwen was known to have been very depressed when the Communists had just come to power. The scar under his chin was probably a residue of a suicide attempt when he was younger. It might have had something to do with a love affair. He had given up his creative writing, and engaged only in historical costume and other research since 1949. What a loss to modern Chinese literature!

Meanwhile, Meng Shouzeng was in trouble. His autobiography writing had put him in agony for almost a week. Many of his drafts had ended in the dustbin. He was afraid that his analysis and self-criticism would never satisfy the authorities.

First of all, he had been working for the YMCA many years. That was under American funding and might cause him lots of trouble. Secondly, he had been involved in Liang Shuming's "Village Education and Reconstruction," a movement competing with the Communists to build schools in the countryside.

Liang Shuming was a prominent Chinese scholar in Mao Zedong's generation. In contrast to the Communist revolutionary approach, he believed in reconstructing rural China through peaceful means. The

Communists viewed him not only as a competitor, but also as a potential enemy.

In misery, Meng Shouzeng confided worries to me. He thought he was definitely a target in the "thought reform campaign," so he was considering leaving the Graduate School without submitting his autobiography. But he admitted pessimistically that if he chose to leave, he might have to pay a big price in the future.

I listened to him with sympathy. The deadline was getting closer. Since I had finished my own autobiography, I became a kind of idle bystander. His beseeching look made me uneasy. Succumbing to sympathy and friendship, I finally stuck my neck out. "Okay. Don't be so sad," I made an offer. "Suppose you tell me about your life. I can try to jot it down for you. Hopefully, it's not too late."

Meng Shouzeng was exhilarated. After working together, he was able to submit his autography on time. But it was a dangerous adventure for both of us. Should Liu Tau or the school authority find out, the two of us would definitely be kicked out and receive severe punishment.

Now it was the end of November of 1950. The weather was getting colder in Beijing and my asthma began to bother me more and more.

One day, before everyone's work assignment was announced, I was called to the administrative office. A well-dressed cadre was waiting there to talk with me. Politely he told me that he already knew Olivia and my background. He asked me straightly whether I would be interested in going abroad again.

That was a total surprise for me. He did not spell out what work he wanted me to do. But since I was not planning to go abroad, I did not ask for details at the moment. I simply explained to him that my wife and I had just come back and that my father was in prison and my mother needed my care. We could not afford to leave them again.

The cadre smiled, informing me that he knew the situation of my parents.

It was not easy to turn down his offer on the spot, so I replied, "It sounds like a great assignment. I'll discuss it with my wife. You know, we came back in May, and we are still studying here. There is a lot for us to learn."

"That's why the Party is choosing you and your wife." The cadre smiled again, standing up and shaking hands with me. "You know, you are privileged to be considered for the assignment. You should let us know as soon as possible through the school's administration."

Olivia and I did not spend much time between ourselves to discuss the offer. We were not and did not wish to become Communist Party members. We had no interest of going abroad to do any work for the Party.

But before I got a chance to give the cadre an answer to his secretive offer, I was knocked down by my asthma. Olivia sent me immediately to the Union Hospital in downtown Beijing in early December.

My failure to give an answer to the cadre must have enraged him and the school authority. In our absence when I was still in the hospital in downtown Beijing, they arbitrarily assigned both Olivia and me to Northwest China to teach in a university.

4

Reassigned to the Cultural Ministry

Founded by the Rockefeller Foundation, the Union Hospital was established in Beijing in the 1920s. It had been the top medical center in China for at least half a century. Even today, it may still be ranked as one of the best clinical centers in the Far East. In Chinese, the name of the hospital is "Xie He," meaning "Harmony."

I stayed there for several weeks in December of 1950. After my asthma attacks were subdued, I went through an operation on my severely infected left mid-ear. Dr. Xu Yinxiang performed the surgery. He did not cut through the back of my ear and therefore left no visible scar.

There were many American trained doctors in the Union Hospital. Dr. Xu Yinxiang was one of them, receiving his medical degree from New York University. He was then the head of the ENT department at the Union Hospital, and he was one of the top specialists in the field.

In the final days at the Graduate School of the North China Revolutionary University, all the students were anxious to know what and where their work assignments would be. Some even tried to make outside contacts. In late November, one of the classmates in Olivia's group, Yan Zhongping, informed Olivia that there was a golden work opportunity for newly returned overseas students.

At the time, Yan Zhongping was a senior history researcher at the Chinese Academy of Sciences. He told Olivia that one of his previous classmates at Qinghua University, Jiang Tianzuo, was now a senior administrator in the Ministry of Culture and was eager to find someone to work in his forthcoming division. Yan Zhongping thought we were the ideal people for the posts, so he had already recommended us to Jiang Tianzuo. He urged Olivia to pay Jiang Tianzuo a visit as soon as possible.

Hospitalization gave me a long needed rest. Most of the tension in the Graduate School faded away temporarily, even though the arbitrary work assignment to Northwest University still caused me some worry.

Reading was a good pastime while on sick bed. One day, Olivia brought me an issue of *Soviet Literature*, a Soviet Union magazine published in English. While scanning through it, I was somehow attracted by a memorial article on the fortieth anniversary of Lev Tolstoy's death. With a pencil and some paper I borrowed from a nurse, I translated it into Chinese.

Olivia came to visit me the next day. She was happy to see that I had recovered well and was able to work on my sick bed. After reading my translation, she gave me a sweet smile, announcing that she would bring it to show Jiang Tianzuo for an interview the next day.

Olivia and I still did not have our own place to live in Beijing. Sister Qiaoyu and brother-in-law Dezhang, however, had helped us find temporary lodging during the weekends. One of their friends owned a courthouse in Shifangyuan in eastern Beijing. Through their arrangement, their friend generously offered us a wing of his courtyard house to use while we were in the Graduate School in the suburbs. After my surgery, their friend extended his hospitality further, inviting us to stay on for my recuperation.

The world seems very small sometimes. Shifangyuan gave us an example of it. At the courthouse one weekend in May 1950, we unexpectedly bumped into a couple we had met in New York City. They were two of the Chinese Student Christian Association (CSCA) organizers. Who would have guessed that now they happened to live in another wing of the same courthouse?

Olivia and I were excited about the encounter. We greeted them warmly as if we were still in New York City. But to our surprise, we found they appeared to be cold. They shook hands with us formally, as if we were new acquaintances. After that, we went on our way, embarrassed.

The landlord was around when the episode took place. He did not know that we had met the couple before, so he explained that those two tenants did not like to socialize with people. He informed us that the two of them were Party members. As far as he knew, the husband was the translator for a top Communist leader.

Olivia and I never expected to meet someone associated with a top Communist leader. Through the encounter, we seemed to have learned a lesson. Now the Communists were in power. All previous personal relationships had to be reassessed. New acquaintances would have to be viewed through new political lenses.

I had met our neighbors at Shifangyuan before in New York City when I participated in some of the CSCA activities in 1949. In that year, I had attended a summer camp organized by CSCA in New Jersey.

The Chinese civil war was then raging ferociously in the Mainland. Antiwar feelings were high both in China and abroad. Many of us in the summer camp had our families back in the Mainland, so we were all worrying about our kin and China.

I remember that I wrote a play at the summer camp. It was entitled *Leaving Shanghai*, portraying the war miseries and people's yearnings in Mainland China. Many camp goers endorsed my play. More than twenty girls and boys put the show on stage. It was quite an experience for us in the summer camp.

However, after returning to New York City from the New Jersey camp, several friends informed me that some CSCA organizers were unhappy about our activities. Suspicious of my background, some organizers had even checked on me. Therefore, my friends cautioned me to be careful.

I was shocked when I received the warning. I found it distasteful, but forgot the whole thing afterward. Now it was summer of 1950, a year after the summer camp. By accident, I learned in Beijing that some of the CSCA organizers were underground Communist Party members in New York City.

A chill ran down my spine. I thought I had been too naive, not only by allowing myself to be used as puppet, but also by putting myself under their surveillance in New York City. The awkward encounter also conjured up more of my memories from the 1949 summer camp.

As I recall, there was a well-dressed man in his fifties always walking around the camp. While we were rehearsing our play, he would stand by with a movie camera. He seemed to have interest in our stage show, shooting reel after reel of film. Since nobody had introduced him to us, I thought he was just a fellow camper fond of taking pictures.

After working at the Ministry of Culture in 1951, however, I was surprised to find his true identity. No wonder he had a movie camera in hand. He was the renowned movie director Cai Chusheng. I had admired since childhood but never had a chance to meet him. After returning to Mainland China, I was even more surprised to find out that he was the Deputy Chief of the Cinema Bureau in the Ministry of Culture.

It was reported that Cai Chusheng had been a Communist Party member since 1927. I was happy to have seen him at close range in 1949. Unfortunately, like millions of upper or underground Communists, he was persecuted thirty years later.

So was the fate of many underground Communists who had returned from overseas. Some of them might have been successful in their career. But some did not fare so well and became victims of the regime. After all, most of them came from well-to-do families. Some even belonged to the richest or the most powerful under the Nationalist regime. They were potential "class enemies" of the indigenous Communists.

Meanwhile, most of the Chinese students who returned from abroad after 1949 had a much harder time than the underground Party members. There were secret dossiers following and shadowing them wherever they went. Their lives in China and abroad were under close scrutiny. They would never have the chance to look into those dossiers or correct them.

Our short stay at Shifangyuan was quite memorable. The well-kept and furnished wing of the courthouse had provided us with a preview of Beijing's living. It had also served as our mailing address from June to December 1950. Without it, we could hardly have kept in touch with my parents in Chongqing. I still remember the hospitality of the house owner, and the services his servant Lao Liu rendered to us over there.

Nevertheless, my memories of Shifangyuan are also associated with some of my agonies, because my parents were in such a dire situation at the time. Sister Qiaoyu had told us that after my father being arrested by the Communists, my mother was scared to visit him in prison sometimes. There was a big bulletin board outside the prison gate. On it, the names of the prisoners executed each day were posted. My mother dared not lift her eyes to look at the board whenever entering the prison gate.

Likewise, in Shifangyuan, we had s similar fear. Olivia and I were often scared when we got mail from Chongqing. We always read the letters slowly, fearing they might be the bearers of horrible news. In addition to my father's unknown fate in prison, my mother had her other troubles in Chongqing.

At the time, the "Land Reform Campaign" was in full swing. Landlords were being either put to death or exiled to labor camps. Their properties were confiscated and their families disbanded.

I knew my parents were not landlords. Although our ancestors had handed down some small lots of land, our family had always lived on teaching and practicing Chinese medicine. My father had left our native town of Omei when he was a child. He had his career in various professions and the military.

The "Land Reform Team" in our native town of Omei, however, disregarded all the facts. In the "Land Reform Campaign," they contacted my mother in Chongqing, demanding her either go back to Omei, or send money to redeem her "sin" as a "landlord." They threatened her with death if she failed to comply.

Mother was afraid and began to send money to appease the "Land Reform Team." But the blackmails continued, and the "ransom" kept rising. My mother gradually realized that she was descending down a bottomless pit. Finally, she decided to refuse further payments.

Thousands of miles away, Olivia and I first thought Mother had good reason to stop the "ransom" payments. But tensions grew higher and higher and we worried about my mother's possible risks. Luckily, my mother's standoff brought results. The ransom scam of the Omei "Land Reform Team" cracked in the end.

In the meantime, Olivia's visit to Jiang Tianzuo was a success. Our translation of the article on Tolstoy impressed him. Learning that we had been assigned by the Graduate School of the Revolutionary University to Sian, he scribbled a memo and asked Olivia to visit immediately the Personnel Bureau of the Central Government.

"This is a request for you and your husband to be transferred to the Ministry of Culture." He handed Olivia a note. "There should be no problem. I'll let you know when you and your husband should report to work."

At the moment, the acting director of the Personnel Bureau was Feng Naichao, who had also been the vice president of Zhongshan University. His office happened to be in walking distance from the Ministry of Culture. Thus, with the approval of the Personnel Bureau, our reassignments to the Cultural Ministry were confirmed.

Olivia was very happy that we did not have to go to the Northwest. Two critical matters in our lives had been settled in one afternoon. But not only had the North China Revolutionary University arbitrarily assigned us to the Northwest, they had also arbitrarily shipped all of our belongings to Northwestern University in Lanzhou. Now, we had to claim our luggage back.

At the time, a round trip between Beijing and Lanzhou took several days. Since I had just been released from the hospital, the burden fell again upon Olivia's shoulders.

The railroad system in Northwest China was quite primitive then. Passenger trains were not well built. Oftentimes, the windows in the passenger cars were not locked properly. Smoke from the locomotive was often blown back into the passenger cars when the train rolled through tunnels. Poor Olivia! She had no experience in riding on that kind of train. The terrible smoke choked her and aroused her asthma. She had to go to hospital when she returned.

Olivia also had asthma? Did I purposely pick her to be my asthma companion? For the first time I learned that Olivia was an asthma veteran.

Her asthma in childhood was even more severe than mine. She had to skip one year in primary school because of it. Now we seemed to understand each other better since we both were at the mercy of "asthma."

Jiang Tianzuo paid us a visit at Shifangyuan during my recuperation. He informed us that a new Literary Editorial Division had just been set up in the Ministry of Culture. He told us we were two of the first staff members and expected us to start work in January of 1951.

Olivia and I were elated to have our first job in Mainland China. Our eight months of wandering seemed to have come to an end. When we reported to work, we found we were indeed the first few enter the offices. Both of us were assigned to a small but cozy and comfortable office, with our desks facing each other.

Jiang Tianzuo briefed us on our first day of work that our new Literary Editorial Division belonged to the Bureau of Art in the Ministry of Culture. It was formed to lay a foundation for a forthcoming publishing house for literature.

Indeed, in the months that followed, more editors were hired for Chinese, Russian and English literature. For Chinese literature, the first group of editors included many from the old "liberated areas," like Fong Zi, Wang Shuming and Nie Gannu. For world literature, the first group of editors such as Ye Junjian, Xu Hejin, Liu Liaoyi and Zheng Baihua were primarily from the big cities such as Beijing and Shanghai.

As soon as we started to work, Olivia and I began to look for a place to live in Beijing. In the 1950s, Beijing had only traditional courtyard houses for rent. The courthouse we chose was in the eastern section of the city. It was in a narrow alley called Beikoudai Lane, not far from our work place. We preferred the north wing, because it faced south and was supposed to be warmer in winters.

But when we went to sign the lease with the landlord, he told us that he had lost his faith in cash. Instead, he wanted us to pay our monthly rent in a certain amount of a special brand of flour. Since the price of the flour was fluctuating, our rent varied from month to month.

That was quite a complex lease. In renting our first house, Olivia and I had not only learned the way traditional Beijing people do business, but also about the fluctuating life they lived under inflation. The unceasing Chinese civil wars had robbed away the people's confidence in the currencies issued by the various ephemeral governments, so people preferred bartering when their interests were on the lines.

Beijing had been the capital of China for many dynasties. It was a sophisticated city with its peculiar culture. Olivia and I were too young to comprehend many of its subtle and complicated customs. For instance, "Beikoudaihutong" meant "North Bag Lane." It was, indeed, a dead-end alley. People could walk in and out. But for automobiles, once they entered, they had to use reverse gears to back out. In Chinese custom, people would be reluctant, if not superstitious, to live in a "bag lane" that was hard to back out of.

Olivia and I were not exempt from some of these superstitions. We had no idea what we would experience when we rented the house in "North Bag Lane." We lived there for more than ten years. But queerly enough, we did gradually have the feeling that we were being "bagged" or "trapped." Neighbors in the alley were particularly sophisticated. We often felt that we were under surveillance. Several times we had tried to move but never succeeded.

Later, after we left Mainland China, the house became a real "bag" or "trap" for our parents. They moved to "Bag Lane" from East Defosi Street. During the devastating "Cultural Revolution," they were ransacked, beaten up, and exiled from the "Bag Lane."

Olivia and I were happy that our office was not in a bag lane. On the contrary, the Ministry of Culture was located in the beautiful campus of the previous American Language Institute in Beijing. It had a gorgeous auditorium, a few elegant garden houses and several rows of beautiful stone buildings. Along the compound paths, and between the buildings, clovers were all over. When flowers blossomed in the spring, the compound looked like a marvelous garden.

Olivia and I were hired to edit world literature needed to be translated from English into Chinese. Olivia and I found our work comfortable and satisfying.

I had always had a special affinity to literature and drama since I was young. It seemed I was destined to take them as my most intimate hobby. In addition to the interest of literature I cultivated at home, I was most fortunate to have an excellent language teacher named Ye Shaojun at Bashu Middle School in 1938.

Known also as Ye Shengto, Ye Shaojun had been a prominent language teacher and author in modern China. His tutoring and guidance inspired a number of our classmates at Bashu to continue writing later on.

Bashu was an elite middle school in Chongqing in the late 1930s. It had many prominent figures in its faculty. For instance, to cultivate students'

42

interest in drama, we were coached by the famous actress Zhang Ruifang and others. Our music teacher was He Luting, one of the most talented composers in modern China, who later became the president of the prestigious Shanghai Music College.

The student body of Bashu Middle School was small. Each class had no more than a dozen students. I still remember how subtle and inspiring the teachers were. For instance, when Ye Shaojun taught us Chinese classics and contemporary literature, he corrected our homework in detail and encouraged us to practice writing by jotting down scenes or events we saw in our daily lives. He often gave us extracurricular assignments to portray a beggar on the street or describe an event we witnessed.

In music class, He Luting's teaching was also delicate and touching. Whenever he taught us a song, he always came to our side, listening to how each of us sang it. Regretfully, Ye Shaojung left Bashu Middle School for Wuhan University in 1939. I was lucky to have been his student for two years. He implanted in me a deep love of literature.

My major in college had been social science, but I was always fond of literature. Social science needs an analytical mind. Literature counts more on strong senses and feelings. I had always been working hard to keep up both of them.

At the Literary Editorial Division, staff editors had little work besides political studies. China and the Soviet Union were then on their sweet honeymoon. Chinese introduction of world literature was primarily following the Soviet line. Most English and American literature was put on shelf except a few classics and leftist publications.

For almost a year, we handled only Russian novels translated into Chinese from English. My first assignment was to revise Zhou Lipo's translation of Mikhail Sholokhov's *Virgin Land Upturned*, a novel on Soviet collectivization in the 1920s.

Zhou Lipo's translation was very popular among the Chinese reading public under the Communist influence. In revising the translation, however, I did not consider the book's previous popularity and circulation. If there were differences between the original text and the translation, I tried to recover the essence of the original text. Unexpectedly, after the revision, the old translation had undergone a major face lift.

As an established writer in Communist China, Zhou Lipo was incensed when he saw the revised text. He couldn't believe that a junior editor would dare to revise so much on his translated work. I did not know how the contention was resolved, but I stuck to my position. The revised text was accepted and went to print in the end.

In Communist literary circles, Zhou Lipo had been quite influential. He had been teaching world literature at the Lu Xun Institute of Art and Literature in Yanan, the Mecca of the Chinese Communists. He was awarded a Stalin prize for one of his novels in the early 1950s. There was a saying in Chinese: "Newly born calves are not afraid of tigers." I could not figure out why as a "calf" I had not been swallowed by the "tiger" in that instance.

The Literary Editorial Division organized a "Conference on Translation" before the end of 1951. Translation was an important media for China to communicate with the outside world. Without it, great religions such as Christianity and Buddhism would not have been able to come to this "middle kingdom." The Communists also counted on it to develop China according to their blueprints.

Under the auspices of the Editorial Division, the Conference was held in the auditorium of the Ministry of Culture. Due to the shortage of personnel, I was assigned to be a secretary to record its proceedings. Looking on the crowd from the podium, I was surprised to find a familiar face in the audience. The more I looked, the more I was sure that he was Ren Genliu, a colleague of mine in Shanghai in 1940s.

I could not refrain from standing up and calling out his name during the intermission. He heard my voice, turned his head, and hesitated for a moment. Then he looked at me and nodded with a smile. Walking up quickly, he shook my hand and introduced me to a few persons following him:

"This is my colleague from before the Liberation," he sounded like the boss of his group. "That's why he doesn't know my real name."

Seeing that I could not understand what Ren Genliu meant, one of his men stepped up and explained: "You didn't know Comrade Ren Rongrong's real name? He is the head of our Publishing House, now the chief of our Shanghai delegation."

For the first time, I learned that Ren Genliu's real name was Ren Rongrong. He signaled his group to leave us alone and started our conversation with a question, "Do you still remember our office at the Board of Supplies?"

Of course I remembered. I nodded in reply, recalling that it was in Shanghai, near Waitan, on the sixth floor of the prominent China Bank Building.

"Remember the guy who always wore an American army uniform?" Ren

Rongrong's voice was gentle and warm. "You know, he was a Nationalist agent. Do you still remember his name?"

I recalled that there was a colleague always dressed in U.S. army uniform, but could not come up with his name. Ren Genliu had apparently targeted the guy as a Communist enemy. But I had not sided with the Communists either at the time. A thought went through my mind quickly: *Ren Genliu might have changed his judgment on me now. Otherwise, he wouldn't talk to me like this.*

"He signed his name as Zhao Tongyi," Ren Rongrong tried to jog up my memory. "You know what? The entire staff was our people. Zhao Tongyi wanted to spy on us. But actually he was under our surveillance." Ren Rongrong burst into laughter.

My memory finally came back. The Board of Supplies had been an agency under Song Ziwen, then the Chief of the Executive Branch of the Nationalist Government. It was set up to receive and distribute the U.S. war surplus. Bribery and corruption had been rampaging. Employees of the Board of Supplies enjoyed special privileges. Two stairways above our office was the China Bank's cafeteria. We had busboys to bring us drinks and snacks.

There were eight people in our unit. All appeared to be well to do, especially Ren Genliu. He dressed well and behaved like a playboy. On his desk, he always kept some English or American novels. Sometimes, he openly translated John Steinbeck's stories during office working hours. Our section chief was a middle-aged woman. Ren Genliu was under her patronage, so nobody dared to challenge or question his work.

I also recalled that Ren Genliu and I had gotten closer to each other. That was before I left for the United States. He knew that I was also interested in American literature, especially John Steinbeck and William Saroyan. We often exchanged our feelings and impressions about their works. Once, Ren Genliu had even invited me to his home. It was a house with a private yard, right behind the busy Nanjing Road. An old man came out to greet me, introducing himself as Ren Genliu's father.

The intermission of the conference seemed to be longer than usual. It provided Ren Genliu and me with more time to chat. With courtesy, I asked him, "How is your father? Remember you once brought me to your home?"

"Oh, that's not my father!" Ren Genliu answered abruptly. "He was only the man hired to raise me." Ren Genliu's tone became solemn. "My father is Ren Bishi. He and my mother were always away for the Revolution."

I was astonished when Ren Genliu revealed his true identity. At the time, his father, Ren Bishi, was the fourth man in the Chinese Communist Party leadership. Many believed that Ren Bishi might become the top Party leader someday, because he was still quite young among the veteran Communist leaders. But he died in the late 1950s.

There was not much to talk about after Ren Genliu's revelation. I could not come up with any comment. Coincidentally, the conference was called into order by the chairperson, so he and I returned to our original seats.

In my mind, Ren Genliu was still the guy I had known in Shanghai more than half a century ago. I have not had another chance to meet him again.

5

Parenthood in Uncertainty

Our first baby boy, David, was born on January 17 of 1952. Olivia and I were elated that we were now crowned with the title of parenthood. Olivia had high blood pressure at the time without knowing it, but thanks to the chief obstetrician of the Union Hospital, Dr. Lin Qiaozhi, the baby was delivered safely. Both mother and son were fine.

David's two grandfathers were overjoyed. They both already had a number of grandchildren. For Olivia's father, David was his first grandson from his daughters' side. In contrast, for my father, David was his first grandson from his only son.

The two grandfathers had suffered greatly during and after World War II. One had been put in a Japanese war camp when Singapore was under the Japanese occupation. The other was still in Communist prison in Chongqing. Yet each of them was delighted to bestow David with a Chinese name.

Olivia's father named David "Yinan." It means, "To remember Southeast Asia." That was a sweet reminder for David that a part of his roots was embedded in Singapore and Malaya. My father gave David his own nick name "Rui." "Rui" meant "Luck." So together with his designated middle name "Li," David's full Chinese name became "Hwang Lirui." Olivia and I were deeply moved when we received those names for David.

The reason Olivia's father was able to give David a name so quickly was because the Communists still maintained good relations with the overseas Chinese. Like the majority of overseas Chinese, Olivia's father had hopes for a new China. In the summer of 1950, when he stopped by the United States on his world tour, he might have been disappointed for not meeting us. But he did write to Olivia and me commending us for "going back to serve the people" after he learned of our return to Mainland China.

After 1952, however, a drastic change occurred. The Communists made an about-face in their policies toward the overseas Chinese. Because most of the overseas Chinese were so-called "bourgeois" to them, they began to apply oppressive measures toward the returned overseas Chinese as well as their families. In response, the warm feelings of the overseas Chinese had held for the Communists quickly went sour.

As the relationship between the Communists and overseas Chinese deteriorated further and further, communication between the families in both places finally broke down. Therefore, for more than eight years, Olivia could neither write home nor receive any news from Singapore.

I liked to collect stamps when I was little and the hobby had stretched into my adult years. I was also interested in photography. My father had given me a black and white German "Zeiss Ikon" for my graduation from college. In 1946, I won a prize with it in a photo competition in Shanghai. Many pictures taken by that camera after 1950 are still kept in our family albums.

Olivia encouraged me to keep up my hobbies. In contrast, she was interested mainly in music. In 1950, the only hand-carried item she brought across the Pacific Ocean was her violin. When we moved to the North Bag Lane in Beijing, among the first items we purchased was a used piano. It was her pet.

For me, my favorite was my book cabinet. It was brand new and served more than one function. In addition to shelving books, I often posted notes or photos on its glass windows. For instance, David, Phillip, Jean and Pauline each received a "welcome home" card on the glass windows when they came back from the hospital's maternity room. The ritual became an everlasting part of our memories.

Regretfully, though, Olivia had seldom played the piano after we bought it. The reason was that the neighbors in the other three wings of the courthouse were not accustomed to Western music. Since she could not freely play the piano, Olivia turned to pass her music interest to the children. Therefore, when David reached the age of four, she sent him to a prestigious private teacher for lessons. After 1955, Mainland China was continuously in turmoil, so there was no more music for Phillip, Jean and Pauline.

Parenting might be a specialty that every couple has to learn by themselves. Olivia and I found it hectic while both working full time. Seeing that we were busy and lacked experience, our friend Meng Shouzeng and his wife came to help. They recommended a live-in baby sitter for David. Her name was Guilan. A bright and tender teenage girl, she took care of David as if he were her baby brother. David was very happy with her for almost two years.

The Literary Editorial Division was our first working place in the "new China." Olivia and I were quite dedicated to our work. Our Division chief Jiang Tianzuo, however, appeared to be even more dedicated than we.

As a cripple, he always limped around energetically in office, anxious to put things in order. It was said that his ankles were maimed by the iron shackles put on him when he was in a Nationalist jail. But he never mentioned his past experience to us. We knew little about his personal life except that he was from Qinghua University and that his real family name was Liu. Everyone seemed to know that he had been very active in Shanghai literary circles before 1949.

Jiang Tianzuo was apparently working closely with Zhou Yan, the Deputy Cultural Minister, in planning the forthcoming publishing house. In 1951, we saw a lot of prospective editors for Chinese and World literature come and go through the Division. But only a few stayed on. Actually, in the ensuing two years, there was little work to do, because the staff was undergoing "thought reform" in a campaign that swept over the country, especially in the literary and cultural circles.

In the Literary Editorial Division, "thought reform" started with the so-called "Daily Life Discussions." Olivia and I were quite naïve to believe that it would not be a big deal for us, because we had already been through "thought reform" in the North China Revolutionary University. But it turned out that we were wrong after attending several "Daily Life Discussions" in the spring of 1952.

Everyone was supposed to air out his or her thoughts and feelings about life in those meetings. Having become a father, I made some complains about the glass bottles we used to feed David with milk or water. Those glass bottles were heavy but extremely fragile. They cracked easily when I rinsed them over hot water, so I had to buy them in dozens at one time to save me trouble.

I thought it was a minor complaint, not relating to any big issue, so I did not expect any criticism. But before my complacency sunk in, my complaint drew in a barrage of attacks. Some in the meeting immediately pointed out with laughter that my stories unbarred my bourgeois thinking and lifestyle. Others admonished me that I was privileged to have milk to feed my baby. Did poor people have problems like that? They said that I had to reform myself and identify with common workers and peasants.

The next thing that Olivia and I were criticized on was our "lack of political incentives." Under the Communist regime, one of the major criteria in checking people's political thought was their attitudes toward the

Communist Party. For young people, the question would be as whether they had the aspirations to become a Party member.

A female colleague had visited Olivia and me at home several times during the "Thought Reform Campaign." Bringing us political brochures, she suggested that we study them first and then attend some classes. The political brochures and the classes were teaching people how to prepare themselves to apply to be a Communist Party member. Olivia and I welcomed the female colleague, talking more on other things and showing no interest in those training classes.

Our failure to respond to the Party's recruitment call brought us, without any surprise, a lot of ridicule in the "Daily Life Discussions." Some felt sorry for us because we were hopelessly petty bourgeois, knowing only how to indulge in cozy family life. Others raised the notch higher. They pointed out that our lack of political motivation reflected our alienation to the Party, which was not only unhealthy but also dangerous.

Olivia and I were really indulging in our own "pitiful, cozy and happy" life, so we did not take the criticisms or attacks seriously. In comparison, our colleague Xu Hejin got a much tougher treatment. Coming from Shanghai, he was a widower in his late forties. Since he had no baby to feed with fragile glass bottles, he told a story about the Soviet advisors as if he were chatting with friends.

In his story, he described how he went to a shopping center in Shanghai a year ago. He saw a truck pull up in front of the stores. A bunch of well-dressed Soviet advisors came down from the truck, dashing toward those stores as if they were boors from the countryside. The scene was unusual, so he stood there watching. After about twenty minutes, the Soviet advisors seemed to have finished their shopping and loaded their truck with all kinds of merchandise. In the meantime, the shelves of those stores had been stripped almost bare.

Never before had anybody anywhere told a story similar to that. Through official propaganda, people believed that the Soviet Union was rich and plentiful, so Xu Hejin's story aroused not only doubts but also amusement. But to the activists, it was nothing but a poisonous heresy. Quickly, the attack on Xu Hejun began.

In that "Daily Life Discussion," Xu Hejun was accused of smearing the Soviet Union, the leader of the socialist camp. An activist shouted, "Yes, there might be a temporary shortage in the Soviet Union. But the socialist system is much superior to the capitalist's. Only our enemies put emphasis on certain temporary difficulties of socialism."

But Xu Hejin was adamant. He insisted that what he said was what he personally witnessed. He did not think socialism should be discussed only in abstract, so he asked, "Why would the Soviet advisors rush to buy things in one shopping tour if socialism means heaven on earth?"

How bold was Xu Hejin! His reply only incited more shouts and attacks. After the "Thought Reform Campaign," he became totally isolated. He left the division without saying goodbye to anyone.

The transition from the Literary Editorial Division to a publishing house turned out to be a daunting process. Because there was still little work to do, I decided to make good use of my office time by getting acquainted with the Chinese Communist literature. There were abundant materials in the Ministry of Culture. Not only were there literary publications from the Communist bases, but also historical documents of the left literary movements in the Nationalist controlled areas.

So I gulped down as many of the Yanan classic novels, poems and essays as I could. The history of the leftist literary movements was full of factional fighting. I had less interest in spending time on those semantic debates or sloganeering practices. But I did find out that since the 1930s, many of the infightings between the leftist literary groups were not entirely caused by any real doctrinal differences. Personal vendetta and agendas sometimes dominated those conflicts.

While I was immersing myself in Communist literature, a mysterious thing happened in the Literary Editorial Division. One day, Jiang Tianzuo, the division chief, suddenly disappeared. No announcement was made as to why he did not come to his office. No staff member knew where he was. The Literary Editorial Division instantly went into limbo. Since no one was giving us assignments, we could only sit idly and attend the required political studies and meetings.

An uncertainty hung over our heads. In the Editorial Division, the name "Jiang Tianzuo" quickly became taboo. Many wondered what happened to him, but none dared to bring the question into the open. Had Jiang Tianzuo been arrested for a crime? I was shocked, to say the least. If Jiang Tianzuo committed political mistakes, he should have been brought to meetings of criticism, but no such meeting was ever held.

As mentioned before, Olivia and I knew very little about Jiang Tianzuo. His sudden disappearance taught us that, under the Communist rule, the fates of individuals were unpredictable, even for the Party members. Uncertainty then became the normalcy. Now our employment was in jeopardy too. We did not know what our next jobs would be.

In the early 1950s, since the Chinese Communists were closely allied with the Soviet Union, the Russian language had become a hot commodity in Mainland China. People rushed to learn Russian for better living. Some English teachers tried hard to change their language skills. The Ministry of Culture, like many other government agencies, had also set up an evening class for employees to learn Russian. Olivia and I enrolled in it in 1951.

The teacher of our class was a Russian in his late twenties, a descendant of a Russian emigrant family after 1917. While teaching Russian to us, he exhibited a strong interest in English, so after learning that Olivia and I had returned from the United States, he often paid special attention to both of us. Whenever he taught us a Russian word, he would ask us to give him the equivalent in English.

Olivia and I had no desire to jump on the Russian language bandwagon. Nor had we contemplated shifting our career. Our interest in English and American literature was rooted. Therefore, under the gnawing uncertainty, we started to translate works into English to sharpen our skills in translation in our spare times.

Since there was almost no work to do in the office, Olivia also gained time to meet with some old friends whom she had not seen after returning to Mainland China. One of them was Shen Yan, a movie director who went with the troupe to Singapore in 1938.

Now after fourteen years, Shen Yan was very happy to see us when I went with Olivia to see him. He asked about our working place, and Olivia informed him of the uncertainty facing the Literary Editorial Division in the Ministry of Culture.

"I wish I had known this earlier!" Shen Yan showed his concern. Then he continued with laughter, "Don't worry! There should be no problem for you. I know several places which would love to hire you two right away." After mentioning a few organizations and agencies, he wrote down our names and address, promising to contact us as soon as he got a reply from the places he mentioned.

Shen Yan's assurance somewhat appeased our uncertainty. Olivia and I plunged back in our translation works again, but two months passed by and there was no word from Shen Yan. We thought he might have forgotten his promise, and we did not feel that we should remind him about our situation.

Slowly, 1952 was drawing to its end. Two new political campaigns that had been launched at the outset of the year were now gradually tapering off. One was called the "Three Anti's;" the other, the "Five Anti's." Both of them were aimed at cleaning up corruption and malfeasances.

In the "Three and Five Anti's" campaigns, business managers and administrators in public agencies were major targets of the Chinese Communists. Party directives and struggle meetings replaced legal procedures. Many famous Chinese entrepreneurs were persecuted. Some of them, like Lu Zuofu, committed suicide.

Lu Zuofu was one of the most successful Chinese entrepreneurs in modern time. His prominent Min Sheng Shi Ye Gong Si (Min Sheng Enterprise) was an important chapter attributed to the modern history of Chinese shipping industry.

Olivia and I were exempted from the "Three and Five Anti's" campaigns, because we had not involved in managerial or administrative affairs. However, while we were working at home one night, there was a knock on our door. Seldom had we had visitors that late. To our surprise, we found Shen Yan standing outside in the cold.

Shen Yan was in rugged clothes and seemed to be in a rush. Without taking a seat, he told us that he had come straight from the railway station. He quickly explained that he had not contacted us because he had been out of town. But he had a very serious matter to discuss with us before going home.

Looking at Shen Yan's haggard face, Olivia and I could not figure out why he acted as if he were in panic.

"What's the matter, Shen Yan?" Olivia became worried.

ShenYan was still standing there. Instead of giving Olivia a reply, he posted a question directly to us, "Do you own a radio?"

Shocked by the query, we were at a loss as to what to say. Olivia ducked her head first. She raised her stunned face and exclaimed, "Oh! That damned Halicrafter! We had never seen it before we got to Qingdao, but it still gives us trouble!"

Shen Yan could not understand what Olivia said, so Olivia told him the story of the Halicrafter radio.

"No matter what, you have to go and claim the radio back!" After listening to Olivia, Shen Yan wanted us to understand the severity of the matter. He paused and shook his head. "You know what? I have recommended you both to several places. They all wanted to hire you, but your dossier indicated that you have brought back a military radio from the United States. Nobody dares to hire you because of that."

Shen Yan left in a hurry. Olivia and I became depressed, but even though we worried about ourselves, we sensed that Shen Yan might be in trouble too. He had just come back from the rural areas. His rugged clothing and haggard look indicated that he might have been exiled to somewhere in the countryside.

Following Shen Yan's advice, Olivia and I decided to straighten out the radio issue right away. The funny thing was that I did not have the receipt from the customs office in Qingdao. Without a receipt, it would be hard for us to claim back the radio that was supposed to belong to us. Therefore, when I went back to Qingdao, I thought the only thing I could do was to locate the old customs clerk. I still remembered that there was a military officer standing behind him when he handled our luggage.

Hope against hope, I encircled around the customs windows after getting into Qingdao's customshouse. I searched each of them with a suspenseful mind. Luckily I caught him finally! The old customs officer was still there. I lined up in front of his window to make sure he was the right man.

The old customs clerk could not recognize me at first. He refused to check my detained radio because I had no receipt. I kept on explaining to him that I had passed through his window two years ago, and now I wanted to claim back my detained radio.

However, he continued to talk to me with a poker face, declining to take up my case. In frustration, I began to recall the whole story, telling him that it was he who had identified the radio brand name as Halicrafter, an item of the U.S. war surplus.

Thank goodness! "Halicrafter" appeared to be the magic word! It struck a cord in the old customs clerk's mind. Instantly he resurrected something from his memory. "Yes. I remember now." He patted his forehead. With a grin, he asked, "Are you the one who had come back from America?"

I nodded in emotion, replying that I had made a special trip from Beijing to claim back my radio. "Two years is long enough for any inspection," I argued. "You people should have released the radio to me long ago. I'm ready to sell it to the government if I am not allowed to own it."

The old customs clerk listened attentively. "I can't get it for you now," he answered with a sigh, clenching his fingers on his lips. "Our warehouse is now in a mess. Nobody can find anything there. Many detained items have been sold or disassembled, especially the electronic merchandise." He spoke with much more confidence than two years ago.

As if being drenched in cold water, I felt helpless and hopeless, but I was determined not to leave the customs office empty-handed this time. Luckily, there was no one standing behind me in the line, so I planted myself there waiting for a solution.

The old customs clerk now realized that he had a stubborn customer in hand. Contemplating for a while, he broke the awkward silence: "You know, comrade, we are now in the 'Three Anti's' and 'Five Anti's' campaigns." He began to talk like a cadre and not an old clerk. "Corruption is the number one enemy we have to wipe out!"

I joined him in denouncing corruption, pointing out that malfeasance was also intolerable. I told him that the "Three and Five Anti's" campaigns were aiming at getting rid of bureaucratic authoritative practices too.

The old customs officer listened with a jerk and seemed to begin to look at me with more reverence. I repeated to him that I would not leave this time without a receipt for my radio. Finally, he leaned forward and smiled. "I understand your anguish now, comrade. Why don't you give me a written request? Let me attach it to our list of the detained items. You'll hear from us about your radio."

If worst comes to worst, I would at least have a promise from an old customs clerk. Nevertheless, I still left Qingdao empty-handed for the second time.

On the train back to Beijing, I could not help screaming to myself, *Oh, radio, radio! Why would you put Olivia and me in such a miserable position?* Thinking about radios, my mind suddenly switched to a high school friend. His name was Lian Rongzhu. He and his family were almost ruined by a radio twenty years ago.

Lian Rongzhu had told me many times about that tragedy. It was in Chongqing, the wartime capital of China in 1939. The city was under heavy Japanese bombing during the Sino-Japanese War. Lian Rongzhu was then a fourteen-year-old boy. At that time, only well-to-do kids could afford to own radios. Lian Rongzhu's family was rich. He was crazy about his radio because it was a newfangled gadget.

One day, in an adventurous spirit, Lian Rongzhu installed an antenna on top of his family's roof. School kids nowadays are free to play with gadgets in their basements, back yards or roof tops in a free country. But that was wartime China. The Japanese bombers were making devastating visits to Chongqing every day.

Neighbors were alarmed to see an antenna sticking out on top of the roof of a house. They suspected the Lian family was assisting the Japanese to pinpoint their bombing targets. With the rage of patriotism, they stormed the Lians' house, destroyed the antenna, and threw Lian Rongzhu's father into jail. When the dust settled, the Lian family was bankrupted. The radio had been a jinx to the family.

To me, Lian Rongzhu was not just an ordinary friend. He had always treated me as a younger brother. While my father was in prison in Chongqing, he and his family had taken my mother into their home, offering their attic as her shelter when most people would keep a distance from a prisoner's wife. Lian Rongzhu's father was sympathetic to my parents, because he himself had once been in prison.

I contacted Lian Rongzhu as soon as I got home from Qingdao. With Olivia's encouragement, I invited him to visit us in Beijing. When he accepted our invitation and came over, he brought with him an oral message from my mother.

It was a piece of good news about my father. My mother wanted us to know that a high-ranking Communist military officer had paid my father a surprise visit in prison, telling my father that he would be soon released. The name of the officer was He Biao, the nephew of the legendary Chinese Communist Marshall He Long.

Father would soon regain his freedom! That was an extraordinary relief for all of us. But Olivia and I also wanted to find out my mother's situation during the last few years. Lian Rongzhu began his reply with a remark, "It's been tough! Very tough! But now things are getting better." As far as he could remember, the most difficult time might have been when my mother caught appendicitis not long after my father's imprisonment.

It was late in an afternoon, as Lian Rongzhu recalled, and he and his wife had to send my mother to a hospital in the suburbs. His wife was pregnant. Both of them could not hold my mother to the emergency room. Luckily, they ran into an off-business rickshaw on their way, so my mother could at least lean on the rickshaw while he and his wife followed by foot. Another lucky thing was that they got to the hospital in time for my mother's surgery.

Olivia and I thanked Lian Rongzhu for his family's help to our parents in their predicaments. In return, he commended us for coming back to take care of our parents in difficult times.

Lian Rongzhu and I had not seen each other for years. There were many fond memories to share when we talked about our old days. Between 1941 and 1942, we were seniors in a high school near Chongqing. We recalled our activities in The Windy Sky, the literary society we organized. During that time, I had had my first romance.

A beautiful and talented girl named Cheng Quanbao joined The Windy Sky. She was fond of literature and stage acting. While in school, she was elected to perform in the prestigious Kangjiantang Theatre in wartime capital

Chongqing. We became very good friends, and she seemed to be deeply attached to me.

A year later, however, I went to college at Wuhan University in Leshan. Since we could no more see each other as often as before, she wrote me more than a hundred love letters. Due to the heavy load of schoolwork, I was unable to write as frequently as she expected. She eventually began to worry. Once, she even asked Lian Rongzhu, our mutual good friend, to accompany her to visit my mother.

Tragically, the murderous tuberculosis Cheng Quanbao contracted snatched her away in 1944. Because I was far away, Lian Rongzhu had represented me in her funeral. When I returned to Chongqing, it was also Lian Rongzhu who had taken me to her tomb so I could express my sorrow and adoration to her.

When Lian Rongzhu was in Beijing, he and I had tried to visit some of our friends in their working places. Queerly, many of our visits ended in failure. We were unable to see many of them if they were working in particular agencies or organizations. Some of the office receptionists were particularly unfriendly. Before letting us in, they often asked us nasty questions or simply turned us away rudely. Time and again, it reminded us that we were now under the Communist regime and that the friends we wanted to see might be in some kind of trouble.

To make up for our failures in meeting friends, Olivia and I decided to entertain Lian Rongzhu at some famous Beijing restaurants. One day, we took him to Quyuan, a restaurant specialized in Hunan cuisine. Hunan was Mao Zedong's native province. He often went to Quyuan to enjoy his favorite Hunan hot dishes. The gluttons also liked Quyuan's bulky chopsticks and big dishes.

Indeed, chopsticks were the first thing that caught the new customer's eyes in Quyuan. Twice as long as ordinary chopsticks, the bulky food-pickers helped the customers to boost up their appetites. The dishes that came in huge plates seemed also to advise the customers: "Eat as much as you can!"

A waiter led us to a corner table to join the gluttons. Before picking up his chopsticks, Lian Rongzhu looked at another table intensely and seemed to have found someone he knew over there. In his excitement, he stood up and dashed to greet a couple sitting at that table. Hurrah! He had found his long-missed uncle. He was ready to swoop down and give his uncle a big hug.

Yet the middle-age man seemed to be exceptionally cold. Turning back to acknowledge Lian Rongzhu's presence, he only nodded slightly and cracked a subtle smile. He immediately returned to his lunch, without even bothering to introduce his female companion to his nephew. Olivia and I had also risen up from our chairs. Courtesy required us to show respect to Lian Rongzhu's uncle. But he failed to take any notice.

Lian Rongzhu's uncle had been a legendary hero in Lian Rongzhu's family. I had heard many times that he had left home for the Revolution when he was young. Lian Rongzhu's sisters and brothers often bragged about him. Now we found their uncle sitting here without showing any emotion toward his nephew.

The situation became awkward. The delicious dishes at Quyuan seemed rotten that day. We could not figure out why Lian Rongzhu's uncle behaved. like that. Was it because he had changed his class status? Had he become snobbish because he was now important in the new regime? Might he be in certain political trouble himself at the moment? No answers to those questions could be found.

Lian Rongzhu received his accounting degree from Chongqing University. He was quite successful in his professional career. The last time I met him was in Guangzhou in 1962 when I was on my way to join Olivia. He was then the chief accountant of a ship building company in Guangzhou.

I hope and pray that he and his family survived the turbulent upheavals of late twentieth century China.

6

The Literature Publishing House

June 21 was the summer solstice. Our second baby boy, Phillip, was born on the longest day of 1953. Mother and son both received good care at a nearby hospital originally called Longfu. It was renamed the No. 4 Hospital for Public Employees and was the designated hospital for our health insurance. Olivia had to rely on it from then on for maternity service instead of going to the Union Hospital.

Phillip had come at a fortunate moment. His grandfather was to be freed soon. His grandmother, out of joy, named him "Ming" from Chongqing. "Ming" was the intonation of one of the four beautiful rivers in our native province Sichuan. Combined with the predesignated middle name "Li," Phillip received the full Chinese name of "Hwang Liming." The change of Grandma's attitude from pessimistic to enthusiastic symbolized the entire family's outlook turning for the better.

David's babysitter, Guilan, left us not long after Phillip came home. She had to leave Beijing with her parents. We hired another live-in babysitter named Xiue from Shanghai. Xiue was also very nice in helping us to take care of both Phillip and David before their grandparents arrived.

In our workplace, the future of the Literary Editorial Division was still unclear. The campaigns of "Suppressing the Counter-Revolutionaries" and the "Three and Five Anti's" seemed to be tapering off. A temporary lull allowed people to catch their breath. Some colleagues in the office even felt relieved that the storms were over. But the lull appeared to be very brief. The trailing "Thought Reform" campaign had entered another phase called "Political Inspection."

It was in the middle of 1953 and everybody was suddenly asked to write an autobiography to unveil his or her past. Olivia and I had had some experience before at the Graduate School of the North China Revolutionary

University. We thought it was a standard procedure to check everyone's background. But this time the "Political Inspection" was different from what we had gone through two years ago.

There was no more so-called "mild breeze and gentle rain" presumably used in previous "Thought Reform" meetings. Instead, hurricanes were often blasted over potential "enemies." The long touted Chinese Communist "Criticism and Self-criticism" formula was discarded. What was needed in the "Political Inspection" was "revelation and confession." And they were to be obtained by whatever means necessary.

To mobilize everyone to confess, a rally was called in the Literary Editorial Division. Since we had only a small staff left, a number of workers from other Divisions were sent in to join us. At the same time, because there was no one in charge of the division, its original figurehead, a famous author named Cao Jinghua, was called back to deliver the keynote speech.

Being a veteran translator of Russian literature, Cao Jinghua was then the head of the Department of Russian Language in Beijing University. He had been associated closely with the Communists since 1930s when he was in the Soviet Union, but he never became a formal Party member. Since he had been in Soviet Union under Stalin's rule and witnessed many of Stalin's cruel persecutions, I was anxious to hear his first hand experiences.

Cao Jinghua was gentle, polite, and soft-spoken. To my surprise, he did not touch on the Soviet Union at all. Neither did he follow the Chinese Communist Party's line to talk about political investigation. Instead, he preached like a modern "Confucian," exalting the merits of "revelation and confession" for self-renewal.

"Practicing self-revelation and confession is like taking a good bath," he opened his keynote speech. "We have to check our thinking constantly." He told the weary audience that, like dirt on our body, our erroneous thoughts might pollute our minds. The way to clean our minds is to check our past, digging out our wrong doings, and immunizing ourselves from contaminated thoughts.

Maybe Cao Jinghua was trying to assure the audience not to worry about "self-revelation and confession," but it was doubtful that he convinced them that day. "Confessions and self-revelations" in Communist "political investigation" were always conducted through coercion. Neither persons under investigation, nor Communist conductors of investigation, would honestly tag "coerced confession and self-revelation" as a practice of so-called "self-renewal."

During the 1940s, Cao Jinghua was in the wartime Chinese capital, Chongqing. It was said that Zhou Enlai was not very happy to see that Cao Jinghua had remained to be a non-Party member. But Cao Jinghua preferred only to be a friend of the Communist Party. He had even maintained that status after the Communists came to power. Since the Soviet Union was the leader of the Socialist camp, the Communists had always honored him as a senior translator of Russian works.

Mao Zedong had observed half a century ago, "Revolution is not a dinner party." To him, there was no room for courtesy and hospitality in political struggles, and he always handled political investigation this way. Therefore, coerced confessions and self-revelations had become the Communist weapons to fight against their alleged enemies. The conventional norms and etiquettes were antithetic to their doctrine but could be used as means to achieve their goals.

Olivia and I were shocked when we went through the ferocious struggle meetings. It was sad to watch people twisting in the political winds. Colleagues from the same office could turn against each other overnight, as did many friends and family members. People always jumped on movement bandwagons for survival. The vicious ones even grabbed the opportunities for their personal revenges or gains.

Targets in "political inspection" generally were not being treated as human beings. Verbal abuse could be as devastating as physical violence. The stormy proceedings probably were aimed at scaring the onlookers. People will always think about their own necks under the created "fear."

It was recorded that during Middle Ages forced confessions had been used as tools by inquisitions in Europe. Had the Chinese Communists created their own techniques in "political inquisition," or borrowed their tactics from somewhere else? It was an interesting question to be answered. But in terms of width and depth, the Chinese Communist ways of obtaining coerced confession might dwarf those used in the Dark Ages in Europe.

Our little, sweet home was always a refuge in our uncertainties. Under the political hurricane and thunderstorms, it also served as our windbreaker and shelter. Olivia and I were aware when we sat as listeners to be educated in those ferocious struggle meetings that we might be the targets in the next round.

Olivia and I had locked ourselves up in our work. We had tried to be as apolitical as possible in the most political environments. At the time, publication had not yet entirely been nationalized. Few proprietors were still seeking authors and translators for their publishing business in Mainland China. Our debut in publication was a book on Lincoln Brigade in the Spanish Civil War in 1936. We translated it from English, and it was published by a private firm in 1953.

At the end of the year, the "political inspection" seemed to have come to a temporarily halt. The People's Publishing House for Literature was properly set up finally. As far as I knew, it was the brainchild of the Deputy Minister of Culture, Zhou Yan. He had put his fingerprints on it from the outset.

For instance, Zhou Yan planned to have the Literature Publishing House located right next to the Ministry of Culture. For that purpose, several rows of buildings were built in a new site, and a special gate was opened to link it to the Ministry's compound. Furthermore, the forerunner of the Literature Publishing House, the Literary Editorial Division, was actually under his direct supervision from the beginning.

But things took a sharp turn since the disappearance of Jiang Tianzao. Gradually, Zhou Yan seemed to lose his grip until he was totally excluded from the helm of running the Literature Publishing House. The reason Zhou Yan was bypassed was because a Bureau of Publications had been also set up prior at the time, so the Bureau immediately took the Literature Publishing House under its jurisdiction.

There might have been a lot of juggling between Communist literary factions. Because the juggling was behind the scenes, no one seemed to know the details. But Zhou Yan might have disappointed when the editor-in-chief position of the Publishing House was given to Feng Xuefeng, a veteran Communist who had been at odds with Zhou Yan since the 1930s.

As an established leftist literary critic, Feng Xuefeng had joined the Communist "Twenty Thousand Li Long March." He claimed that he had served as a special liaison between the Party and Lu Xun, the author most revered by the Communists. Therefore, in terms of seniority and achievement, he considered himself much higher than Zhou Yan in the Party as well as in the literary circles.

Zhou Yan and his group were also active in Shanghai in the middle of the 1930s. They happened to have been severely criticized by Lu Xun before they fled to Yanan. It became a sore spot on their backs ever since. Now Zhou Yan and his group were Mao Zedong's men in charge of literature and art. But as long as Lu Xun remained the saint in Communist literature, the sore spot on their backs continuously made Zhou Yan and his group uncomfortable and vulnerable.

In his quest for power, Mao Zedong had praised Lu Xun as a saint, the greatest author in modern China. Following his suit, the Chinese leftist literary circles had put Lu Xun on the lotus throne of modern Chinese literature. Thus, many had scrambled to be recognized as Lu Xun's true disciple after his death. Chief among them was the leftist literary critic Hu Feng and the veteran Party member Feng Xuefeng.

However, as soon as Lu Xun passed away, Mao Zedong established the *Lu Xun Institute of Art and Literature* in Yanan to attract Lu Xun's followers in the 1940s. Paradoxically, the man he appointed to head the Lu Xun Institute was Zhou Yan, who happened to be the very underground Communist leader Lu Xun opposed and hated in Shanghai. Therefore, when Zhou Yan came to Beijing as the Communist literary czar, some of the self-claimed disciples of Lu Xun's would not honor or listen to him. Thus, an old wound was reopened, and a time bomb was set in the literary circles to explode.

Feng Xuefeng was at the apex of his career in early 1954. When he assumed the presidency of the People's Publishing House for Literature, he also served as a Party secretary to the Writer's Union. In addition, while Ding Ling was editing *Wenyibao* (*Art and Literature Monthly*), Feng Xuefeng sat in her Board of Advisors.

At the same time, Feng Xuefeng published his *Recollections on Lu Xun* to affirm that he was Lu Xun's most trusted disciple. There had been schedule meetings at the Cultural Ministry for the subordinate agencies to report their operations. But in avoiding Zhou Yan, Feng Xuefeng never bothered to attend those meetings or to get instructions from Zhou Yan.

Thus, in a way, Zhou Yan was cut off from his "brain-child," the Literature Publishing House right after its coming into being. Neither did he have a say in its organization nor could he direct its policies and operations.

When Feng Xuefeng took over the steering wheel of the Publishing House, he gave the printing duty to a staff he brought over from the Triple Alliance Book Store, an established underground Communist publisher in Shanghai. For editorial work, he not only hired a new staff from various quarters, but also made an organizational change by establishing a special department to edit and publish Lu Xun's works.

The emphasis on Lu Xun was, of course, another way of jacking up the importance of Lu Xun and his claimed disciples, but its implications went much further than a policy of the Publishing House. As underdogs in Lu Xun's works, Zhou Yan and his group might feel Feng Xuefeng's move was a threat to their leadership positions.

In addition to Lu Xun's works, Feng Xuefeng replaced the entire editorial staff. Very few editors were retained from the old Literary Division. Surprisingly, Olivia and I were among them. Both of us were assigned to work continuously on world literature. While I would edit translations on American titles, Olivia was supposed to handle the introduction of Scandinavian literature.

In organization, Feng Xuefeng divided the editorial staff into five departments: 1) Contemporary Chinese Literature; 2) Classical Chinese Literature; 3) Russian Literature; 4) World Literature; and 5) Lu Xun's Works. Each department was subdivided into groups to deal with specific times or areas of the literature in the whole world. In the meantime, an Editor-in-Chief Office was set up to coordinate editorial works of the entire Publishing House.

Olivia and I had worked at the Literature Publishing House for more than ten years. There were still memories lingering in our minds, some fond and some sad. After half a century's departure, sometimes I am still able to visualize some of our colleagues. For the whole Publishing House, there might be three editorial departments worth mentioning besides our own World Literature Department.

First, all the editors in the Department of Classical Chinese Literature were professionals, but the department head, Nie Gannu, was an unusual Communist. And one of its editors, Shu Wu, had triggered the campaign for "Wiping Out All Hidden Anti-Revolutionary Elements."

Nie Gannu was a veteran Communist Party member since the 1920s. He had been a cadet of the famous Nationalist Huangpu Military Academy. In early 1930s, he went to Moscow, and had attended Oriental University. Yet, as a man, he was eccentric and unyielding, always maintaining an independent stand of his own. He chose to be a freelance writer before his Party came into power. But he seemed always running foul of the Party disciplines. Thus, he had been exiled and put in prison many times in his life.

Shu Wu was a talented young author, formerly a follower of Hu Feng, another disciple of Lu Xun. Nie Gannu recruited him to work as an editor in the Classical Chinese Literature Department. For some unknown reasons, however, Shu Wu turned into an informer after breaking with his mentor Hu Feng. After receiving Hu Feng's letters secretly submitted by Shu Wu, the Communists immediately branded Hu Feng and his followers as an Anti-Communist clique.

Thus, when Mao Zedong launched his campaign of "Wiping Out All

Hidden Anti-Revolutionary Elements," our Publishing House became sort of the eye in a hurricane.

The other editorial department worth mentioning was the Department of Russian Literature. As far as I could remember, female editors seemed to have outnumbered their male colleagues. Most of them had special and prominent connections. For example, there were the wives of Marshall Chen Yi and General Chen Xilian; the daughter-in-law of the Minister of Culture Shen Yanbing (Mao Dun); the daughter of Cao Jinghua; and last but not the least, Zhou Yan's girlfriend. But they should all be commended for their professional excellence. While working as editors, they always maintained low profiles.

As mentioned before, the Department of Lu Xun's Works enjoyed a special status in the Publishing House. One major function of those editors was to provide footnotes to Lu Xun's polemic works. When it came to the controversy between Lu Xun and Zhou Yan, the footnotes to Lu Xun's remarks on Zhou Yan and his group naturally became a delicate but contentious issue.

In his writings, Lu Xun had always been relentless to his enemies. He had ferociously attacked Zhou Yan and his group in 1937. Half a century later, reading the sarcastic remarks, one might feel that it was overdone, and question the vengeful manner of the bickering. But at the time, it was a life-and-death struggle within the left literary circles in Shanghai. It seemed unbelievable that the old bickering was rehashed in 1955 with the same vengeance, and was even expanded to a much larger life-and-death struggle.

As mentioned, Mao Zedong had been using Lu Xun as a banner in the late 1930s and established the *Lu Xun Institute of Art and Literature* in Yanan. But ironically, a prominent journalist, Zhao Chaogou visited Yanan in 1944. In his reportage, Zhao Chaogou was curious as to why he could not find Lu Xun's works in any of the Yanan bookstores. He had found writers were silenced in their criticism of the Communists in Yanan. He had tried to meet a courageous writer named Wang Shiwei who had been airing out grievances in Yanan. But he only knew that Wang Shiwei had been struggled against but did not know Wang Shiwei was secretly being killed by the Communists afterward.

Not until twenty years later did Mao Zedong reveal his true feelings about Lu Xun. During the "Cultural Revolution" from 1965 to 1975, it was reported that a group of writers and artists had asked Mao Zedong once in Shanghai: "How would Lu Xun fare if he were still alive today?"

Mao Zedong's reply was quick and straightforward: "If Lu Xun were still around, he would either have to shut up or be locked up!"

That was a scary comment the Chinese intellectuals never expected to hear. No Communist newspaper dared to print his remarks of revelation in the 1960s. Even down to today, the Chinese Communist Party does not acknowledge that it was a Mao Zedong's scheme to set up the *Lu Xun Institute of Art and Literature* in Yanan to attract the left-leaning Chinese intellectuals during World War II.

In 1955, Lu Xun was still under Mao Zedong's patronage. Nobody had thought Mao Zedong would repudiate Lu Xun ten years later, so the self-proclaimed disciples of Lu Xun continued their quarrels with Zhou Yan and his group, thinking they were under the protection of Mao Zedong. Blinded by their belief that they would never be viewed as the Communist's enemies, the Lu Xun followers even appealed to Mao Zedong for his help to continue to praise and worship Lu Xun. Tragically, as soon as they restarted their quarrels, Mao Zedong immediately threw them into the political arena and branded them as Anti-Communists. Hundreds of innocent intellectuals were implicated. They all fell into the trap and became victims in the purge.

Feng Xuefeng had held Lu Xun's banner high, and so had Hu Feng, another self-proclaimed true disciple of Lu Xun. For a while, they appeared to be two strong challengers of Communist leadership in the literary field. But soon Zhou Yan and his group fought back. First, when the chief and vice editors of *Wenyibao* (*Art and Literature Monthly*), Ding Ling and her associates, were branded as an anti-Party clique, Feng Xuefeng was implicated. His prestige, power and influence diminished quickly.

At the time, few in the Publishing House knew what had happened. But ever since late 1954, Feng Xuefeng failed to show up at his Editor-in-Chief office. He also seemed to have lost his positions in the Writers' Union and other literary organizations. Not long afterward, another famous literary critic named Wang Renshu formally replaced him as the head of the Publishing House.

Actually, long before Feng Xuefeng and Ding Ling were persecuted, Mao Zedong had wanted to be the supreme commander of Chinese cultural life. He started to put his imprints on products in literature and art right after he came to Beijing. In 1951 and 1952, his first alarming shots were fired at two popular movies entitled *Wu Xun the Beggar* (*Wu Xun Zhuan*) and *Anecdotes from the Qing Palace* (*Qing Gong Wai Shi*).

In his barrage of criticism, he blasted *Wu Xun the Beggar* for its portrayal of a beggar as a savior in the old society and condemned the *Anecdotes from the Qing Palace* for its nostalgia for the dynastic rulers. In order to discredit the screen writer, the director and the players in *Wu Xun the Beggar*, he even dispatched his wife Jiang Qing to dig out Wu Xun's real life.

Jiang Qing was Mao Zedong's third wife, who had been a third rate movie star in Shanghai in the 1930s. When she married Mao Zedong in Yanan, she was prohibited to meddle in politics by the Chinese Communist Party. But she resented and was defiant to the restriction. Right after entering Beijing, she became a member of the Supervising Board in the Bureau of Cinema. By dispatching her under a pseudo-name to discredit Wu Xun, Mao Zedong opened the door and unleashed her to mess up politics in Communist China further.

After Mao Zedong's first shots against the two movies, persecutions spread all over the literary circles. More and more talented stars such as Zhao Dan began to be disgraced. At first, public opinion was split when *Wu Xun the Beggar* and *Anecdotes from the Qing Dynasty* were banned. There were even dissenting views within the Chinese Communist Party. But Mao Zedong quickly silenced the dissenters and tightened the censorship on all media.

It was mind boggling to understand why Mao Zedong put so much of his attention and energy on cultural affairs. He seemed to be very much interested in literature but was antagonistic to intellectuals old and young, so he put all literary circles under his personal watch. China was desperately in need of reconstruction after so many devastating external and civil wars. Yet, personally he liked to indulge in poetry and polemic writings. Publicly, he concentrated on humiliating and reforming intellectuals, and controlling the literary activities of the entire country.

From the early 1950s on, the Chinese Communist Party had begun to tout the so-called "Mao Zedong Thought," paving the way for the "Mao Zedong Cult." His writings became 'political bible." While reading his works in a study session one day, I accidentally came across his famous poem "Qin Yuan Chun Xue" again. I had read it before, but I overlooked its underlying aspiration and meaning. Suddenly, an epiphany answered many of my questions and doubts.

Qin Yuan Chun Xue was a poem Mao Zedong wrote in mid 1940s. In it, he reviewed the great Chinese emperors of the past. With poetic rhymes, he gave some of them credits in military conquests, but he felt sorry for their lacking of literary talents. For those who did have certain literary achievement, he lamented that they were short of personal gallantries.

Therefore, Mao Zedong concluded in his poem that a great emperor should have both military and literary talents, as well as personal gallantries.

In the end, he proclaimed that the greatest emperor was yet to come. What an ambitious proclamation! No wonder he thought that a ruler should not only have military conquests, great literary talents, but also the ability to be a gallant playboy.

From Mao Zedong's personal history, there might be clues to explain why he had been antagonistic toward intellectuals while aspiring to gain the highest fame in literary pursuit. Records showed that he began to cultivate his grand ambitions when he attended a teacher's school in Changsha. After that, he went to the Chinese capital of Beijing (then called Peiping), and worked as a clerk at the Beijing University's Library.

Fate might have played some cruel mischief on him there. Some of the prominent students and scholars, not foreseeing Mao Zedong might become a "great Chinese emperor" in the future, might have intentionally or absentmindedly belittled him. It was a pity that the slightness had haunted him in his life. It was also a pity that all Chinese intellectuals had to pay the price for those who had belittled Mao Zedong many years ago.

Mao Zedong had taken his revenge after he conquered all of Mainland China. He was dictatorial. But why would so many Chinese writers and artists keep on plunging themselves into his persecution machine? When the Communists took over all Mainland China in 1949, most writers and artists were jubilant, especially the young and the idealistic. They thought a new era had dawned and that utopia was in sight. Even Hu Feng, the literary critic who had differences with the Communists, proclaimed in his euphoria: "Time has just begun!"

Yes, "Time has just begun!" many young Chinese writers and artists echoed. Like drunkards on binges, they believed that the new regime would embrace them and reward them for their support. While some of them might have felt sour after their hot faces were met with icy pats, a majority of them remained hopeful. Had Stalin not said once that writers and artists were the "engineers of human souls"? They tried to boost up their own spirits. "Engineers of human souls!" That's a great title!

Old and established writers and artists might not have been so naïve. Some jockeyed to the forefront but retreated soon after. Most of them seemed to have taken a wait-and-see stand. At the same time, the sages and the most talented, like Shen Congwen, were preparing to quit creative writing altogether.

The Chinese Communists had applied literature and art as tools to achieve their goals. In contested areas, they had been using The Writer and Artist

Union to enlarge their united front operations. In areas under their control, the same unions became their organizations for propaganda and thought control.

Mao Zedong needed a flowering literature and art to decorate his regime after he put them under absolute control. The Writer and Artist Union was his factory to manufacture those literary products. Literary careerists were anxious to meet his demands in order to have an "iron bowl" job. But Mao Zedong's whims were ephemeral. The union operatives also had their constant infightings. Therefore, campaigns and persecutions never ended in the literary field.

When Feng Xuefeng's fate hung in the wind, the Publishing House was only able to publish very few new titles. Reprints of old classics and anthologies from the Chinese and world literature became our major duty. The Chinese Communists had a two-circle system of publication and distribution since the Yanan days. One was for the "inner circle," the other for the "outer circle."

"Inner circle" meant the leadership and elites in the Communist Party. "Outer circle" meant the general public. Within each circle, there were different levels of reader's eligibility. The Publishing House was obliged to fulfill the requests of the most privileged, even if the requests were works of pornographic or controversial nature.

In my memory, not until the arrival of our new head Wang Renshu did the Publishing House become steady. Editorial plans were drafted and put into operation. The publication of Chinese and world literature became systematic. For instance, for American literature, only leftist authors were allowed to be introduced before. But now Walt Whitman, Mark Twain and a number of eighteenth and nineteenth century American authors had all been put for publication.

Olivia and I now had more work to do in office. It gave us a lift in our spirits. At home, we also found more incentive to enhance our skills in translation. Therefore, we began to have more of our own translations published. Among them were Albert Maltz's *The Underground Stream* and James Aldridge's *Sea Eagle*. With several colleagues, we also experimented to translate together Charles Lamb's stories of the *Odyssey* and some Indian novels from English into Chinese.

Looking back, that was an exceptionally tranquil period for work. I remember that the joint translation practice had even gone beyond the Publishing House. One day, an editor named Si Konggu from the Drama Publishing House unexpectedly came to offer me a contract to compile an anthology of world renowned one-act plays. Drama happened to be my favorite, so I accepted his offer on the spot.

By coincidence, our old friend Zhong Rexin visited us from Guangzhou that week. I mentioned to him the project and invited him to join me. He had been studying drama at Yale University, so he was most willing to participate. In excitement, he further recommended two friends to join the project. One was Wang Zongyan, his colleague at Zhongshan University. The other was Fang Shuchun, his friend then teaching philosophy at Beijing University. He advised me to contact the latter as soon as possible.

After Zhong Rexin left, I went to visit Fang Shuchun in the Langrun Garden of Beijing University. It was the first time we ever met. I found him living in a forlorn yard and was somewhat downcast. But as we discussed the translation project, he became spirited, telling me that he loved the project. Before I left, he promised to do some research on world renowned one-act play, and send me a bibliography quickly. He even joked with a rueful smile that the project had cheered him up.

Unfortunately, a political thunderstorm struck again in mid 1955. The world one-act plays project died before birth. For some unknown reason, Si Konggu disappeared for quite some time. Another political campaign was in full swing. Everything turned upside down, and we seemed to be in another terror again,

A year later, when the political sky cleared up, I wished to contact Fang Shuchun to resume the interrupted project. But when I got to his premises, I was stunned to learn that he had committed suicide in 1955.

Why would Fang Shuchun leave the world drastically? Nobody was able to give me a satisfactory answer.

7

Reunion with Grandparents

For nearly five years, my father was in Communist jail, and my mother had been hiding in a friend's attic. During and after the Sino-Japanese War, they had lost their homes one after another. Now they were coming to live with us. They might be excited to meet their daughter-in-law and see their two little grandsons for the first time.

While preparing to welcome them, Olivia and I were still under the ominous shadow of the Halicrafter. The Qingdao customs office finally notified me that they were ready to release the radio, but they asked me to pick it up from their office in Tianjin instead of Qingdao.

The Halicrafter had been a curse to us, so to avoid further complication, I went to Tianjin immediately. Before signing the release paper, I took an initiative by telling the clerk that I really did not need the radio. I formerly offered to denote or sell it to the government. The clerk checked his file, shook his head, and said: "No, you have to take it back. Here is the release paper. Certain parts of the radio have been removed."

For the first time, I got the chance to touch and have a close look at the radio. The Halicrafter was a big, dark gray rectangular radio. Like holding a hot potato, I brought it back and laid it down in a corner of our bedroom. I swore not to touch it again.

However, Olivia was curious about the radio she had never seen before. Not knowing my feelings, she plugged it on one day. Her test lasted at most a few minutes. But still, several policemen stormed our premises that night. In their shocking search, one of them grabbed the radio and wanted to take it away for inspection. I told him that the radio had already been inspected, but the policeman insisted, "We want to make sure that the customs office did it right." After I produced the release paper, they still argued. But in the end, the official document blocked their attempts to take it away.

Under the Communist rule, people were afraid of staying close to their relatives, especially when someone was in political trouble. Seldom would people dare to stay with their kin who had just come out of prison. Class lines were drawn in every group and most family. People would feel lucky if they were not forced to struggle against their kin or friends.

But those misgivings were irrelevant to us. Olivia and I had returned to Mainland China with a determination to take care of our parents. Our love toward them outweighed the cowardly considerations. If the police's shocking visit had affected us at all, it only enhanced our wish to have our family reunion as soon as possible.

Yes, we were aware that we had been under around-the-clock surveillance. We knew that our neighborhood was part of the surveillance network. Yes, we had been told to report regularly to our working unit and the local police about our parents' movements. Yes, we understood that by maintaining our blood ties, we would have to foreclose our advancement under the regime. And yes, we had to be prepared for a lot of other unforeseeable hazards in the future.

A dream finally came true! Father and Mother arrived in Beijing in late 1954. Born respectively in 1899 and 1898, they were still in their mid-fifties at the time. When I had last seen them ten years before, they were in good spirit and health. Now their graying hairs and weary looks seemed to have added more than ten years to their ages.

The family reunion was so happy and precious for us. Olivia and I did not want to talk about what Father and Mother had gone through. We did not ask Father specifically about his sufferings in prison, nor did we encourage Mother to recall her agonies when she stayed alone in the Liang family's attic. Of course, we never wanted Father and Mother to know the troubles we had encountered with the Halicrafter radio.

David and Phillip, the two grandsons, kept their grandparents busy instantly. Olivia was very considerate and made a brilliant decision. She handed over all of the household management to Mother when Mother settled down. The burden seemed to take away a great deal of our parents' time to think of their past traumas.

Mother began to find in Olivia another daughter. She seemed also to feel she was back to a home of her own, so she resurrected her energy, rolled up her sleeves, and resumed her role in taking care of all of us in the family. It might be hard to find a family of three generations living together like ours under the Communist regime.

Father was one of the most handsome and intelligent men among his peers. Amiable, gentle, noble, with impeccable manners, he had always been liked by people around him. He had always been dressed in dignity, be it olive drab, conservative suits or mufti. But when he came out of prison, he changed his outfit. Instead of tailor-made suits, he now wore the traditional Chinese shirts and pants.

The sufferings in prison seemed to have made some imprints on Father. Now he had become more taciturn than before. But after he settled down with us, I found that his personality and outlook had not changed at all. He seemed to have faced the drastic change of his life with his born dignity. Seldom had he complained about his fate. There was graciousness in his adjustment to his deprived new environment.

In his entire life, Father had never been out of work before. After coming to us in Beijing, he remained interested in reading and studying. He became very close to his grandchildren, playing and coaching them whenever they went to him. He had been a perfect father for my sisters and me. Now he was a perfect grandfather to his grand children.

Father was different from some of the traditional Chinese parents. When I was a kid, he often chatted with me privately as if I was his young friend. I was anxious to have the opportunity to have heart-to-heart talks with him after he came to Beijing. But circumstances had changed. Our house was congested. The grandchildren were our focus. It was only possible after Olivia and most of our children left in 1962.

Because Father was now more tacit, I could not but help recall the days when he had been opinionated. Father was quite outspoken during World War II. At the time, he was working for the Nationalist government. He was upset whenever he saw injustice or corruption. I had witnessed some of his outbursts when I came home from boarding school. Once, he became angry because a high-ranking officer tried to sneak a man into his office.

"Do you think I should fire someone to make room for that guy's relative?" he asked mother, as if she could provide him with an answer. "You know, people have to make a living. They have to feed their families. How can I go against my conscience to do something like that?"

Mother had her routine answer under similar circumstances. She would ignore father's sentiment and say, "Finish your dinner, please. The dishes are getting cold." After a while, though, she often added, "Look, don't criticize too much. I am afraid that you might get into trouble one day."

Now Father was not at work. There was no demand for him to do things against his conscience. Therefore, he seemed to be less opinionated. When he saw something unfair or corrupt, he would shake his head. If pressed to offer an opinion, he might give a soft comment: "That's not good. Things will get better. Deviations are minor compared to what we have achieved."

That was s standard comment the Communists wanted people to make when they witnessed something bad under their regime. But as far as I could observe, father's inner heart remained against evil and injustice. It was hard for him to refrain from speaking out. At crucial junctures, he would hold up his convictions on right or wrong.

Father liked to hold David and Phillip on his lap. When I saw David or Phillip hunching on his back, my mind often flashed back to how I rode on his back to school one day. At that time, our family was in Chengdu. Three generations of us were living together in a large courtyard house within a walled compound. The street's name was Zaojenmiao. A beautiful creek rippled under the shaded trees outside. It was my favorite play area.

Kids in our family started educations early. One day, Father asked me to take a walk with him. Seldom had I been allowed to go outside, so I was excited to hold Father's hand, marveling at the streets bursting with people. But before long I became exhausted and kept on asking Father how far I had to go. Father looked down with a loving smile. "We will be there soon," he comforted me, lifting me up onto his back. "Don't worry."

Father did not want to tell me that he was sending me to a school, because he was afraid that I might be scared by school at the age of five. Hunching on the back of Father all the way, we finally arrived at the prestigious Shude Elementary School. The principal was very nice to us. After a brief test, he pinned my nametag onto his office wall. That was how I started my formal education.

Afterward, Father went to work in Nanjing, the capital of the Nationalist government. Mother brought my sisters and me to join him. At the time, my grandfather was teaching nearby. Following our family's tradition, Father sent all his children to his father for school and family education. Therefore, I lived with my grandfather for a year before returning to my parents.

I remembered that our house in Nanjing was at the Yinyu (Silver Fish) Alley, nearby the Zhongyang (Central) University. There was a mini-sized soccer field close to our house. At the edge of the soccer field, we could enter the university freely through one of its side entrances. Many of my sweet memories were associated with theYinyu Alley, the soccer field and the campus of Zhongyang University.

In our family, home education had been considered important. Each day, therefore, there would be some "family homework" waiting for me after school. One of the required courses was Chinese calligraphy exercise. I was asked to copy our family tree again and again until I could memorize many names of our ancestors. To learn classical Chinese poems and essays, Father taught me through several of the most important anthologies.

Father's patience and gentility in teaching was unmatchable. He was both strict and tender. When a day's home study was over, he would always bring me outdoors, mount me onto my bike, and send me off to the university gate. He encouraged me to play soccer on the nearby field, but he restricted my biking only within the university campus.

As a child, I could not understand why I was not allowed to ride my bicycle on the streets. Father's consideration was probably for my safety. Father might not have known that his restriction had brought me many fringe benefits. First, by constantly playing in the university campus, I got to know the head of the receiving room in the university library. After he learned that I was a kid interested in stamps, he saved a lot of stamps from the big packages he received. That made me a child envied by my fellow stamp collectors.

Second, I became a nine-year-old friend to the guard at the side entrance of the university. He was a veteran from the Nationalist army and had many fascinating battle stories. I often glued to him when he recalled the civil war against the Communists. "Oh boy!" He used to start his battle stories with an exclamation. Then he proceeded with more exclamations, "Those red soldiers were ghosts! They often popped up out of the blue. But in a twinkle, they vanished. There was no way you could get them!"

Father also wanted to build up my diction skill when I was young. I remember that he urged me strongly to enter a speech tournament when I got into junior high. I was hesitant to compete with senior high schoolmates. But he kept on urging me to have more confidence.

Unfortunately, he was hospitalized two days before the tournament in my school. In order to coach me continuously, he advised me on his sick bed and arranged a rehearsal for me in front his doctors and nurses. I received only a fourth prize in my speech competition, but without Father's coaching, I would not have had that intensified starter on my voice and diction.

As the gates of my memory opened up, recollections of Father continually came back to my mind. I still remembered vividly, at the outset of Sino-Japanese War, how Father and Mother evacuated my sisters and me from Nanjing. At first, they sent us to our grandparents in nearby Jurong County.

It was on the morning of August 15 of 1937, the day the Japanese started to bomb Nanjing. During the Japanese bombing, my sisters and I hid ourselves around the railway station. The Japanese pilots were very arrogant. They came down so low that we could even see their faces. The railway station was in a mess. Not until late that night could we arrive in Qiaotouzhen, the town where our grandparents lived.

Father was then working at the Nationalist military headquarters. In the first phase of the War, he had been dispatched to various war theaters. Mother had no reason to stay alone in Nanjing, so she quickly joined us in Qiaotouzhen. However, the invading Japanese army advanced rapidly toward Nanjing. Very soon, it became clear that Jurong County might be the next battleground.

Therefore, almost at the last minute, Mother brought grandmother and all the family members to escape to Hankou through the Yangzi River. Tragically, Grandfather decided to stay behind to take care of his college.

The river boat on the Yangzi River was compacted with refugees. Each inch of its deck was occupied. People had to bribe to get on. There were nine of us. In addition to my three sisters and me, Mother also brought with her my grandmother, youngest uncle, my aunt and her newly wed husband. Thanks to God! Mother managed to get us all on board one by one. The nine of us arrived in Hankou after midnight the next day and went to a family friend's home.

At the time, Hankou was the hub of evacuees from eastern China. The nine of us arrived there after midnight the next day. No one knew where we should go after Hankou, so we went to a family friend's home first.

A real miracle occurred at that juncture. Only several hours after our arrival, Father suddenly appeared at the door of our family friend's house. He had just evacuated to Hankou, and had learned from another friend of our escape, so he rushed to us immediately. Father was tremendously relieved to see us out of danger, but Grandfather's staying in the war zone caused him new worry.

From military sources, it was reported that Jurong County had already fallen into Japanese hands. Communications were cut down. The Japanese army was poised to take Nanjing. Its next target would be Hankou, the bottleneck of Chinese evacuation. After meeting us, Father did not think we should stay on there, and decided to send us upstream the Yangzi to go back to our native province Sichuan.

Now the Nationalist military headquarters was in Hankou. Father stayed with his colleagues in a makeshift lodge. Only in off-duty hours could he come to see us for a while. However, it was incredible that he made the travel arrangements for all of us to go to Chongqing by boat in two days.

Before we embarked on our river journey, Father dropped by one evening to check on our preparations. Casually, he found my shoes were worn out. He bent over to hug me and said gently, "You can't leave Hankou like this. Let's go buy a new pair." He bought a new pair of "Paja" shoes, an expensive brand from Italy. Up until today, whenever I see the name "Paja," it instantly brings back memories of Father's love.

Finally, boarding time arrived. Everyone was happy that we would sail upstream to Chongqing and leave the war zone farther behind. Father came to see us off at the river front, but when numbers were counted, we suddenly found that our youngest uncle was missing. He had stayed with Father the night before, so we thought he would come by himself.

Father was devastated with disbelief. With grandfather in war zone, he felt that it was his utmost duty to take care of the whole family. His youngest brother was only sixteen years old then and needed his protection. Since his youngest brother was with him in his official makeshift lodge, he immediately rushed back to the lodge after sending us off.

But again, to his disbelief, the only thing he found in his makeshift lodge was a note left by his youngest brother saying that he was going overseas through Guangzhou. It was wartime and battles were waging on many fronts. Military officers were not allowed to leave their posts without permission. But Father was so anxious to get back his brother that without a second thought of military discipline, he went to the railway station in no time.

Following his youngest brother's route, he took a train heading south all the way to Hengyoung. At each stop, he used the station's loud speaker to call his brother's name. He hoped to find his youngest brother and persuade him to come back, but no one answered or responded to his calls.

Father fell ill after his chase ended in failure. Confined in bed with a high fever, he almost lost track of the war events. The Japanese forces were encroaching on Hankou. When he awoke in his makeshift lodge two days later, he found his bodyguard had fled with his wallet and belongings. Hankou would fall to the Japanese. He was ordered to evacuate to Chongqing immediately.

In the meantime, through Father's arrangements, those of us who went upstream of the Yangzi regained our security and normalcy quickly. Father's good friend Wang Zhifei, who I always called "Uncle Wang," met us at the Chongqing wharf and immediately put us under his care. Through his splendid lift, we were instantly transformed from war refugees to honorary guests.

As the chief engineer of a big military factory in Chongqing, Uncle Wang Zhifei had considerable influence around the city. During the late 1920s, he had been working under Father, when Father was the head of the Guiyang Power Plant in Guizhou Province. Therefore, following traditional Chinese values, he always respected Father as his boss. Grandmother, Mother and all of us stayed in his residence almost a month. He treated us with impeccable courtesy and rendered us help in our needs.

For my schooling, Uncle Wang Zhifei wanted me to have no interruption, so he helped me to enter the Bashu Middle School immediately. Bashu was then the best secondary school in Chongqing. In reflection, I had learned much more there than in other high schools I attended. Chongqing was then China's wartime capital, and it had a severe housing shortage problem. When Father joined us from Hankou later, however, Uncle Wang Zhifei leased to us one of his downtown houses.

The elegant three-story house was located on Laojie (Old Street). In the hilly city of Chongqing, a multi-floor house often had its top floor on one street and the rest on other streets. The layout of the Laojie house was exactly like that. Each floor had two suites and a patio, which led to different streets. Since we rented only the top floor on Laojie, we always called it the Old Street house.

During 1939 and 1940, the Japanese bombed Chongqing daily. Mother evacuated to the suburbs. My sisters and I were in boarding schools. But Father stayed in the Old Street house to work in his nearby office. Since that was an ideal location, some of Father's colleagues also moved in to keep him company.

During those bombing days, I often went with Mother on weekends to the Old Street house. The Japanese bombing had devastated the whole neighborhood. What were left were mostly skeletons of the houses around. Many broken walls still stood up here and there. There was a tall one specifically towering over us. But by a miracle, our rented Old Street house somehow retained intact.

It was in the fall and the rainy reason had started. One late Friday afternoon, Father was still in office when we got to the Old Street house. The incessant rain dripped lazily and wrapped the sky in a mist. Everything seemed saggy and sticky. Most of the room windows of the Old Street house were facing a shared patio. If one stood on it, a part of the Yangzi River would come in sight on a sunny day, but all was blurred that weekend.

Mother went to the market for groceries, and I stayed alone in Father's study. While scanning things at Father's desk against the window, I saw a stocky man in military uniform come onto the patio from the other suite of the house. Sauntering on the patio for a while, he peeked through the window and found me. "Hi, young man!" he called. "Your father still not home?" A big smile came across his face.

I told him that Father was still in office, and we were waiting him for dinner. The military man paused, looking at me attentively. "Come out, young man," He waved after a while, as if wishing to rescue me from my boredom. "Come on to my room. I have treats for you."

In politeness, I followed the stocky man to his room in the other side of the house. Without telling me who he was, he offered me candies and peanuts, and started to quiz me as if he knew me: "My young friend, have you read the *Story of the Three Kingdoms*?" That was a popular Chinese historical novel depicting the exciting events of 300 A.D. School kids would be ashamed if they did not have some knowledge of it. I answered in the positive and stressed that I had browsed it twice.

The military man nodded with a grin of satisfaction. "Then tell me, young man," he leaned over and began to pepper me with questions. "What strategies did the three kingdoms use most in wars against each other?"

At the age of thirteen, how could I be expected to know military strategies? I stammered and could not come up with a ready answer. The stocky military man was amused. "Then, tell me this. How did the three kingdoms use the natural elements to fight their enemies?" He rephrased his question. "You know there are fire, water and wind, don't you?"

Thanks to those clues, I slowly came up with some famous battles that used fire, water and wind between the three kingdoms. The man patted me on the shoulder with hearty laughter. "Don't you know, my little friend, your father is great!" He suddenly changed the subject. "Your father has made very valuable suggestions on our air defense. You must have heard the warning sirens and seen the colored balloons that warn us that the Japanese planes are coming. Your father was involved in designing those systems!"

Father seldom talked about his work at home. Those stories were fascinating to me. The stocky military man tried to impress me even more. "You know what, my young friend? Your father has been sent to test our first self-made water bombs. That was a few months ago. A special car took him to Leshan and back. We all admire him in our office. You should listen to your father at the staff meetings. His study and forecast about the European war was excellent …" Regretfully, Father had returned from office. I was called back for dinner before the military officer finished his talk.

The rain intensified from drippings to downpours that night. It came down in sheets sometimes. A catastrophe was poised to happen the next day.

Father was accustomed to sorting his mail on Saturdays. A letter dumbfounded him that morning. It came from his friend, offering some information about Grandfather's death. We already knew that Grandfather had been murdered by bandits in 1938, but we did not know who the bandits were. Father had been incensed for not being able to get the facts. He showed me the letter and called aloud to Mother, asking her to come to read and share the new information.

Mother was cooking in the kitchen at the other side of the house. The only route from our suite to the kitchen was through an entrance hallway. After some delay, she finally came over from the kitchen while complaining that Father had interrupted her cooking. But before she could sit down after her arrival, a thunderous bang shook the whole house. The whirling wind of dust instantly covered our room.

Someone was screaming in the other suite. Father rushed to the patio and saw his colleague holding onto a window frame. I followed Father and found it was the military officer I had talked to the day before. His room had sunk and there was no floor for him to stand on. His feet were dangling dangerously in the air.

The military officer was holding onto his window sill. Father used all his muscles to pull out him from the window frame. It was amazing to see the stocky military officer's strength. He had jumped in the air to hold onto the window sill when the floor collapsed underneath of his feet. His forehead was bleeding. Mother came to help put bandages on his wounds.

At that moment, nobody knew what had happened. Father looked around and found the damaged wall that had been overlooking our house was gone. Apparently, it had fallen on our house. Mother suddenly recalled that she had been in the kitchen before what happened. Where was the kitchen now? She became aware that Father's bodyguard was assisting her in preparing our lunch. She immediately asked us to find the bodyguard.

The military officer was lying on the patio. Heeding Mother's call, he raised his head and responded, "There is no kitchen left. It sunk with my room. The entire hallway has probably collapsed."

We began to yell for help. The two lower floors of the house must have damaged by the same catastrophe. Rescuers came to attend the injured first, and then they brought us out through a ladder landing on another street. They confirmed that our entrance hallway and kitchen had vanished. After searching through the rubbles, they finally found the body of Father's bodyguard.

That was one of our tragedies in the Sino-Japanese War. Father and Mother believed that the letter informing us of Grandfather's death had saved Mother's life. She would have gone down with the kitchen if Father had not called her for the letter.

Father went overseas as a military attaché after 1942. He wrote to me frequently when I was in Wuhan University. Once he sent me a watch in the most difficult period of the war. Most of us ate and clothed poorly in college, depending primarily on subsidies from the government. Pocket money was a trump card for most of us in our student life.

To convert the watch into cash, I went to a flea market first. There were simply no watches for sale, so nobody could quote a price for me. Then I went to a store selling the used merchandise. The owner asked me to price it myself. In a bold move, I set the price of my watch as 200 yuans. It was a big figure at the time. Unbelievably, however, the watch was sold within an hour. Thankfully, the money provided me with a new jacket. It also enabled me to visit local restaurants many times with friends.

Father was still overseas when World War II ended. He accomplished one of his cherished goals by locating his youngest brother in 1945. After learning his brother was in the Philippines, he immediately sent two thousand U.S. dollars, asking an American friend to sponsor his youngest brother to go to college in the United States.

When I graduated from Wuhan University, Father returned from his overseas assignments. After a brief trip to Xikang, I went to Nanjing and found a big and comfortable new home. It was in Chengge Old Alley, an elegant and quiet neighborhood in the center of the Nationalist capital. Father and Mother had welcomed my grandmother to our house after the war. To my surprise, the first thing he gave me was a wardrobe. It was a reminder that now that the war was over, I should say goodbye to my old apparel.

At that time, my two elder sisters Hwang Chun and Hwang Lian and their families were in Shanghai. My second brother-in-law Wan Changtai introduced me to work at the newly formed Board of Supplies. My father's old friend Zhu Ziwu happened to be the head of the department of storage and transportation over there, so he quickly transferred me to work in his department.

But Father wanted me to proceed with my education. As he had done for his youngest brother, he sent another two thousand dollars to his old

American friend to sponsor me to have graduate studies in the United States. Two thousand U.S. dollars was a hefty sum for a college student in the mid 1940s. I shall always be grateful to Father for sending me to the land of freedom and opportunity.

When Father came to Beijing at the end of 1954, I wanted to share many unforgettable memories with him. There were things I wished to report to him and get his advice about. He probably had many things to tell me too.

But as mentioned before, our living space was small, and the goings were tough. Not until six years later, after Olivia and four of our children left for freedom, did I get the chance to talk to Father privately in depth.

8

Happiness Under Hardship

On February 5 of 1955, I came back from the old Longfu Hospital in the afternoon. With excitement, I reported to Mother and Father that Olivia had given birth to a baby girl. They smiled radiantly and inquired about Olivia's condition. I told them that Olivia and the baby were doing fine and would be home in a few days. Mother and Father were ecstatic and in a mood of celebration.

David was playing around by himself. Phillip was crawling and tossing in Grandfather's lap. They looked curious but could not comprehend what was going on. Mother had my belated brunch ready. While bringing noodles and appetizers to me, she kept on murmuring to Father, "Did I tell you that I knew we would have a granddaughter this time? I never miscalculate a birth!"

Holding Phillip in his arms, Father edged closer to my seat and asked, "Have you and Kailan given thought about the baby's name?" Father and Mother only called Olivia by her Chinese name. According to Chinese tradition, the grandfather was the one in a family had the honor of naming his descendants.

"Kailan's family is from Hainan Island." I began to brief Father about Olivia's considerations. "Even though her family has settled down in Malaya and Singapore for a few generations, they still take Hainan as their native land. Hainan is called 'Qiongzhou' in Chinese. Kailan wishes to have the character 'qiong' in her baby daughter's Chinese name."

Father nodded in contemplation with a broad grin. While he was brooding, I made a suggestion. "You have designated 'Li' as all your grandchildren's middle name. How about we call our baby girl Liqiong? Qiong is homonymous with Jean. We may call her 'Jean' in English."

Father beamed with delight. "Don't you know 'Qiong' means 'beautiful jade' in Chinese?" He stood up and walked around with Phillip. "Liqiong will be a beautiful name for our little baby girl. Please tell Kailan her choice is excellent!"

As the family grew bigger, our living quarters on Bag Lane seemed to become smaller. The front porch was spacious but inside was congested. Other than our mid-sized bedroom, there was only a large living room and a tiny kitchen.

When our parents arrived, Olivia and I partitioned our large living room by a big piece of canvas hanging from the ceiling. The inner part served as the sleeping quarters for our parents. The outer part became a multi-purpose area. With a small set of sofas in one corner, it survived to be a small living room. After putting a big table and few chairs in its middle, it became our dining and working place. Then with the piano sitting in another corner, it could be taken as our music room. Finally, should guests come for an overnight or so stay, we would put mattresses on the floor to accommodate them.

Olivia's cousin Meifeng was then in Beijing. She had once brought a group of her friends to our house and enjoyed our guest accommodations. Some forty years later when she visited us in Washington, she still remembered fondly the melody of my father's snoring through the partitioning canvas.

There was no plumbing or sewage system in Bag Lane courtyard house. All tenets depended on a single faucet for water in a corner of the courtyard. Thus, each household had to fill up its vases and containers each day. Since there was no sewage, used water was dumped at a few designated spots. Therefore, hauling buckets in and out was a daily chore for all residents in the courthouse compound.

That was our way of life at the Bag Lane house. It was congested and inconvenient, but we all seemed to be happy and contented. The hardship had not bogged Mother down at all. She resumed her specialized cooking and made various kinds of pickles and beans. In addition to the fabulous dishes she cooked, we all enjoyed very much the special meat pancakes she made.

Groceries in Beijing had been under tight control since the Korean War. Many staples and delicacies disappeared. Once in a while, though, various kinds of fruit, such as the tangerines, would reappear for a while and then vanish. Thus, grocery shopping became a kind of hide-and-seek game.

In addition to taking care of the grandchildren, Mother was the one in the family who hunted for groceries. She had to buy items when they were available even if they were not in immediate need. Without a refrigerator, however, she could only buy dried or canned food. There was no storage facility in the house, so the only place for her to store anything would be underneath our beds. Poor Mother and Olivia! They often had to crawl on the floor to search for their needed items.

After giving birth to Jean, Olivia's asthma attacks unexpectedly flared up badly. When the weather turned colder, she could hardly stop her severe coughing. Since medicine from the hospital did not help, many friends suggested that she consider alternative treatment. There were renowned Chinese traditional doctors in Beijing. Some had even served in the Qing Dynasty Court before. One friend recommended Olivia to a doctor named Xiao Longyou, one of the most outstanding four.

Traditional Chinese medicine has served the Chinese people for thousands of years. It was embedded in Chinese culture, emphasizing the relationship between man and nature, applying chiefly herbal medicines. My grandfather was a "layman physician" in traditional Chinese medicine, and he had been pretty good at it, so I was not uncomfortable visiting a traditional Chinese doctor at all.

Dr. Xiao Longyou lived in his clinic. His living room was impressive. I was attracted by the beautiful Chinese couplets and paintings hanging against the walls. While I was trying to read something on one of the couplets, a man walked in with a bodyguard.

Well dressed in a tailored tunic, the man nodded to us in courtesy and quietly took a seat in the waiting area. But his bodyguard seemed to be edgy and swaggered around to show that his boss was somebody. Seeing that Olivia was the person ahead of his boss, he talked to the receptionist, and he wanted his boss to be attended before her.

"What are you doing, you stupid dummy?" His boss became embarrassed and annoyed. "You think we are still home?" The man ordered his bodyguard to be quiet.

In admonishing his bodyguard, the man used Sichuan dialect. Sichuan was my native province, so the dialect immediately aroused my attention. I looked at the man more closely, and I suddenly found that he was none other than Liu Wenhui, one of the most famous Sichuan warlords. Liu Wenhui had become the Governor of the Xikang Province after being chased out from Sichuan Province. I happened to know his niece, and I had once visited Xikang Province myself.

While we were waiting in line for the doctor, I took the initiative to introduce myself to Liu Wenhui, and I inquired about his niece's well-being. Liu Wenhui was surprised and delighted to learn that I was a classmate of his niece Liu Yuanshen. He informed me that Liu Yuanshen was presently studying at the Marxist-Leninist Institute in Beijing, and he seldom heard from her now.

When I told Liu Wenhui that I had visited Xikang Province in 1946, he became animated and asked me about my trip. Regrettably, before we could continue to chat, Olivia was called to see the doctor, so I had to leave. It was a pity that I never had a chance to see him or his niece Liu Yuanshen again.

However, the encounter with Liu Wenhui brought back my memories of Xikang. I had taken the trip in the summer of 1946, right after I graduated from Wuhan University. I was stuck in Chongqing at that time, preparing to go to Nanjing to join my parents, but no transportation was available. Hundreds of thousands of people were still waiting to get back to their homes after the end of World War II.

Dr. Wan Quansheng, a close family friend, happened to be in Chongqing with his wife at that juncture. Both of them were working in Xikang and were ready to go back with two truckloads of medical supplies. They invited me to have a free tour of Xikang. I had never seen the hinterland of China before. It would provide me with an excellent chance to go to somewhere near Tibet, so I accepted their invitation with excitement.

Dr. Wan Quansheng was the head of the health department of the Xikang Provincial government, and also the chief of the Kangding Hospital. On our way, we stopped first at his home town Yaan, the border city between Xikang and Sichuan.

Xikang was then a de facto independent area, out of control of the Nationalist Government. Opium was openly sold in the markets. There was a wealthy neighborhood in Yaan called the Banyue Pond (Crescent Pond). It was said that one did not have to go far to look for opium. Right in Crescent Pond, there were tons and tons of the stuff. Great amounts of opium were regularly shipped under the escort of military regiments.

However, Liu Wenhui was not an ordinary warlord. He might have harbored a much higher ambition. When the Nationalist government was at war with the Communists, he had given the Communists a free hand in his controlled areas to conduct clandestine activities against the Nationalists. There had been a long and secretive relationship between him and the Communists that could be traced back to the mid 1930s.

I was surprised to read various Communist publications in Kangding, the provincial capital of the Xikang Province. Broadcasts from the Communist base in Yaan could also be heard in Kangding. Apparently, Liu Wenhui and the Communists had a common goal of overthrowing the Nationalist government.

Liu Wenhui had controlled Xikang Province for more than twenty years. He had not yet gotten the chance to rule the entire country although he had certainly entertained the goal. On our way from Yaan to Kangding, we met many local politicians and military officers at various stops.

Some of the local politicians were attracted by Dr. Wan Quansheng's two truckloads of medical supplies. They stopped us and held up the trucks more than once, claiming that they were all Liu Wenhui's men, so they were entitled to a share of the "spoils."

As one of them said, "We all work for the governor, so we ought to get a part of what he gets!"

Dr. Wan Quansheng did not have enough clout to fence off the blackmails. Thus, a number of wranglings took place. During the bargaining, one local politician bragged that he had been a loyal lieutenant of the governor for years. "Don't you know that? We are all fortunate to work under the future ruler of China!" He lectured Dr. Wan Quansheng. "You should closely study the governor's countenance! The fortune tellers have assured us that the governor is a born emperor!"

Nevertheless, after opening up some of the medical packages, the local politicians found that they had no real need for those supplies. Besides, it was hard for them to learn how to use the tricky equipment, so they finally allowed us to continue our journey.

Governor Liu Wenhui published a book in 1946 entitled *Ten Speeches on Building New Xikang*. I was in the audience when he delivered one of those speeches. As far as I could recall, it was a fanfare full of pomposity in the Provincial Government's auditorium. When Liu Wenhui entered and left the auditorium, a band always played marshal music in high volume. During his speech, the audience applauded cheerfully whenever he made a pause. His theme on that day was: "One day, Xikang should be the 'Switzerland' of China."

Xikang was a mountainous region with rich resources. Liu Wenhui's speech was visionary. It could have been a blueprint to develop the area if it was not merely a political platform. In our journey, we had climbed the famous Erlang Mountain, where the Chinese Communist Red Army had also gone across in their long retreat in 1930s.

There was a song entitled "The Erlang Mountain" composed by the Communists in memory of their "Twenty-Five-Thousand-Mile Long

March." In and outside of China, I was still able to visualize the Erlang mountain slopes and their colorful wild flowers. Beyond the Erlang Mountain, the lofty Daxue Mountain still stood in my vision.

Climbing over the Erlang Mountain, we reached the Luding Bridge over the Dadu River, another historic site of the Communists' Long March. It was said that a critical battle had been fought on the suspension bridge over Dadu River. Today's deafening action movies with their ear splitting sound tracks might be able to recreate the exciting battle scene. But when we walked over the bridge, all was quiet and calm.

Xikang had many small lakes with crystal waters. Local people called them "haizi," meaning the "little seas." I started my horseback riding there. It was such an enjoyment to ride along a trail beside a beautiful "haizi" and watch the Tibetan caravans passing by. Kangding was the doorway to Tibet, so Tibetans came and went through the area every day with their caravans.

There was a huge cauldron, I remember, hanging in front of an eatery on the outskirts of Kangding. Freshly cooked beef and mutton from the cauldron were served there. A group of local friends urged me to go and enjoy the spicy "meat breakfast." I went with them with excitement every morning. But after a week, my nose began bleeding. I thought it might have been caused by the high altitude of Xikang, but the doctors thought my nose bleeding might have something to do with the meat. Thus, I reluctantly gave up my meat breakfast.

Kangding had a small theater and a photo shop at the time. I went to the theater once, and I enjoyed a Sichuan opera performed by a troupe from Chengdu. As for the photo shop, I became its constant customer.

The owner of the photo shop was a pleasant and knowledgeable man. I learned from him many things about the Tibetans and their religion. He had sets of pictures depicting how a little boy was chosen to be a living Buddha. Another set of pictures showed the proceedings for the boy to assume his living Buddha's title at a monastery. Fascinated by the pictures, I bought two complete sets from the owner, and I left them home as part of my treasure trove. Unfortunately, they were discarded when Father went to Communist prison in Chongqing.

In the year of 1955 back at home in Beijing, Olivia had been continuously suffering from her asthma attacks. After various treatments in hospitals failed, the Chinese medicine also did not help very much. Therefore, for a year she was almost entirely confined at home. But while she was absent in the office, another political upheaval started. The newly erupted turmoil was called the "Wiping Out All Hidden Anti-Revolutionary Elements

Campaign." Paradoxically, Olivia's sick leave exempted her from some horrible encounters.

Once again, the literary circles were the targeted area, and the People's Publishing House for Literature had become the epic center of the political earthquake. Because Shu Wu was an editor of our Department of Chinese Classical Literature, the head of the Department Nie Gannu was immediately implicated.

Hu Feng had been considering himself as the most important disciple of Lu Xun. He had written a 300,000 words long letters to the Communists to complain about their literary policies. The Communists were anxiously looking for a wedge to break up and wipe out Hu Feng and his group, now they found it from Shu Wu.

Mao Zedong was livid at Hu Feng's criticism. Under his order, the Communist Party organ *People's Daily* published the letters Hu Feng sent to his followers one by one. Prefaced to each of the Hu Feng's letter, there was an Editor's Note written by Mao Zedong himself, branding Hu Feng and his group as "hidden anti-revolutionaries." Gradually, as the purge intensified and widened to become a nationwide "Wiping Out All Hidden Anti-Revolutionary Elements Campaign."

Most people did not know Hu Feng wanted to discuss literary policies with the Communists in 1953. Neither could they understand the hair-splitting differences on literature and art between Hu Feng and Communists. To them, the campaign was nothing but another round of political inspection and persecution, except for the people working in literature and art. They faced a life-or-death trial.

Many established literary figures and organizations crumbled overnight. "Counter Revolution" was now a crime under Communist law, so the debate on literary issues was no more an academic exercise. Anyone who disagreed or expressed variant views on Communist official literary policies would end up in jail or exile.

In our Literature Publishing House, the existing chief Feng Xuefeng had been already relegated to a figurehead in early 1955. However, when the "Wiping Out All Hidden Anti-Revolutionary Elements Campaign" started, he was called back to mobilize the Publishing House staff.

I remember Feng Xuefeng behaved strangely that day. His clothes were tattered and his hair was rumpled. When he stepped onto the podium to mobilize the audience, he shouted to denounce the counter revolutionists. He looked so enraged that his face turned red. Saliva kept on shooting out from his mouth when he condemned Hu Feng and others. He appeared to be a completely different person.

I also remember that in order to convince the audience, Feng Xuefeng repeated again and again one sentence: "If we don't wipe out those hidden counter revolutionists today, hundreds of thousands of our heads will be chopped off by them tomorrow!" Those words had somehow registered in my mind, because they sounded not like his usual vocabulary. As the campaign got more ferocious, the same sentence was repeated by other Communist operatives, so it was most likely a standard Communist script, not Feng Xuefeng's own words.

Why did Shu Wu betray Hu Feng and make so many literary figures victims of the Communists? Half a century has elapsed and the reasons are still unknown. Maybe only Shu Wu himself could answer the question.

In the editorial departments of our Publishing House, in addition to Nie Gannu, the notable victims included Niu Ding, a poet and editor of contemporary Chinese literature, and Lu Ying, a literary researcher stationed in our official compound. Some colleagues suddenly disappeared without a trace.

As the mesh spread wider and wider, no one could be sure that he would not become a target of the campaign. Once again, political inspections intensified. Each person's background was under double or triple checks. All staff members were reorganized into mix groups to attend the struggle meetings.

I could never forget a horrible scene in one of our group meetings. An old administrative clerk was struggled and arrested in front of us. For almost an hour, one campaign operative kept on pointing out that among us there was still one person who had not confessed his counter-revolutionary crime. Since nobody except the campaign operatives knew who the target was, a hush descended on the whole room. Many ducked their heads to avoid attention. Some even began to panic, fearing that he or she was the alleged culprit.

Two more public security officers walked into the meeting room. The tension escalated even higher. After a lull, several activists in the campaign stood up. "Look, who is trembling?"

One of them yelled. "Look whose face has turned pale?"

Another one shouted, "He has committed crimes, but he doesn't confess!"

Like a tightened string before snapping, a few in the meeting were so frightened that they began to tremble, including the unnamed target. His face looked like a sheet of white paper. At the last moment, as in a stage show, one public security officer stood up and announced the target's name, accusing him for being a landlord and assisting the Nationalists during the civil war. The victim was handcuffed and led away in front of us.

At the terrifying scene, I could not help reviewing my own situation. I had a feeling that I was isolated and that I might be a target sooner or later. The next day, as predicted, I was called to the campaign office. In my mind, the Halicrafter radio had finally put me in grave jeopardy. But to my surprise, a campaign operative only questioned me about why I had associated with persons with diplomatic passports of the Nationalist government in the United States.

That was a vague question with complicated implications. My answer to the campaign operative was that, as a student, I had no means to check the passports of the ones I met. But instantly, I became aware that I had been under surveillance of certain underground Communist agents in the United States. They must have compiled a dossier on me. The campaign operative made no comment on my answer, but he asked me to come to the office at dawn the next day. I was scheduled to attend the city-wide outdoor struggle meetings in the ensuing days.

Outdoor gigantic struggle meetings were held in the city's parks. Campaign targets from various places had been sent there to learn. I remember I had to go to our Publishing House before sunrise to be escorted to those struggle meetings. When I got there, however, it was too early to leave, so I was told to wait alone in my own office. While campaign operatives and some activists conducted their meetings in separate rooms, I felt like a lonely defendant waiting for trial.

Trucks were ready to bring us to the struggle meetings. When mounting time came, all the potential targets stood on a sidewalk. I found that there were half a dozen of us. It gave me a kind of consolation that I was actually not alone. The campaign operatives began to line us up. Each potential target was sandwiched by two activists, one in the front and one at the back. We were instructed to remember our position and never go astray.

I did not know the guy ahead of me, but I was sure the female colleague behind me was an editor from another department. She happened to be Zhou Yan's girlfriend. Thanks to her I stayed in place! She helped get me back on line whenever I took a variant direction.

Obviously, the purpose of sending potential targets to gigantic struggle meetings was to show them their destiny if they chose not to "confess."

People might care more for their own lives when watching others being tortured or executed. It is said that the Czar of Russia had once scared the Russian writer Fyodor Dostoyevski by putting him before a firing squad. In those gigantic struggle meetings, I did feel like I had been put before a political firing squad.

When I was a student in Wuhan University, Professor Yang Renbian had offered a course on the French Revolution. I had sat in some of his lectures dealing with the Reign of Terror. In the "Wiping out All Hidden Anti-Revolutionary Elements Campaign," I could not resist an urge to compare it with the Reign of Terror in the French Revolution.

Interestingly, as a potential target, I had a chance to witness how a real target behaved under persecution. Since the "Wiping Out All Hidden Anti-Revolutionary Elements Campaign" started, I heard that Nie Gannu had been detained in his office. No one expected that he too would be sent to the outdoor gigantic struggle meetings. Each time he was the last one to be escorted out of his office. In the early morning, in his sleepy walks, he always brought his bedding with him as if he were being transferred to another prison.

Annoyed by his sloppiness, the campaign operatives always snatched away his bedding before putting him on the truck. They did not like the way Nie Gannu was comparing struggling meetings to prisons. I did not know Nie Gannu personally, but I had once played Chinese chess with him when were in the Literary Editorial Division. He was eccentric, but a genuine human being.

I never figured out why the Communists would persecute Nie Gannu so severely. He had been sent to prison in the 1960s and 1970s. Neither could I understand why the Communists had to brand Hu Feng and his followers as counter revolutionaries. Hu Feng and his followers had long been Communist sympathizers. Their group was small, numbering not even more than a hundred. They never had the structure of a real organization. But the Communists had chosen to use their sledgehammer to kill flies.

Because Hu Feng's group was tiny, Mao Zedong added Hu Shi and his followers to his enemy list. Hu Shi was one of the most important cultural leaders of modern China and had a profound influence in Chinese academic and literary circles since 1919. At the time of the "Wiping Out All Hidden Anti-Revolutionary Elements Campaign," Hu Shi was in the United States. Therefore, the campaign against him was actually aimed at his spiritual followers who remained in Mainland China.

Hu Shi had been corresponding with a lot of people since 1919. Unfortunately when he left Mainland China, he left his belongings in Beijing, including his private correspondence, so the Communists acquired a treasure when they seized Hu Shi's letter collections in 1949. Through the letters, they found many prominent Chinese intellectuals had corresponded with Hu Shi. But those prominent Chinese intellectuals were completely in the dark, without knowing the Communists had their records while being struggled against in the Campaign.

More than forty years later, the Communists unabashedly published Hu Shi's private correspondence. Only until then did many prominent Chinese academic and literary figures realize that they had been in a trap all these years.

During the "Wiping Out All Hidden Anti-Revolutionary Elements Campaign," I never talked about my situation at home. Father and Mother had come to live with us only a year ago. Olivia was sick. I did not want to disturb them.

My family was my sanctuary. Amidst the uncertainties, Olivia and I were expecting to welcome another family member next summer.

9

The False Thaw

Pauline was born on July 22, 1956. Upon her arrival, an unexpected political "thaw" had set in. Suddenly, political suppression seemed to be something of the past. The tension that had hung over all of us lifted overnight. In their disbelief, many people found it easier to breathe than before.

Grandfather took the initiative to give his newly born granddaughter a Chinese name. "Since the baby's sister had adopted a character from her mother's native island," he mused, "why not give the baby girl the character 'Po' from Singapore, where her mother grew up, and call her 'Lipo'?" Olivia agreed to the suggestion wholeheartedly. She decided to name our new baby girl "Pauline" in English because "Po" and "Pau" are close in pronunciation.

Pauline had a long way to go before she could recognize what was going on. She could not know that her mother had gradually regained her health after asthma began tapering off. Her grandmother was elated to add one more granddaughter under her care. At the same time, her grandfather's life had taken a turn for the better. He had put on a new tunic, rekindled many of his interests, and resumed some of his social activities. His language skills in German, English and Russian could now be put to use because he had been hired by a translation agency.

Pauline also could not know that her brother David had started to learn the piano and that her second brother Phillip was taught Chinese characters by Grandfather at home. Of course, she had no way of knowing that her parents were more relaxed at work and now several of their translated books were displayed on the shelves of the bookstores.

Actually, the reversal of the Reign of Terror to normal life was not unique in China. It was part of what was called the "thaw" in the socialist camp in 1956, starting first in Soviet Union, and then spreading to Eastern Europe. China under Mao Zedong was only reluctantly following suit.

Nevertheless, the Chinese Communists suddenly put on smiling faces and loosened the nooses and yokes they placed on the population. The Chinese intellectuals were bewildered and could not figure out why the Communists made such an about-face. I was puzzled too by the drastic change.

One day I went to the library to scan the foreign newspapers. Accidentally, I came across a copy of the *Worker's Daily*, the official organ of the American Communist Party. It was permitted to circulate in Mainland China, because it was a communist publication. In it, I was astonished to find the report Khrushchev delivered at the Twentieth Congress of the Soviet Communist Party.

Like being struck by a thunderbolt, I was shocked when I read the crimes committed by Stalin. Khrushchev was then the general secretary of the Soviet Communist Party. If his report was true, it meant that the whole world had been blinded and that we had been living under false propaganda all these years.

I could hardly stand still after reading Khrushchev's report. Stalin had been worshiped as god in the Communist world for so long. Now his crimes had been openly exposed. He was falling from his throne in disgrace. I was anxious to share the information with others, but the Chinese Communists never published Khrushchev's report. Nobody had been informed of Stalin's crimes. I could only search for more information by myself.

Khrushchev's report reminded me that I had been secluded. I had majored in political science and international relations in college, but I had given them up ever since my return to Mainland China. In "thought reform," the only information people could get was from Communist newspapers, but the Communist newspapers were mostly engaging in propaganda. I felt ashamed to let myself be cut off from the outside world.

Now the *Worker's Daily* seemed to have brought me out of the cocoon. I told myself that I should read more foreign newspapers such as the *New York Times*. But foreign newspapers were under extremely tight control by the Communists. The only place for me to find foreign newspapers was the editorial office of the *Translation Monthly* magazine.

I knew the editor of *Translation Monthly* Xiao Qian because he was one of our translators, so I went to his office to have a try. To my disappointment, however, they had only the Sunday literary supplements of the *New York Times*, not its daily newspaper. And the supplements in their possession were incomplete and outdated. More than that, all approved readers were only permitted to scan them at specific times and in a particular room. I could not help being frustrated when the room closed before I could finish my scanning of a specific "ancient" issue.

The unhappy experience triggered some of my not-so-far-off memories. I recalled that, only six years ago, nobody ever had any difficulty buying newspapers in New York City. Sometimes, people only found it hard to dispose of the heavy bundles after scanning them. Now here in Beijing, I was not even allowed to finish my scanning of the outdated supplements. What an irony!

In Communist China, only the powerful and the privileged could have a chance to read "capitalist publications." While reflecting on my predicament, I could only blame myself for getting into this disfranchisement. With no way out, I let myself drift back to the old routine. In resignation, I tried again to duck my head in my work, paying little attention to the political winds whirling outside.

Khrushchev's report had started de-Stalinization in the Soviet Union. In contrast, the general Chinese public was entirely in the dark. The high echelon of the Chinese Communist Party leadership put up a tranquil facade. Half a century later, however, we learned that they were very nervous and busy in that year. More than twenty volumes of documents and news digests had been translated for the inner circle of the Communist leadership to monitor the reactions of the world towards de-Stalinization. .

What were the Chinese Communist's real feelings toward de-Stalinization? Mao Zedong was obviously unhappy about it from the outset. He was afraid that once de-Stalinization started, many Communist dictators would fall. Sooner or later, it would be his turn. He decided to prevent that from happening whatever costs.

At the outset, Mao did not challenge the de-Stalinization move of his "Big Brother" in the socialist camp. He even made a complete about-face by abruptly terminating his ferocious "Wiping out All Hidden Anti-Revolutionary Elements Campaign." That was a notice to the world that he was following the Soviets to make a "thaw" in China. To publicize his new move, he ordered the Chinese Communist Party to show a friendly face to the intellectuals.

I remember that Zhou Enlai took the first move. In the summer of 1956, he gave a big report to leading intellectuals, redefining the role played by intellectuals in the Chinese revolution. Contrary to previous Chinese Communist doctrines on intellectuals, he praised the intellectuals' contributions, acknowledging that they had been treated wrongly sometimes.

He emphasized that intellectuals were indispensable in building socialism in China.

In his long speech, Zhou Enlai promised that the Chinese Communist Party would follow a "Four Not's" policy. From then on, cadres were not allowed to do four things in the revolutionary ranks. First, they should not "grab someone's tail" to put him in trouble. "Tails" referred to the long braids men wore in the Qing Dynasty. Grabbing a man's tail meant that he had found his fault and would not release him. Second, the cadres should not "cap a hat" on someone's head to label him with titles of the enemies. Thirdly, they should not "hit someone with sticks." That meant people should not be heavily attacked or punished in the revolutionary ranks. Lastly and most importantly, the cadres should not "dig out the roots" of their fellow comrades to struggle against them.

In the audience, there were victims of Communist tactics in the past. Zhou Enlai's talks made them felt good but were too good for them to believe. They did not know what was going behind the scenes, but they doubted that Zhou Enlai and the Communist leadership could keep their promises.

Their experiences told them that "grabbing people's tails," "capping hats on people's heads," "hitting people with sticks" and "digging out people's roots" were the trademark practices of the Chinese Communist Party. No one from the Party had ever openly repudiated those practices. They wondered how the Party could change its operational codes overnight.

About the same time, Marshall Chen Yi gave a talk at another gathering of intellectuals. He had just been appointed Vice Premier and Minister of Foreign Affairs. As a former student from France after World War I, he specifically addressed those students who had just returned from overseas. He knew that many of them had suffered in political campaigns or been put on shelves at their working places. To show sympathy, he used his personal observations and experiences to soothe their wounds and feelings.

"Did you know that Chairman Mao had also been put on a 'cold stool' many times?" he told the audience with a grin. "One was in the mid 1930s when he was in the central Soviet areas." With some humor, he described an episode in the early history of the Chinese Communist Party. "We all know that not until we reached Zunyi in the Long March in 1935, did Chairman Mao become the Party's indisputable leader, so don't be afraid of being put on a 'cold stool' temporarily. Resilience is important! Besides, even cold stools can turn warm if you sit on them long enough!"

Some laughter erupted from the audience. Chen Yi was delighted to get the joyful response. "Let me tell you frankly," he continued lightheartedly. "I have not only been put on a 'cold stool' but also put in jail and gone through a lot of rough treatment. A guy once tried to squeeze a confession out of me by beating me and then holding a hammer over my head. I told him that he could beat me again but not with the hammer. 'You know,' I said to him, 'each of us has only one head. If it's gone, it's gone. You can't get my confession without my head.'" The audience enjoyed and applauded his humor.

Zhou Enlai and Chen Yi were trying to regain trust from the intellectuals. They obviously wanted to put the intellectuals at ease and rekindle their enthusiasm under the Communist rule. In the meantime, a series of new policies were announced to "thaw" the academic institutions and literary circles. Universities and colleges were told to offer degrees to the students. The idea of letting the scholars run the academia was put out for public discussion.

In our Publishing House, we were suddenly asked to draft a personal plan to advance toward socialism. Previously, "housing adjustments," "vacations," and various "material incentives" had been branded as capitalist means of exploiting the workers. They were taboos never to be mentioned, but overnight they were hailed as socialist entitlements. Now each editor was supposed to have an annual vacation of one month. While enjoying the unexpected benefits of the new incentive systems, nobody seemed to be bothered by the old theoretical tenets.

Olivia and I were puzzled by the hullabaloo. We would not dispute the notion that there might be delicious cakes on the "Communist moon." But nobody ever knew what those moon cakes looked and tasted like. We preferred to work on things solid and valuable on earth. As one proverb says, "One bird in hand is better than ten in the woods." So we remained concentrated on our work both in the office and at home.

It was now early November and Beijing became chilly at night. I often stayed late to read or translate in the office, because it was quiet over there. Our office attendant, Lao Li, was diligent and considerate. When he saw me working late, he would add more fuel to the room furnace instead of cleaning it out for the next day.

One night, I was in my office working at my desk. The only light in the room was from my table lamp. Quiet and tranquil, it was a perfect venue for work. All of a sudden, I felt my shoulders grabbed from behind. A familiar voice greeted me. "Hey, Lao Hwang, you are really working hard! I never expected to find you in your office so late."

I was familiar with that voice, so I was not as scared as I should have been. It was Zhang Ruji, one of my best friends! We had not seen or heard from each other since we parted in New York City seven years ago. He had returned to Mainland China before me, but he was not working in Beijing. I never expected to see him especially so late in my office.

Zhang Ruji explained his unannounced visit by saying, "You know, I seldom write letters. Whenever I want to go, I just go. Your wife is very nice. She drew me a map to lead me here."

Among our friends, Zhang Ruji had been regarded as a bit eccentric. Sometimes, he appeared to be quite conceited. He often showed no patience in listening to ideas or remarks he considered superficial. Thus, he was hard to chat with or get along with by many others. Very queerly, though, he and I seemed to be able to understand each other quite well, so we became close friends.

Both Zhang Ruji and I were from Wuhan University. He was an economics major and a year ahead of me. In school, we acknowledged each other's presence, but we never got acquainted. At the time when we were still college students, he did not seem to be interested in regular student activities. He often behaved as if he were superior to others because he already had started to write editorials for a few well-known newspapers such as the *New People's Daily (Xinminbao)*.

Zhang Ruji had an uncle who served as the Nationalist Government representative to the International Labor Organization. Under his uncle's sponsorship, he went to the United States in the 1940s. He came to see me when he passed by Shanghai, and we immediately became friends. I still remember that he left a bunch of Reynolds ballpoint pens with me and another schoolmate. He wanted us to sell those pens to support student movements then spreading across Mainland China. That was the first time I got the impression that he was no longer aloof to events outside of his domain. His actions indicated that he wanted to be involved in real life.

As soon as I arrived in the United States, Zhang Ruji wrote to me very frequently. In his letters, he revealed to me his intellectual loneliness. He told me that he had lost interest in graduate studies. He was working full time as an editor for the old Chinese daily *World Journal* in New York City. He also confided to me that he felt like living in a cultural desert, and he desperately wished to see a green vista, so he invited me several times to go to New York City to have a heart-to-heart talk.

I was then working for my M.A. degree at the University of Maryland. Not until early 1949 did I get the chance to see him when my advisor Dr.

Steinmeyer first brought me to a conference on NATO in Philadelphia and then to Long Island to visit his friends at the United Nations Secretariat.

Dr. Steinmeyer took me to the United Nations because my M.A. thesis was "A Study of the Tripartite System of Representation in the International Labor Organization." He strongly encouraged and wished me to work at the forthcoming U.N. headquarters. At the time, the current U.N. building was not even in its blueprint stage. The U.N. secretariat staff was working in a compound of U.S. Marine iron-corrugated houses along the Long Island seashore. Dr. Steinmeyer must have been very disappointed because I did not follow his advice afterwards.

On the other hand, Zhang Ruji was very excited to see me when I dropped by. He asked me to stay with him in New York City for two more days, showing me a publication called the *Journal of Chinese Students in the United States* and insisting that I become a member of its editorial board. He also beseeched me to move to New York City quickly, so that I could take over the journal's chief editorship after he left for Mainland China.

All of that was a surprise to me. I had just received my M.A., and I was not sure where to go to continue my graduate studies, so I only promised Zhang Ruji and other editors of the journal to be a contributing author. But a twist in my life occurred. In the summer of 1949, I was accepted by Columbia University. When I went for my scholarship interview, I met Zhang Ruji again in New York City.

Zhang Ruji was as happy as I was for my admission to Columbia. This time, he kept me in New York City for more than a week. In addition to the journal's editorial work, he wanted me to be its correspondent attending a summer camp organized by the Chinese Student Christian Association for a week.

I had never planned to stay out of Washington for so long. I did not have the things I needed for camping in the countryside, but Zhang Ruji and friends would not let me go. Embarrassingly, after getting into the summer camp, I had to beg a guy to drive me to get items needed for outdoor life.

Zhang Ruji was theoretically minded. He loathed dealing with trivial matters or sentimental things. On the night he came to see me in my office, we strolled along the streets in Beijing streets for almost three hours. Neither of us talked about what we had encountered after coming back to Mainland China. But both of us seemed to assume we knew what the other had gone through. Neither did we exchange our views on the Communist system. Both of us also seemed to understand what the other felt. We just walked and walked along the Chang An Boulevard and enjoyed delicious snacks in a few eateries.

Nevertheless, a discussion came up when we talked about our mutual friend Li Bingxiang. It concerned with the question: "What is the best thing we can do under the current circumstances?" Zhang Ruji commended me first for my concentration on translation and not practical politics. He told me that he had met Li Bingxiang a few days ago in Nanjing, and they had a debate on the subject.

Li Bingxiang was now a leader of the Chinese Democratic Union. Because he was very active and interested only in politics, Zhang Ruji had questioned him: "Do you prefer to welcome and see people off every day at the railway station or engage in some solid work in building the country?"

Obviously, Zhang Ruji was reminding Li Bingxiang that there might be things more worthwhile to do. But Li Bingxiang did not seem to get the point, so he answered, "To build the country, a lot of work has to be done. People need to be rallied, cheered up and organized too!"

I could understand that Zhang Ruji was cautioning Li Bingxiang that under the Communist regime, only Communists were allowed to rally, cheer up or organize the people. But apparently he did not cool down Li Bingxiang's zealotry in Communist politics. I remember that, in that very year of 1956, Li Bingxiang had written me a number of letters, encouraging me to participate in the "Ming Fang Movement." His letters had brought me back to the old days we were in Wuhan University.

Li Bingxiang and I had both majored in political science. We also belonged to a student paper called the *Contemporary Critics*. He was the society's first president, and I took over his post after he graduated. At the time, we were all admirers of the British political system, and we believed the Fabian Society was a model for organizing the intellectuals.

In 1945, our political science department had a "Mock British Parliament" project. Li Bingxiang played the British Prime Minister, and I acted as the Opposition Leader in the British Parliament. He had his fake cabinet, and I had my bogus parliamentary members. College students liked to have fun. We had the energy.

Staged in the university auditorium, the mock British parliament had two sessions. Schoolmates of other departments had been invited to participate. Li Bingxiang and his "cabinet ministers" pompously presented their policies and programs. The Opposition succeeded in poking their loopholes. A vote of "non-confidence" finally brought down the fake Prime Minister. At the end, the fake Opposition claimed victory.

Li Bingxiang and I became closer after the mock British parliament exercise. He was older than me and often treated me as his younger brother. "You know, it's hard to be able to think, talk, and write at the same time," he had advised me more than one time. "These are born gifts. You should develop them and put them to use."

Li Bingxiang knew that I believed in democratic political principles and systems. In Wuhan University, we both had associated more closely with teachers and schoolmates who affiliated with neither the Nationalists nor the Communists. We generally called ourselves the "third force" or the "third way believers."

In 1944, the Chinese Democratic Union had been quietly set up. Li Bingxiang probably joined it right away. He urged me to do the same thing, but I had doubts in Chinese practical politics at the time. I told him that the Nationalists had tried to recruit me, and the Communists had also approached me, but neither of them had convinced me. As for the third parties, I did not believe they could have enough room to operate either under Nationalist government or Communist regime. Sooner or later, they would probably split up or fall into the two big parties' orbits, so I would like to try my best to be an independent political thinker or practitioner.

Li Bingxiang did not argue with me, but he never gave up his attempt to convince me to join his rank. I remember that he had specifically sent a friend to see me in Shanghai after he joined the Chinese Democratic Union. I was then working at the Board of Supplies.

Dressing like a banker, his friend carried a shiny brief case when he came to my office. I invited him to coffee at the top floor of the China Bank, and he briefed me on the political situation. He asked about my view on the outlook of China, and I gave him a pessimistic answer. Then he pulled out some documents from his brief case.

"Have you read these directives from the Central Committee?" He handed me those document. I was somewhat embarrassed after a quick scan of the title pages because they were internal papers of the Chinese Democratic Union. I gave the documents back to him and told him apologetically that I was not member of his Union. The man was stunned. Chuckling in disbelief, he said, "We thought you are our member!"

Li Bingxiang was a good-hearted man, but he seemed always restless and needing to involve himself in something. As a politician, I believe he could be successful in most political systems except that of the totalitarian. Perhaps by destiny, he was branded in 1957 as a "Rightist" by the Communists. I was deeply saddened when I read some of the "condemnations" against him in the newspaper. The tragedy happened about a year after his debate with Zhang Ruji. I prayed that he had survived the Communist persecution.

Zhang Ruji spent a week in Beijing. He had never met Olivia before. His interest had not been in anybody's family life, but he congratulated Olivia and me heartily for our marriage. However, we lost contact again after 1956. As he said, he was not a letter writer. I also seldom wrote letters in Communist China.

Forty years later, I heard that he had suffered a lot, but he seemed to have survived all the persecutions. I learned from a mutual friend that Zhang Ruji was teaching at the Jilin University. The good news about him was that he had finally gotten married. I prayed that he fulfilled his goals in those turbulent years.

1956 was supposed to be a year free of any political campaign, but Mao Zedong could not live without it. Just for spreading out the "thaw" that had forced upon him, he wanted to rely on political movements. His top lieutenants, Zhou Enlai and Chen Yi, had already cajoled the public. Yet the public did not seem to have responded with enthusiasm, so he became impatient and decided to launch a campaign to arouse public attention.

This time, he started with the Chinese Communist Party itself. Alleging that the lukewarm response of the public was caused by the mistakes of certain Communist Party members, he launched a "rectifying" campaign within the Communist Party. Normally, in a nominally "multi-party" country, a party rectifying itself should be its own business, but this was not the way Mao Zedong wanted it. He demanded the entire country, especially the satellite parties, participate in the campaign.

In early 1957, Mao Zedong claimed that he had had a new discovery as a Marxian theoretician. He announced at a State Supreme Council meeting that political conflicts were unavoidable in any society. But in a socialist state, there were two types of political conflicts: one between the people and their enemies, the other among people themselves. He emphasized that the two kinds of conflicts were different in nature. Therefore, they should be handled differently.

In the same State Supreme Council meeting, Mao Zedong admitted that the Chinese Communist Party was infected by "bureaucratism, factionalism and subjectivism," so he asked for the public's assistance to rid Communism of those "Party diseases."

The public was perplexed by the announcement. In their memory, the Chinese Communist Party had never admitted its wrong doings in the past.

They could not understand why Mao Zedong suddenly made the Communist Party a target of a campaign. As the saying goes, "Once burned, people would hesitate to get near to a fire." So the public remained silent after the agitation.

Mao Zedong was embarrassed. He could not stand the public quietude, but it was hard to break the awkward silence. At that juncture, to his surprise, he got unexpected assistance from a prominent scholar.

The scholar was Fei Xiaotong, a world-renowned sociologist and a leader of the Chinese Democratic Union. In an article published in February 1957, he offered an explanation as to why the public responded so coolly toward the Communist calls. He related the inertness of the public to the chilly political weather. In his opinion, the political climate in Mainland China at that moment was like the weather in "early spring." Spring should have brought warmth. Bur early spring was still quite chilly. Before the true political spring arrived, people might not be ready to speak out.

The article was widely read and aroused public interest across the country. Mao Zedong immediately caught the lifesaver thrown to him. He began to act as the supreme protector of free speech. He sharply blamed some middle-echelon Communist cadres for suppressing public opinions. The scapegoats had been his loyal subordinates. They were stunned by his flip-flop. Some of them, like a Communist administrator Ma Hangbing committed suicide right after being brandished.

Curiously, Mao Zedong' role as the protector of "freedom of speech" still did not convince the public, so after some frustration, he took another demagogic move in February 1957. In order to draw people to air out their true thoughts and feelings, he purposely created a "fake political spring" by launching the new "Ming Fang Movement."

"Ming" and "Fang" were two terms Mao Zedong borrowed from the golden era of ancient Chinese history. "Ming" meant to let a hundred schools of different thought contest. "Fang" called for letting a hundred different flowers bloom. Putting them together, "Ming" and "Fang" spoke of "freedom of expression" in Chinese.

Like dumping gasoline on a fire, Mao Zedong's "Ming Fang Movement" finally caught public enthusiasm. Many Chinese intellectuals, old and young, finally incited and began to answer his call. So by promoting "Ming Fang" he seemed to have killed two birds with one stone. First, he had substituted the foreign jargon "thaw" with a genius Chinese term "Ming Fang." Second, by calling for "hundreds of different schools of thought to contest" and "hundreds of different flowers to bloom," he tried to match his totalitarian rule with a golden era in ancient Chinese history.

In early 1957, the schemes and motives of Mao Zedong were unknown. People were fascinated because they seemed to be enjoying a freedom that could only be found in 220 B.C. in Chinese history. Never had the Chinese culture flourished so colorfully as after that golden era. When Mao Zedong proposed to bring the golden era back, no one could argue against his proposal.

At first, people spoke out gingerly. As their enthusiasm grew, they became bolder and bolder and spoke louder and louder. Their long held vigilance began to loosen up. The bravest stuck their necks out. They finally plunged into the mud pit of "Ming" and "Fang."

An unprecedented purge was waiting for the victims at the snare.

Olivia at Manhattanville College of the Sacred Heart in New York City, 1949.

One of my photos in New York City, 1949.

Above: Our first date at the Tavern on the Green in Central Park, New York City.

Left: Our wedding held at the China Institute in New York City on March 18, 1950.

After classes, a group of Chinese graduate students lining up in front of
Columbia University's Library, 1949. I am third from the right.

The world literature editorial staff of the People's Publishing House of Literature in Mainland China, 1959. Olivia is the second from the left on second row, and I am at the right end of the second row.

My mother, Liu Wen-shi (1898-1995), on the left and my father, Hwang Tze-an (1899-1966), on the right. My mother survived the "Cultural Revolution" (1966-1976) in Mainland China and joined us in the United States in early 1980. My father was united with us in 1954 while we were in Mainland China, but he did not survive the "Cultural Revolution" in 1966.

Taken on the front porch of our rented house
in the North Bag Lane, Beijing, in early 1956.

A family portrait in 1959 before the "Great Famine" hit hard.

Left: My father-in-law, Quek Shin (1884-1955). I never had a chance to pay respect to him in person. Olivia saw him last in 1946.

Right: My mother-in-law, Pan Yu-ing (1903-1929), died when Olivia was only four years old.

Right: My brother-in-law, Quek Kaitee (1904-1980). As Olivia's eldest step-brother, he took on the responsibility of caring for Olivia throughout her childhood and adult life.

Left: Professor Chen Xu-jing (1903-1967), a prominent Chinese scholar and educator. He was one of the best friends of Quek Kaitee, and also a fatherly figure to Olivia and me.

Olivia and the children, finally united in Hong Kong, 1963.

A family reunion in Hong Kong, 1963.

10

"Ming Fang" and "Anti-Rightist"

Looking back, I was extremely lucky to have my first, but also my last, annual leave in Communist China in 1957. I was particularly lucky to have that vacation scheduled in May and June when the "Ming Fang Movement" reached its climax. The relentless "Anti-Rightist Campaign" started as soon as my vacation ended.

Thanks to the one month "annual leave," I was exempted from many critical meetings. Had I been in the office during those days, I would have fallen into the political traps. More importantly, the God-sent vacation enabled me to change my routine for a short period. That change widened my vista and provided me with an opportunity to witness many things in the "Ming Fang Movement."

The weather in Beijing was glorious that May of 1957. The crisp air, the bright sunshine, as well as the blue sky all beckoned me to go outdoors. Since I was away from my desk, I felt like exploring the good tea in Beijing parks. Therefore, I stopped by a few teahouses and eateries every day.

Surprisingly, I found the parks were more crowded than before. Even on weekdays, the teahouses and eateries seemed to be congested. A carefree atmosphere encompassed the resort areas. Many dissenting views could be heard when you walked around. It did not seem dangerous now to express different opinions. The ominous political campaigns seemed to have gone with the wind.

At a teahouse, I picked a nice, small table. I was planning to read under the sky, but I was distracted by a lot of noise. Turning my head, I found the nearby customers were reading and discussing something. What they read, however, were not books but newspapers about the latest development of the "Ming Fang Movement." Like it or not, I became the only "ignorant bookish person" in the teahouse.

Looking around further, I noticed that the teahouse was in fact not a quiet place. Some customers exchanged newspapers as if they knew each other before. Nobody would dare to talk so freely in public in the past, so I thought they must belong to a group coming to the park for tea.

But my guess was proven wrong. During the next days in the same teahouse, I saw some of the same tea drinkers. They came and left individually, at various times, and went different directions. That meant that they were random customers, so I drew the conclusion that they were most likely casual customers, probably on vacation like me.

Nevertheless, those tea drinkers had interrupted my vacation. No matter who they were and where they came from, their behavior made me aware that I had lost touch with the outside world. Like a student lagging behind, I felt that I should catch up, so I altered my routine quickly. Instead of bringing books to the teahouses, I bought daily newspapers on my way. At various newsstands, I also looked for the back issues, trying to keep myself as updated as possible.

Now I was no more a bookworm at the teahouses. My change might have caught the eyes of some fellow customers too. They were impressed when they saw me bringing some of the back issues of the newspaper to the teahouses. Soon I was inducted into their casual discussions among tea tables.

Under the Communist rule, people were not supposed to trust anybody else. Since early 1950s, they had learned not to talk with strangers. It would be incredible for anyone to unveil one's thoughts to an unknown person. But at the height of the "Ming Fang Movement," people seemed to have loosened their vigilance.

The people I met at the teahouses talked quite freely, but they never exchanged with one another their names, addresses or work places. Anonymity was still an insurance policy for everyone. However, human beings are social animals, and they need someone to talk to once in a while. Unless the listener was a policeman in uniform, they were not afraid of airing out some of their thinking.

Among the subjects most people often discussed during the "Ming Fang Movement" were the widespread persecutions that had occurred during the last few years, especially in the terror of 1955. Many victims tried hard to have their cases reopened and verdicts redressed. At the teahouses, some tea drinkers often exchanged horrible stories about various campaigns.

I thought I had witnessed enough terrors, but the firsthand or secondhand stories I heard at the teahouses shocked me into numbness. For instance, there were many suicide cases in colleges, universities and other academic institutions I had never heard of. All those stories made what happened in our Publishing House the tip of an iceberg.

"Don't worry!" I remember a fellow tea drinker commenting on the suicides in various colleges. "The students are young and daring. They won't be scared in the long run. Here is a story I heard from a friend."

The story told by our fellow tea drinker happened in Beijing's suburbs in 1955. After the "Wiping Out Campaign," a college student posted an open letter on a campus wall. In longhand writing, he listed the crimes of the Communists, especially those horrible persecutions in the "Wiping Out Campaign" in 1955. The student said he was fearless in accusing the Communists because he knew he would die sooner or later.

Our fellow tea drinker said that his friend had passed that wall by chance that day. He was shocked when he read the open letter. Quickly, a crowd gathered in front of the wall. People elbowed their way to the front to get a closer look. After reading the accusations, all of them fell into stunned silence. But before long, a number of Communist cadres arrived. They dispersed the throng and tore down the posted letter.

In the month of May 1957, Mao Zedong kept on fueling the "Ming Fang Movement" while alerting high echelon lieutenants to prepare for action. As reported by the major Communist newspapers, nine metro cities were ordered to organize public forums on May 4, 1957. Four days later, the Central United Front Department of the Communist Party formerly invited the leaders of its satellite parties to speak out in the meetings of the "Ming Fang Movement."

Thus, under Mao Zedong's direction, the "Ming Fang" show got closer and closer to its climax. In retrospect, it was surely a Machiavellian masterpiece. The Communists first set up an "invitation only" forum to draw out the leaders of their satellite parties. "Invitation only" meant it was an honor and privilege to the participants.

But very soon, the "invitation only" turned into a "required presence," an obligation for the celebrities of the satellite parties to attend and speak out in thirteen sessions of the forum. The verbal proceedings of each session were major news items of the day. I could hardly recall a time when I had ever been so overwhelmed by newspapers.

In addition to Communist media, there were a few old newspapers, which reappeared. I spent a great deal of time reading them too. First, *Wenhuibao (The Wenhui Daily)* in Shanghai was reorganized. Under its original editor-in-chief, Xu Zhucheng, it gained back its reputation as an independent paper. Second, the Communists allowed *Guangmingribao*, a Beijing daily, to become the official organ of the Chinese Democratic Union. Chu Anping, the renowned former chief editor of the liberal weekly *Gwan Cha (The Observer)*, was appointed to be the new editor-in-chief of the *Guangmingribao (The Light Daily)*.

Wenhuibao had been influential under Xu Zhucheng since World War II. After 1949, however, it became a Communist newspaper. Now with Xu Zhucheng returning to its helm, many readers were jubilant. Similarly, with Chu Anping in charge the *Guangmingribao*, many readers were excited to see what independent stand the old daily would take.

As May of 1957 drew to its end, the pace of "Ming Fang" accelerated. At the teahouse, a fellow drinker brought a piece of exciting news not yet printed: "Big letter posters appear at Beijing University." At the time, nobody had ever seen a "big letter poster." The fellow tea drinker said that he was curious. I told him, "Me too!"

Beijing University had always been a barometer in modern Chinese history. Ideas and actions originated from there always had great impact on Chinese politics. After a brief chat, he and I decided to go together even though we hardly knew each other.

It was certainly an adventure for both of us. When we got there, it was late afternoon. The university was in a festive mood and was bursting with people. It was hard to differentiate who belonged to the university and who came from outside, but all seemed to share an unexplainable excitement.

My fellow tea drinker turned out to be a good guide. We first squeezed through the auditorium, then the dining halls, and finally one of the dormitories. The big letter posters were hand scripted on big sheets of used paper. Hanging in the air or pasted on the walls, each of them was a piece of "Ming Fang."

Some of the posters aired grievances against political control and persecution. Others criticized the Communist educational policies. Many offered ideas and views on how to improve political and academic affairs. There were cartoons, too, mostly ridiculing the bureaucrats running the university.

As I recall, amid the din of the crowd, I suddenly felt like I was back in my college days. Time seemed to have stopped. The scenes were similar and familiar. Many issues remained the same. Things had definitely not improved up to now.

During World War II, there were many student movements. Then, the university and college campuses were full of steam. After the communist takeover in 1949, there seemed to be no more student movements. But the Beijing University campus was now alive again at the end of May in 1957.

Democracy and science had been two continuous demands in Chinese student movements since 1919. Forty years had passed, and the demands were still there. Under the Communist regime, democracy was farther out of reach. From the big letter posters, I felt that there was a strong pulse of ferment to renew the old demand.

Indeed, beginning in June 1957, rumors had it that there was campus unrest in Beijing, but students were not able to organize as before under Communist control. They were waiting for a leader. Once organized, they would most likely go from their campus to the streets. Therefore, the Communists were extremely nervous. They had already been scared by the unrest in Poland and Hungary in 1956.

In the explosive atmosphere, Chu Anping delivered a frontal attack on the Communist leadership. After being appointed as editor-in-chief of *Guangmingribao*, he spoke at the forum provided by the Communists, and he directly challenged Mao Zedong and Zhou Enlai.

Chu Anping pointed out that China's problems under current regime derived from the Communist assertion that they owned the whole country. He told the audience that there was no way for China to have democracy unless the Communists gave up their attempt of ruling everything under the sun.

It was June 1 of 1956. Chu Anping's succinct and sharp remarks brought more criticism on the Communists. Mao Zedong was pushed back to a defensive position, and the imminent student unrest also caused him worries.

The satellite parties had many members in the faculties of many universities and colleges. They had a stake too if the student unrest spilled over to the street. Thus, six of their leaders got together on June 6 and offered their assistance to the Communists in dealing with the explosive situation.

But to their astonishment, their offer was rudely rejected and brushed away. Instead of taking them as helpers, the Communists branded them as the cause of all campus unrest. Thus, when the "Ming Fang Movement" turned into the "Anti-Rightist Campaign," the same six academic members of the satellite parties, including Fei Xiaotong, were branded as "Rightists." It was certainly an irony for those celebrities of the satellite party. They received only punishments, not credits, from the Communists.

For many Chinese intellectuals who had lived through the latter half of the twentieth century, June 8 of 1957 might have been a critical date in their lives.

On the surface, the "Ming Fang Movement" was still in full swing, but the tone of the Communists made a sudden and sharp turn on that day. Alleging that a person who was friendly to the Communists had been threatened, the Communist official organ *People's Daily* bluntly asked in its editorial: "Why did this happen?"

That was a portent that something serious was going to happen! Curiously, at that moment, the news reminded me of an episode in the Weimar Republic in German history. The Nazis had used the Reichstag fire to ascend into power in the 1930s. We did not know whether the alleged incident was true, but Mao Zedong used it to launch his "Anti-Rightist Campaign." People took it only as another of Mao Zedong's habitual flip-flops at first. But this flip-flop had serious long-range consequences.

Following the eighth of June, more editorials were cranked out by the *People's Daily* each day. A systematic and ferocious counteroffensive began to attack those who had aired their views during the "Ming Fang Movement." First, there was an editorial entitled "Workers Speak Out." Then, "The Peasants and Other Trade Organizations" appeared in the *People's Daily* to condemn the so-called Rightists.

On the tenth of June, the "Ming Fang Movement" formally turned into the "Anti-Rightist Campaign." The prescheduled forums for the satellite party leaders to "Ming Fang" were conveniently transformed into struggle meetings against the leaders themselves.

The Communists had infiltrated the satellite parties from day one of their existence. Some of the satellite party leaders were actually underground Communist members, so every satellite party's move had not only been under the Communist's watch, but also followed the Communist's direction.

Now in the satellite parties, the underground Communist members were struggling against those non-Communist members. The real relationship between the Communist Party and its satellite parties was bared. It had been nothing but a farce.

In the "Anti-Rightist Campaign," it was estimated that more than 800,000 Chinese intellectuals had been purged. They were the cream of Chinese intelligentsia. After being capped as a "Rightists," they became outcasts under the Communist regime. They lost their dignity and livelihood. Their families also were degraded to "untouchables." Most of them ended up either in jails or in labor camps. The cruelty of the purge could only be matched by the Holocaust in Germany or the Gulags of the Soviet Union.

Did Mao Zedong have a premeditated scheme to trap the Chinese intellectuals in 1956 and 1957? The question has been raised ever since the

"Ming Fang Movement" turned into the "Anti-Rightist Campaign." "Yes, it was a scheme," Mao Zedong himself once bluntly answered, but he unabashedly argued that his scheme was not a "yinmou" (secret plot), but a "yangmou" (open plot).

In heated debates, Mao Zedong even proudly admitted that his "Ming Fang Movement" was a stratagem, aimed at luring out the "niu" (oxen), "gui" (devils), "she" (snakes) and "shen" (gods), so that he could terminate them altogether. Niu, gui, she, shen had been the names he habitually appropriated for his enemies.

But history was not a parsing game. No semantic maneuvering could change an "open plot" into a "non-plot." No matter how strenuously they tried to rewrite history, Mao Zedong and his lieutenants were responsible for the crimes they committed.

My vacation was abruptly terminated when the "Anti-Rightist Campaign" began. I was called back to the office on the tenth of June and found the Publishing House was already in a vortex. In the "Ming Fang" movement, under the Communist cajole and encouragement, some colleagues had aired their grievances about the cruel treatment they received from the Communists in the past. Now the Communists turned the table, insisting that what they had done was correct and necessary, and those who complained harbored ill feelings toward the Party.

Once again, the Chinese Classical Literature Department became the battleground. This time, it was not because of Hu Feng, but because a number of its editors were satellite party members. Those affiliated with Min Ge (Revolutionary Committee of the Nationalist Party) and Jiusan Xueshe (September Third Society) were accused for their "political ambitions."

But in the Publishing House, the most important "Rightist" title went to Feng Xuefeng, our former editor-in-chief. The last time I had seen him was two years ago when he made the mobilizing speech for the "Wiping Out Campaign." Because he had been a veteran Communist and had special status in the literary circles, the struggling meetings against him were held at the "All China Federation of Art and Literature Workers." I was sent with a group of editors to those large-sized struggle meetings.

When it came to Feng Xuefeng's turn, the auditorium of the Federation was fully packed. There was a special table and a chair set in the middle of the auditorium for Feng Xuefeng alone. Among the attendees, there were Deputy Minister of Culture, Zhou Yan, and other big shots in the literary circles.

As soon as the large-sized struggle meeting started, some exposed Feng Xuefeng's relationship with Hu Feng, and others attacked him for his involvement in Ding Ling's "Anti-Party Clique" activities. But sitting motionlessly at the table, Feng Xuefeng did not utter a word throughout the first day.

That was quite a special struggle meeting. Usually a target was supposed to answer questions on the spot, but Feng Xuefeng did not respond to any accusation, nor had accusers demanded him to confess anything. Many had expected Zhou Yan and his lieutenants to challenge Feng Xuefeng on other issues, but they did not do it either.

The next day, Feng Xuefeng was called upon to speak. He remained in his chair; pulling out a piece of paper from his pocket, he read a brief statement. His voice was low and the statement did not connect to the "Anti-Rightist Campaign" at all. What he said was that he had been in the "Long March." When the Red Army reached the Shaanxi Province in 1935, the Party sent him back to Shanghai. Premier Zhou Enlai personally handed him a transmitter, instructing him to work underground and restore the Party's connection with Lu Xun.

The audience was hushed. After listening to Feng Xuefeng's narrative with deference, the chair called no more speakers, and the struggle meeting came to a close. Nevertheless, Feng Xuefeng was branded as a "Rightist" afterward. His impressive dossier did not seem to help him much. Neither did his protector and mentor Zhou Enlai render him any assistance to save him from persecution.

Xiao Qian, a famous author and newspaper reporter, was the next target. In contrast to Feng Xuefeng, the struggle meeting against him was more dramatic. As a journalist, Xiao Qian had been in Europe during World War II. He married in England before returning to China after the War. He and his English wife had a son named Tie Zhu. Later on, his English wife left him and he remarried to Mei Tao. In the eyes of the Communists, he was a rotten bourgeois journalist under Western influence.

Olivia and I knew Xiao Qian because he often came to our Publishing House. His third wife, Wen Jieruo, was one of our colleagues in the World Literature Department. I still remember when Xiao Qian visited us at our home in 1953. That was right after he and his second wife Mei Tao had divorced. He confided to us why he made the decision and told us that he was planning to marry our colleague Wen Jieruo.

Xiao Qian's interest was quite broad. In addition to journalism, he had been engaged in creative writing for years. In his zeal to join the Communist "literary army," he and his newly wed wife moved into the dormitory of the

Communist Writers Union. For him that might not have been a good decision because the Communist literary bureaucrats had always considered him an enemy. The near vicinity to those Communists in charge of the Writers Union might have caused him miserable sufferings thereafter.

In struggling against Xiao Qian, the campaign operatives focused chiefly on his personal life. The first person who came to attack him was his second wife, Mei Tao. She called Xiao Qian a hypocrite, accusing him of always "straddling on two boats at the same time." Using her own experience, she exposed Xiao Qian's disloyalty in her vendetta. From then on, the struggle meeting became a soap opera. The audience seemed to enjoy it, so the campaign operatives let the show go on quite long.

The next person who came up to struggle against Xiao Qian was Ye Junjian, a member of the Art and Literature Workers Federation, who happened to have been in wartime London with Xiao Qian. Ye Junjian's attacks on Xiao Qian were also quite personal. Using a few episodes in London, he illustrated how hypocritical Xiao Qian was among the Britons. He alleged that Xiao Qian had even used pets to gain favors from them. The audience also enjoyed watching two "bourgeois literary figures" fight with each other.

During the "Anti-Rightist Campaign," Olivia had still not fully recovered from her illness. In addition to office work, there were more things for her to take care of at home. First of all, because Father was dragged into the "Anti-Rightist" pit, Mother began to worry about Father's new predicament, Olivia had to console them.

Secondly, David and Phillip were approaching preschool age. Both of them needed more attention. They had been taught by Grandfather at home. Now Olivia had to take over some of Grandfather's duties. It was incredible that Olivia could finish her translation of Olive Schreiner's *The Story of an African Farm* in 1957.

In retrospect, Father's new predicament traced back to the false "thaw." The "Beijing Translation Society" that had hired him was not really a business organization. It was a "labor reform" agency set up by the Communists. Run by a Communist agent previously under the Japanese occupation and Nationalist regime, it belonged to the Communist secret service apparatus.

In 1956, the Society offered father a good position, encouraging him to resume contact with some of his old colleagues. To utilize Father's language skills, they gave him an assignment to translate the Swiss educator J. H.

Pestalozzi's classic novel *Leonard and Gertrude*. Father was delighted to use his German language again, but he soon fell again into the Communist trap.

Like all agencies and societies under Communist regime, the "Society" used "political studies" to check on the out-of-prison employees. Father had always been a straight talker. We did not know what he spoke about in the "Ming Fang Movement," but he was branded a "Rightist" during the "Anti-Rightist Campaign."

Father used to play with his grandchildren at home. He was their favorite grandfather. However, toward the end of 1957, he became tacit again like when he had first come to Beijing. The energetic spirit he had regained in the last three years evaporated. We found him retreating to a corner every time he returned from meetings at the "Beijing Translation Society." On top of it all, he was beginning to lose his appetite and weight.

Mother was the most worried. We could hear that she often questioned Father as to what had happened to him. But Father invariably kept his lips tight. One day, Mother finally spoke out. "I knew that guy was no good! Why did you bring him home for dinner so often?"

The man Mother mentioned was a priest who also worked at the "Beijing Translation Society." Without a family to live with and no church to preach to, the priest had become Father's confidant. Father tried hard to duck Mother's question. When pressed hard, his answer was that he believed the priest was really not a bad man.

"He betrayed you! He informed the authorities what you told him!" Mother was upset. "Isn't it true? How can you still call him a good man?"

"He has been under tremendous pressure!" Father defended his friend in a low voice. "He has no way out!"

Mother was not convinced. She did not want to hear any more, so she picked up Jean and Pauline and walked away.

Olivia and I did not know how to comfort our parents. Now Father had become the victim in the new campaign, and he suffered a lot in his work place. The best thing we could do was to make the family as a shelter in the storm.

Before the end of the "Anti-Rightist Campaign," Mao Zedong divided his victims into six categories. Those in the "number one category" would get the most severe punishment. By descending order, the "number six category" victims might be treated more leniently. But the tag of "Rightist" carried the same weight on each bearer.

Mao Zedong wanted to conduct his political persecutions in his "scientific" way. He liked to use a "5% formula" to calculate where his enemies were. In 1955, he prescribed that 5% of the population were "Anti-Revolutionaries." In 1957, he also proclaimed that 5% of the intellectuals were "Rightists." Therefore, 5% was the quota the Communist Party functionaries had to meet in producing "Rightists."

In Chinese Communist history, "left" rather than "right" had been the golden motto to be followed by the functionaries. Since Mao Zedong had branded 5% of the intellectuals as "Rightists," the Party's operatives dared not to produce less that 5% of the people in their units as "Rightists." How did those Communist operatives meet Mao Zedong's prescribed quota? Ridiculous but horrible stories were abundant.

For example, it was reported that there was a Work Unit trying hard to dig out "Rightists." After numerous struggle meetings, however, it was still short of one "Rightist" to meet the required 5% quota. The deadline was rapidly approaching. The head and deputy head of the unit met together. They were afraid of the severe penalty they would get if they could not meet the 5% quota.

"God damn it!" The head of the unit lamented. "We only need one more to meet the 5%. Only one more! We've tried hard, but we can't find another one."

An awkward silence came up. The deputy head capped his chin in his hands for a while. After a long contemplation, he raised his head and said with a rueful smile:

"It looks like that one of us has to go…. It's either you or me!…Maybe I should volunteer to be damned!"

The head of the unit could not believe what he heard. Meanwhile, his deputy continued, "You know, I am not married….I have less family burden…and it might be easier for me to go through the ordeal!"

After another pause, the deputy head summoned his courage and made a bold offer. "O.K., comrade! If you promise to take care of my mother, I shall volunteer to be the Rightist for our unit!"

The story was bitterly sarcastic. Like millions of tragedies in Communist China, we probably will never be able to know their endings.

Father was fragile after the "Anti-Rightist Campaign." There was no way he could resign from the "Beijing Translation Society." The humiliation and slavish treatment exacted further tolls on his health and spirit.

He fell into illness in 1959, and he had a surgery for his respiratory problems that year. Since then, his health had never recovered.

11

The "Great Leap Forward" into Starvation

Mao Zedong was forced to stop the "Wiping Out All Hidden Anti-Revolutionary Elements Campaign" and make a "false thaw" in 1956. As soon as the political air got warmer, however, he reversed his "Ming Fang Movement" and launched the "Anti-Rightist Campaign."

However, his addiction to political campaigns was still not satisfied. When the "Anti-Rightist Campaign" was still going on, his whims twisted further, and he plunged Mainland China into another series of fanatic adventures. He called them the "Three Red Flags Movement."

There was a background to these flip-flops. In the middle of the 1950s, a leadership vacuum seemed to have emerged in the international Communist movement. After Stalin's death, the unfledged Soviet leadership was not yet fully consolidated, but the Soviet Union was still the head of the socialist camp.

Mao Zedong had no respect for the greenish Soviet leadership. Their de-Stalinization offended him, so unabashedly he wanted to grab the leadership of international Communism from their hands.

The new Soviet leadership did not flinch from Mao Zedong's challenge. Slowing down their aid to Communist China, they wished to rein in the "little brother." But their pressures backfired. Mao Zedong was livid by their slights.

When the Sino-Soviet rift opened, he adopted a "self-reliance" domestic policy and showed a defiant attitude towards his "big brother" while engaging in ideological dispute with the new Soviet leadership.

Internally, however, Mao Zedong was in hot water. After the flip-flop from the "Ming Fang Movement" to the "Anti-Rightist Campaign," China was in ferment for change. He badly needed to divert the public's attention to other concerns.

Riding on the rising nationalistic feeling of the Chinese population, he put forward his blueprint to build a totalitarian utopia in China. Through a hodgepodge of funny, capricious and wild projects, namely "Double the Steel Production," "Great Leap Forward toward Socialism" and "Organize the Country into Communes," he wanted to catapult China directly into Communism.

History had recorded that the so-called "Three Red Flags Movements" almost ruined China. The "Double the Steel Production" movement was Mao Zedong's first pet project. He believed that a nation's strength was represented by its steel output, so he ordered to double China's steel production in 1958.

Many experts might have seriously doubted that his goal was achievable, but Mao Zedong had mandated the goal to be the nation's top priority. He gathered a group of alchemists to his aid. They scorned the myth of modern technology, claiming that steel could be produced by any ordinary home-made furnace. Promoting the alchemists' claim, Mao Zedong mobilized the whole population to produce steel.

Thus, the whole country was quickly overwhelmed by the frenzy of steel production. In rural areas, the strong peasants were dispatched to the wooded hills to collect timber to be fuel. After building furnaces, they became "steel workers" overnight and began to turn crude iron into something they called "steel."

Under the mobilization, the call for doubling the steel production had also put workers of all trades in urban and industrial areas into the same frenzy. The call to produce steel had also become the top priority in our Publishing House in 1958. We were asked to dedicate our energy, time and resources to achieve the goal. While strong hands were building and mending the home-furnace, the rest of us were supposed to boost their spirits and supply them with the necessary raw materials.

Pitifully, there was no iron mine in the cities. Crude iron soon became a precious metal. To supply our steel workers at the furnace, many of us had to donate our utensils or other iron artifacts from our homes.

"Steel Production," however, was only one of many Mao Zedong's whimsical projects. He also wanted to immediately increase the agricultural output. As alchemists came to his aid in steel production, different agriculturalists offered different methods of seeding and tilling to double or triple the farm production. Accepting their advice, Mao Zedong raised the target of agricultural production of the country to a sky-high level.

But increasing industrial and agricultural production was only one part of Mao Zedong's agenda. In realizing his totalitarian utopia on earth, he also wanted to organize China into a country of communes and transform the entire Chinese population into "workers, peasants and soldiers."

Several years ago, hundreds of millions of Chinese peasants had just been hurdled into agricultural cooperatives. Now Mao Zedong found it far too slow. Blaming his agricultural lieutenants for taking "mincing gaits" in collectivization, he ridiculed them, saying they were walking like lily-footed ladies. He ordered them to merge the millions of agricultural cooperatives immediately into mega-size communes.

Thus, in one stroke, Mao Zedong brought small towns and villages in rural areas under big jurisdictions. The scattered Chinese peasants' lives were put under one unified control. In urban areas, the commune structure was different, but the goal was the same. Henceforth, the lives of workers of all trades would be under that same overall unified control.

Mao Zedong was a lover of struggles. He proclaimed that there was endless fun in struggles. Not only in struggles against his class enemies, but also in struggles against nature itself. In 1957, he had begun to persecute his enemies among the Chinese intellectuals in the "Anti-Rightist Campaign." In 1958, he bombarded his Nationalist enemies across the Taiwan Strait.

Now he turned his attention to nature and made it a new target on the radio screen of his mind. He was known not to be a good friend to pets, be it a dog, a cat, a bird, a fish or a horse. He seemed to have had some special quarrel with the sparrows in the past. Thus, as if conducting a symphony orchestra, he suddenly swung his baton at the sparrows, accusing them of eating up crops and food. His ragtag orchestra thereby immediately launched a "Termination of Sparrows Campaign."

Instantly, the little sparrows became prey to the campaign. I did not have a chance to witness their fate in the countryside. But in Beijing, it was an odd and crude scene. In order to exhaust the sparrows, gong, drums, loud speakers and thunderous music were applied. There was no way to catch or kill the sparrows until they came to perch on a tree or rooftop.

The sparrows had no way to fight back against the human onslaught. Their only escape from the genocide was flying. In the cities, they certainly could not fly forever in the sky. Once they returned to earth, they met their destiny. But in the countryside and the wilderness, their numbers insured their survival. So the "Termination of Sparrows Campaign" failed along with the "Great Leap Forward Movement" in the end.

It became an irony that years later, the Chinese Communists reversed their verdict on sparrows. They found that by pecking away many pests in the farmland, sparrows were actually beneficial to agriculture. Therefore, like rehabilitating some of their previous enemies, they welcomed back the sparrows after trying to terminate them altogether.

In the "Great Leap Forward Movement," productivity was supposed to accelerate everywhere. At the Publishing House, our output in 1958 was also more than doubled. Olivia and I had put in extra hours at work like our colleagues. However, in addition to her editorial duties, Olivia also had extra manual labor assignments. Periodically, she had to go for manual labor at places like the Shisanling Reservoir, the Badaling Commune, and the Shijinshan Steel Foundry.

"Manual labor" was Mao Zedong's prescription for the Chinese intellectuals in their "thought reform." He wanted to remold them by forcing them to work with their hands, feet or shoulders instead of their brains. At the time, however, tools available for manual labor in Mainland China were chiefly hoes and shovels. Earthmovers, utility trucks, or backhoe diggers were unheard of. One could only use a shovel to move the soil by hand, and basket the dirt away by shoulder.

Olivia was a dedicated worker everywhere, even in her manual labor assignments. She won many awards for her labor. However, due to overworking and long exposure to cold, she once got pneumonia after working at the Shijingshan Steel Foundry in 1958. That put her in the hospital.

I myself had been a constant visitor to the hospital because of my asthma, so I was exempted from the long manual labor assignments. I was only sent on a one-day manual labor assignment such as at the Shisanling Reservoir. But to make up for my exemption from the manual labor, I had taken more duties in the office.

During 1958 and 1959, in the "Great Leap Forward" period, the Chinese Communists invited many foreign literary figures to visit Mainland China. That added to my workload. For example, Dr. William Du Bois, a renowned American educator and author, happened to come to Beijing with his wife in 1958.

Under the Chinese Communist "United Policy," our Publishing House published the Chinese translation of Dr. Du Bois's *The Soul of the Blacks*. As the editor of his book in Chinese translation, I was sent to visit them and attended several of the receptions for them. Dr. Du Bois's wife, Shirley

Graham, was also an accomplished author, so we had had quite a pleasant time chatting.

As far as I could recall, there were other writers who came to Beijing from the outside world. Before, our Publishing House was not permitted to communicate directly with foreign visitors. But this was the "Great Leap Forward" period! The Chinese Communists were anxious to show their "achievements" to the outside world; so we were suddenly allowed to see some foreigners.

At about the same time, the Publishing House started another project to honor Rabindranath Tagore, the Indian Nobel Prize winner. His one-hundredth birthday was coming in 1961. Since Tagore had been popular in China since the 1920s and some of his works already had Chinese translations, the Publishing House planned to publish a ten-volume memorial collection to celebrate his one-hundredth birthday. I was very interested in Tagore's works, especially his only full-length novel, *Gora*, so I volunteered to translate it into Chinese in my leisure time.

My translation of *Gora* came out when Tagore was commemorated in Mainland China. It was printed in two forms, one as an independent book, and the other as volumes eight and nine of his memorial collection. I never expected to receive any honor or prize under the Communist system, but surprisingly, I got a top reward from the Publishing House in 1959.

The "Great Leap Forward" was Mao Zedong's attempt to quicken China's modernization, but he mixed up politics and economics. Instead of following economic rules, he preached again and again that "politics should take command of everything." But political command under him was nothing but his whims.

His lieutenants understood what he meant by "politics should take command of everything." In order to protect their turfs, careers, and their own lives, they used false statistics to satisfy Mao Zedong's vanity, instead of reporting to him the catastrophic consequences of his "Three Red Flags Movement."

Gradually, fabrication became the vogue of the day, rumors replaced facts, and fantasy overshadowed reality. The Communist operatives competed with each other in the cheating game. First they tried to con Mao Zedong and others. Then they conned themselves. Pretty soon, the whole country was intoxicated in the binge of the "Great Leap Forward." In the euphoria, people willed things from being "false" into "truth."

That was exactly what happened from 1958 to 1960 in Communist China. The mass media spread pompous projections day and night. For instance, it was reported that a commune peasant was asked, "How many crops can you reap?"

The peasant replied, "Whatever you want!"

Another peasant joined in, saying, "The thing to worry about is not what you can get, but what you dare to say you can get!"

Food had been under rationing ever since the Communists came to power. But suddenly the rationing was loosened in late 1958. For a while, it appeared unbelievable that food became plentiful in the cities. Groceries were running like free markets, and restaurants enthusiastically added new entries to their menus. They even stayed open until midnight to accommodate the late customers.

According to news reports, scenes seemed even more grotesque in some of the rural communes. The slogans were: "Communism Is Heaven on Earth!" "Communes Are the Bridges to Communism!" To illustrate how communes were the bridges to heaven, a number of communes had already set up cafeterias and nursing homes. The former was to free housewives from cooking at home. The latter was to take care of the elderly and the invalids.

Some communes even offered free meals to the returning strong laborers to compensate for their work in steel production or dam construction. Would the strong laborers decline the offer of free lunches and dinners? Of course not. The slogan was, "Stretch out your stomach, buddies! Eat as much as you can!"

Finally, the "Great Leap Forward' spun out of control. Its skyrocketing statistics became waste paper. The bubble of "Communism Is Heaven on Earth" burst. In the rural communes, they folded up the nursing homes and cafeterias after they found themselves bankrupt. When the Communist cadres went to look at the farmland, they were shocked to find that there was no crop that year because of the desperate shortage of labor hands and wrong farming techniques. An unprecedented catastrophe hung over the whole country.

Like numerous masked burglars, famine began to sneak into Mainland China. We did not notice it in Beijing because we were still under the illusion that everything was fine. But suddenly, the food shortage was apparent in early 1959. The shelves of the groceries were empty. Essential staples became harder and harder to find. A new rationing system was imposed. How much food could a person get a month? It depended on age, sex and type of work if no privilege was claimed.

Olivia and I had never encountered famine in our lives. We had only read about starvation in books before. We became true appreciators of the meals we received every day after the starvation. Famine taught us many other lessons. For instance, how individuals would fare differently under the test of starvation. It told us a lot about the thin line between human beings and animals.

The Chinese Communists never openly admitted their responsibility for the famine. They falsely claimed the calamity was caused by bad weather, but evidence showed completely otherwise. It was one thousand percent a manmade catastrophe. More than twenty million Chinese people, according to a conservative estimation, perished in that famine. Three generations of Chinese, at least, were impacted by the calamity.

As Olivia and I witnessed that people affected by starvation might first lose their energy and vigor. Then their appearances might begin to undergo a number of changes. Their faces might become bloated, eyes glazed, and bodies swollen. They were warned that it would be fatal to let the swelling reach their heads.

Curiously, the mind of a starving person was still active. They could not help but ask what went wrong. At first, few would dare to say that the glazed eyes and the swollen face were caused by starvation. Some even tried to divert the subject, blaming their illness on water, salt or other contamination. But before long, they had to accept the truth and admit that famine was the cause of all their troubles.

How to deal with the starvation in famine? Mao Zedong benignly came out at last. He admonished people to eat more vegetables, pumpkins and melons as if those food items were still available. But vegetables, pumpkins and melons were as scarce as the basic staples. His chief propagandist Hu Qiaomu viewed the dire situation more seriously. "Why not tell people to eat tree leaves?" he advised the Communist leadership. By digging out World War II documents, he said that he had found that Hitler had ordered the Germans to eat tree leaves in similar circumstances.

Hu Qiaomu turned out to be a slow learner. People did not have to follow Hitler. They had started eating tree leaves long ago. In the countryside, people under famine stuffed their stomachs with other plants and insects. Urban dwellers had less or no access to tree leaves, plants, insects or animals. They could only cling to their rationing coupons.

Therefore, disharmonies sometimes occurred at homes, especially when in-laws were living under the same roof. Tensions went high when everyone wanted to make sure that they got the full amount of food their rationing coupons indicated. At the same time, in order to discourage food consumption, the cafeterias resorted to some unconventional practices.

I still remember there was an invention called "Shuang Zheng Fan" (Double Steamed Rice) in the famine period. By soaking the raw rice in water before steaming, cafeterias could make the rice bigger and heavier. Thus, people would get a lesser amount of rice from their rationing coupons. Furthermore, the so-called "double steamed rice" was tasteless. People were disgusted and protested. In our cafeteria at the Publishing House, they stopped the dishonorable practice after two days of experimenting.

In times of famine, money might lose its power when there is no food to buy. But it could help tremendously if somehow food was still available. First, it was highly honored in the black markets. Second, it could buy rationing coupons or special overpriced food items. Above all, it could certainly buy connections if one knew the channel to get to the source of food.

The Chinese Communists had set up "special supply centers" for foreigners and "high price stores" for the rich. At the "high price stores," one could buy candies, cookies or beer at ten times the regular prices without rationing coupons, so money was still the trump card under those circumstances.

Olivia and I were fortunate to have some extra income through translation. The royalties from our translations usually amounted to ten times our salaries. That was a tremendous help to our growing family. With those royalties, we were also able to support a number of our relatives. But believe it or not, no matter how large our royalties were, we could never get them in full.

Big chunks of our royalties were usually instantly transformed into government bonds when we received them. The cadres in charge at our Publishing House were extremely keen. When they issued the checks to us, they invariably pressed us to buy government bonds. To buy or not to buy government bonds was a political test Olivia and I could not afford to fail. We never redeemed one penny from the bonds we bought.

Also, we were constantly in debt in 1959. Olivia had to borrow money from the labor union to meet our needs each month. Nevertheless, thanks to the borrowed money, sometimes we were able to buy the expensive cookies when famine hit us severely. The cookies from the "high price stores" were mostly stale, but they helped to calm down some of the gnawing feeling in our empty stomachs during the wintry nights.

The Communists had abolished land ownership long ago. Whether the ownership of intellectual property should be allowed in communism was now an open question. During the "Great Leap Forward" movement, there were debates about the legitimacy of "royalty" and "revenue" from "intellectual property." Some even asked, "Should intellectual property ownership be allowed in Socialism and Communism?" Very strangely, however, the debate was cut short.

Olivia and I never counted on royalties, and we doubted that the copyright system would last long under Communist rule. But after so many ferocious campaigns, the copyright system remained intact. It took quite some time for us to realize that in Communist China, the ownership of intellectual property had Mao Zedong as its protector. He had been the biggest intellectual property owner in Communist China. No one dared to touch the ideological issue of intellectual property in Socialism or Communism.

Mao Zedong's works had been published and reprinted into hundreds of millions of copies. He must have received an astronomical amount of royalties. It was mind boggling to understand why he did not give up his copyright or ever donate his royalties to any philanthropic organizations.

At home during the famine, Father's respiratory problem got worse. He was bogged down day and night by his unstoppable coughing. Our congested premises had no space for him to take a real rest. One of his friends voluntarily leased him a room for his recuperation. Mother had been taking care of David, Phillip, Jean and Pauline. Now she had to move with Father to attend his health.

Instantly, we faced a critical problem. Olivia and I were both working full time. Sometimes she had to go for manual labor for a full week. No one could stay home to take care of the children. We definitely needed to hire a nanny. But one nanny would not be able to take care of all four of them.

During the famine, it was well known that kindergartens were better off places. They enjoyed special status in food rationing. Olivia and I never wanted our kids to leave home, but that was the only option we had. After visiting the kindergarten of the Ministry of Culture and studying its live-in conditions, we finally decided to send Phillip, Jean and Pauline there for a short period. We hired "Nanny Chen" to take care of David, because he had to stay home for elementary school.

At the time, Phillip, Jean and Pauline were only two to five years old. Parting with them every Sunday evening was heartbreaking. Fortunately, they stayed there for only half a year. When Phillip started school, they ended their exiles. We still have a picture showing Phillip bringing his two young sisters to the kindergarten. Another photo shows Jean, Pauline and Phillip in a park enjoying their ice cream bars. A third picture portrays how they piled up on a tiny bike with their eldest brother David.

When David was at home for school, the famine hit us really hard. Olivia was out of town for manual labor. One day, I came home from the office with a half empty stomach. David was having his dinner with Nanny Chen. All he had was a bowl of gruel rice with some pickles in it. That had been his meal for the last few days. His stomach was growling with hunger. He cried at the table, and he refused to eat.

"Honey, finish it!" Nanny Chen was cajoling and urging him. "This is what we have today. Come on. Be a good boy and finish it." She pulled out some slips from her pocket. "See? Here are some food coupons. My son just came back from the army yesterday. He gave me these coupons. I'll buy some flour and make pancakes for you tomorrow. Lick and clear your bowl, honey!"

Seeing that I was standing by, Nanny Chen initiated a conversation. "Ah, Comrade Hwang," she started with a sigh. "Everybody is minding their stomachs these days. But there is no food!" She let out another sigh. "I often think it would be nice if we weren't born with our stomachs! That would keep us out of all these troubles! Now I find it's more difficult to take care of David than raising my son. It's not easy to be a nanny these days!"

Nanny Chen was a widow from the countryside, and she had overcome lots of hardships. I thought she was asking for a pay raise, but she continued in a different tone.

"Well, Comrade Hwang, do you think only the city folks are starving?" She changed the subject abruptly. "No! You city folks don't know that people are dying in the countryside. My younger sister is in a commune. She came to see me the other day. She told me that starvation in villages is hundred times more serious. People like to die in the city, rather than starving to death in the commune!"

I was dumbfounded to hear what she said. However, she went on before I could make any comment. "Let me tell you. The cadres in the communes forbid anyone to leave!" She began to lose control of her wrath. "So people can't come to the city to die! We have been following Chairman Mao. He is our God! But now many say that Chairman Mao is good except one thing! He kills too many people. He lets too many starve to death!"

I never expected Nanny Chen would dare to say things like that. She was probably fearless because she had a son in the army.

The whirling wind of the "Great Leap Forward" had been blasted everywhere. Finally, it blew into our courtyard. Since early 1959, our landlord had suddenly ceased to appear. A Housing Bureau agent took his place in collecting monthly rent. What had happened to our landlord? Was he in trouble? Had his property been confiscated? We wanted to find out, but the city rent collector only shook his head. He did not provide us with any information. Maybe he really did not know.

Meanwhile, tenants of the east and west wings quickly moved out and a group of traditional Chinese musicians from Shanghai moved in. They told us that they belonged to a newly formed dance troupe. The courthouse was supposed to be their training center and their boss was a famous old dancer named Wu Xiaobang.

That was a total surprise to us! We could not figure out what was going on until Wu Xiaobang showed up one day. Without amenity, he announced that he had just formed a dancing troupe and planned to bring some traditional Chinese dance accompanied by Chinese music to stage. He said that his project was funded by the government in the "Great Leap Forward Movement." He wanted us to move out because he had rented the courthouse.

Wu Xiabang's attitude was rude and his words blunt. I instantly rebuffed his demand, telling him that I had a legal lease for the north wing of the courthouse. Wu Xiaobang was swaggering. After getting the rebuttal, he still kept on wanting me to move, saying that my workplace should have a dormitory for me. Tired of giving him any reply, I only showed my lease contract to his staff.

The dispute with Wu Xiaobang lasted almost half a year. During the deadlock, his musicians bombarded us day and night with their awful music. Fortunately, Father had left for his recuperation. Pauline, Jean and Phillip were also lucky to stay temporarily in the live-in kindergarten. Otherwise, they would also be polluted by the unbearable noise.

Things took an unexpected turn in early 1960. Before our confrontation with Wu Xiaobang was resolved, we suddenly had newcomers come to live with us in the Bag Lane. Again, our premises became congested. Even if Wu Xiaobang offered settlement, we would not be able to move.

Our newcomers were my niece Xie Lilin and nephew Xie Likun, the second daughter and son of my eldest sister Hwang Chun and her husband Xic Jiasong. They were both teenagers. When their father and mother were exiled by the Communists to the Northwest in 1959, they stayed behind in Shanghai by themselves. One day, Likun fell from the stairway and received a head concussion. Olivia and I were alarmed, so we brought them to Beijing right away.

Sister Hwang Chun and her husband had been living in Shanghai for years. Anyone familiarized with Russian history might have noticed that

Stalin had relocated the Russian population a lot by exiling the "undesirables" far away. Other Communists, like Mao Zedong and Pol Pot, had done the same and even more. My brother-in-law Xie Jiasong and my sister Hwang Chun might have been targeted.

Olivia and I worried about their exile. Before their departure from Shanghai to the Qinghai Province, we had beseeched Mother to go to Shanghai and advise them not to bring all their children along, so they only went with their youngest daughter, Xie Libin.

It was extremely fortunate that a dancing troupe in Beijing began recruiting young trainees not long after they reached the Qinghai Province. Libin was talented and interested in dancing. When she came to Beijing, Olivia brought her over for an audition.

The dancing troupe was run by the military and the training program was for the most talented. In the interview, the judges took Xie Libin as Olivia's daughter. Libin was very lucky to be admitted on the spot. The dancing troupe not only brought her back from the Qinghai Province, but also led her to a very successful career.

12

The Complicated Overseas Ties

The last time Olivia had heard from her home in Singapore was 1952. We had received a letter full of love from Father-in-law, bestowing David with the Chinese name "Yinan." He seemed anxious to meet all of us. But Mainland China abruptly sealed off the relations between the returned overseas Chinese and their families abroad. News from the outside world was censored, and personal communication was disrupted.

A tragic change thus took place. After their power was consolidated, the Communists began to suppress those overseas Chinese families that had remained in China. In response, the overseas Chinese abroad adopted an unfriendly attitude towards the Communists. Caught in between the conflicts, many overseas Chinese family members became victims. Olivia lost her family connection in Singapore.

Following the tenet that "the ends justify the means," the Chinese Communists had always applied whatever means necessary to achieve their goals. No moral consideration was allowed to enter or interfere in their operations. They only used the overseas Chinese to exert their influence abroad and seize their power at home.

For instance, before they had entirely taken over Mainland China, they were very sweet to overseas Chinese. It was well known that during World War II, a prominent overseas Chinese named Chen Jiageng was attracted by Communist announced goals. He went to Yanan from Singapore and donated trucks of medical and other supplies to them. Ironically, the ambulance he donated turned into Mao Zedong's personal sedan in Yanan later on.

Once solidly in power, the Communists had gone after many overseas Chinese families in the Mainland, targeting them as potential enemies and confiscating their homes and businesses. Olivia had not been affected because she did not own any land or property at the time.

As previously noted, a twist had come with the "false thaw" of 1956. The Communists had suddenly softened their policy, turning a warm face toward overseas Chinese families. Once again, they put their "united front" policy in full display.

Olivia was surprised to be contacted by the Overseas Chinese Bureau. A female cadre came to brief her about the situation of her family in Singapore. She encouraged Olivia to reconnect with her family. In her briefings, however, the cadre casually informed Olivia that her father had passed away in 1955.

That brought a terrible shock to Olivia! She was resentful to learn of her father's death from the Communists instead of from other sources. She realized that she had been blocked from the outside world under the Communist rule.

Mourning her father in tears, Olivia did not want to be used as a tool for the so-called "united front" policy. Instead of reconnecting with Singapore, she only recollected with deep love her connection with her father. Meanwhile, the visits of the female cadre had also resurrected many memories of her early life. For the first time since we had met and married, she shared with me in detail many of her stories.

Olivia told me that her father had always been busy and often away from home. The few occasions for him to see the family together had been when he was at the dinner table. None of the children had had the opportunity to get close to him individually.

During those occasions, Olivia recalled that her father would lecture them on how to be good people. Sometimes, he would tell stories from Chinese history. One folk hero he often talked about was the legendary Guangong. Olivia's father took him as a model of fidelity and loyalty.

Olivia considered herself to be the luckiest because she had once gotten a chance to be close to her father. That was early 1946 in Shanghai. She had been at her father's side alone for several weeks. At the time, her father happened to have left Singapore to attend the National Congress of the Nationalist Government. Olivia was in her freshman year majoring in electric engineering at Jiaotong University.

For Olivia, the sojourn was an everlasting sweet memory. She told me that her father had been very proud of her as a girl enrolled in the most prestigious university of technology in China. Her father stayed in a business partner's mansion. Olivia described how happy her father had been when she brought him the daily newspaper every morning. Her father had also taken her to some of his social gatherings. Once, at a banquet, he even asked her to make a toast on his behalf. Olivia had never touched alcohol before. She got rashes from the drink right away.

The more Olivia reflected the past, the more she felt her father's love was irreplaceable. In 1950, she had once been afraid that her father might get mad at her because she did not wait for him in the United States after our wedding. But when we went back to Mainland China, her father had written to congratulate us for going back to "serve the people" in China. That was not a casual comment. Olivia had read the letter over and over accepting it as her father's encouragement.

Then came early 1952. When her father had been informed of David's birth, he had bestowed upon David the name of "Yinan." In memorializing her father now, Olivia realized that "Yinan" was more than just a name given from him. David was her father's first grandson from his daughter's side. "Yinan" meant "keep Southeast Asia in memory." Olivia felt that her father had sent his descendants a message: "Never Forget Southeast Asia."

In order to relay her rekindled memories to me, Olivia found it convenient to start with World War II at wartime Chongqing. We both had gone through the war in Chongqing when we were teenagers.

Olivia told me that she had fled Singapore in 1941. Her father had sent her and her elder sister Helen by plane to Burma right before the Japanese invasion. Many members of the extended Quek family led by her Elder Uncle Juchuan had also escaped through another route afterward. Only her father had remained behind in Singapore, intending to look after the family business. Unfortunately, he had been put into a Japanese prison camp throughout the war.

All the Quek evacuees had gone to Chongqing, the wartime capital of China. Olivia emphasized that they had been extremely lucky because her eldest brother Kaitee was there. As if by God's will, he had already established the Zhongyuan Paper Factory in the Sichuan Province with its headquarters in Chongqing. Therefore, when the Quek evacuees arrived, they did not have to worry about their lodging, schools or livelihoods.

Being the eldest son of Olivia's first mother, Kaitee was almost twenty years older than Olivia. Trained as an engineer in Germany, he had come home in the early 1930s supposedly to assist his father in business. But he had voluntarily taken up the responsibility of taking care of all his younger stepsisters and stepbrothers. All of them, especially Olivia, were his beneficiaries. Olivia sincerely believed that in her childhood, she might not have survived without her brother Kaitee. Therefore, she always felt that Kaitee was like a fatherly brother.

Olivia's own mother was her father's second wife. Tragically, she passed away before reaching thirty. Olivia was only three and in poor health when left motherless. At the age of seven, she suffered from severe asthma. Fortunately, brother Kaitee had come home at that very juncture, and he immediately took Olivia under his care.

When she came to this part of her heartfelt memory, Olivia recited it with deep emotion. She described with gratitude how brother Kaitee had taken her daily to doctors for eye treatments and vitamin shots. Brother Kaitee had even sent her to Malaya when her asthma became uncontrollably severe. As a little girl of seven, she could not comprehend why she should stop going to school and stay with some unknown relatives in the hilly countryside. She recalled with a chuckle that she had wailed and clung to brother Kaitee's leg when he dropped her off. But thanks to brother Kaitee, her asthma had subdued for at least ten years after staying one whole year in the countryside.

To Olivia, her experience in Chongqing illustrated again brother Kaitee's devotion to the whole Quek family. She believed that the Quek girls and boys in her generation were blessed to have him in Chongqing. There were only a few good middle schools around. Without the direct support of brother Kaitee and his friend Professor Chen Xujing, the Quek girls and boys would definitely have not been able to attend Nankai High School, one of the top high schools in China.

Wartime meals at Nankai, though, had not been very tasteful. Olivia recalled with laughter how the Quek girls and boys had gathered at brother Kaitee's headquarters of the Zhongyuan Paper Company. It had been the rejuvenating center of all the Quek youngsters every weekend. They went there to refill their stomachs, listen to music, play games, and get their badly needed supplies. Olivia often announced proudly that she had learned how to play contract bridge from her brother Kaitee.

In the summer of 1943, Kaitee came up with a special project. Olivia remembered that she had been asked to accompany Professor Chen Xujing and his family to tour Omei Mountain. The whole trip had been arranged and funded by brother Kaitee to offer them a vacation. The Omei Mountain was marvelous. However, Olivia recalled, as they climbed, the temperature dropped rapidly. At the mountaintop Jinding, it was freezing. Her asthma had flared back that night.

Omei happened to be my native town. I had been raised in Nanjing but went back to the Sichuan Province in 1938. In the middle of 1940s, I had visited Omei twice, and toured the Omei Mountain. I was interested to hear about Olivia's experience in Omei, so I chimed in, "Where did you stay at the mountaintop?"

Olivia was not prepared for my interruption. She paused a little while and clapped her hands: "Of course, I remember it! I believe we stayed at 'Woyunan' that night. I remember it was a nunnery."

"Ha! That was also the place I stayed at Jinding!" I also clapped my hands. "I got an asthma attack that night too! 'Woyunan' means 'Nunnery Lying on the Clouds.' But I was able to watch the 'ocean of clouds' under the moon that night. Were you?" Olivia had been very sick during her stay and had been confined to her bed, so she did not answer the question. Nevertheless, our similar experiences at the Omei Mountain brought us unstoppable giggles.

There were more stories of brother Kaitee from Olivia. She told me that Kaitee was tender in heart, gentle in manner, and reserved in nature. To her knowledge, Kaitee had never bragged about the good things he had done for his family or his friends. He had also been the one who quietly planned and sent Olivia and her younger sister Flora to the United States in 1946.

Professor Chen Xujing was a prominent scholar in China. He also came from Hainan Island. Olivia had gotten to know him better through the tour to Omei arranged by her brother Kaitee. She found that both her brother Kaitee and Professor Chen had similar temperaments. She took both of them as father-like brothers. I came to know Professor Chen later through Olivia, and I was fortunate to get close to him. I witnessed how he treated Olivia as a dear niece/sister.

Olivia happened to have had two cousins, Meifeng and Jinfeng, living in Beijing in the 1950s. They were two of the Quek evacuees from Singapore during World War II. They shared many of her memories of wartime Chongqing. Whenever they got together and talked about their wartime experiences, brother Kaitee and Professor Chen Xujing's names were frequently mentioned.

Meifeng and Jinfeng were daughters of Olivia's elder uncle Juchuan. Occasionally, Olivia had lived with them when they were young. As soon as the news of Mainland China's famine reached Singapore, their mother kept sending them food supplies. In order to find out about their well-being, their mother also dispatched their nanny, Sister Qing Xiang, to Mainland China to find out their real situations in early 1959.

That was a kind of general practice for many overseas Chinese families. Without her parents around, Olivia did not expect anyone to come to see her.

After her father's death, she intuitively sensed something might have happened to her brothers, so she did not expect to hear from her brothers as well.

But Sister Qing Xiang knew Olivia when Olivia was a little girl. She had also been in wartime Chongqing with the Queks. Therefore, she came to visit Olivia in Beijing. She was very happy to see Olivia, telling Olivia many things about her home in Singapore but curiously little about Olivia's brothers. There seemed to be a riddle in Olivia's family that Sister Qing Xiang would not dare to crack. While listening to Sister Qing Xiang, Olivia mindfully did not ask about her brothers or send them any message.

Olivia had had a nickname "Yinggutou" ("Hard Bone") at home in Singapore. When she was young, she appeared quite stubborn sometimes. She liked to stick to what she deemed right. She had faith in her siblings' love, but she would not ask for assistance under any circumstances.

Several months after Sister Qing Xiang's visit, however, a big package of staples came to Olivia. In the package, there was Chinese farm produce sold to Southeast Asia and re-imported into Mainland China. Food items such as rice, flour, sugar and cooking oil were badly needed under the famine. Olivia appreciated the timely assistance. She was anxious to send a "thank you" letter to whoever rendered her a hand in dire hardship. But embarrassingly, she found no sender's name or address in the package.

Thus, there came another riddle. Why would her brothers not want to acknowledge if they were the senders? Olivia guessed that Sister Qing Xiang's visit might have something to do with the package. Someone in Singapore might have sent her that package in anonymity.

The unknowns in Singapore kept on bugging Olivia for a few months. She was confident that her brothers loved her, but she could not understand why they kept silent. She tried hard to crack the riddle and to understand why she was rejected and ignored by her brothers. In the end, she had to accept a hard fact that someone in the family had attempted to cut her off.

Amidst the enigmatic situation, a letter unexpectedly came to Olivia from Malaya in July 1961. Olivia was very excited because the letter was sent by an old sister-in-law, San Sao. San Sao was the wife of her cousin Kai Kee, the third son of her uncle Quek Ju-chuan. She was in the same age group as Olivia's own mother and had always treated Olivia as her own daughter. Olivia had grown up with San Sao's two daughters Ailin and Ailan. They had been very close to her, considering themselves not aunt and nieces, but dear sisters.

However, San Sao's letter consisted of only a few lines. She said nothing but urged Olivia to come home immediately. The message was short and straightforward, warning that Olivia would regret for life if she did not go back as quickly as possible.

It was a shock to Olivia. She never expected to get such a warning. San Sao's brief letter did not mention Olivia's brothers, but alerted Olivia that something had happened in her family. "Go home right away!" was strong advice. "Regret for life!" was a serious warning.

No one would like to "regret for life." For a week, Olivia was in agony, trying to figure out the meaning of San Sao's warning. One day, she dragged me away from my desk. "I want to tell you something you don't know." She sounded serious. "You should help me to decide whether I should go back to Singapore right away or not!"

For the first time, she told me that she was a shareholder of her family's company. Although her father had named his company Quek Shin & Sons, he had given each of his daughters a certain amount of shares in it. She did not know exactly how many shares she had, but no matter how small her share was, she was a shareholder anyway.

With a deep sigh, Olivia said that she had never given a thought about her shares in her family company. She always wanted to work hard, supporting herself and her own family. Since returning to Mainland China, she had forgotten all together about her shareholder status at home.

I knew nothing about Olivia's family's company or of Olivia's shares in it. I had no experience or interest in business all my life. "Shareholder" was an alien term to me, so I listened to Olivia, but could not make any comment.

"Now the problem for me is giving San Sao an answer. To go or not to go—I have to make a quick decision!" Olivia pressed to get my opinion.

Many things Olivia confided to me were unknown to me before that time. We were expecting to have another baby before the end of that year. Under Olivia's quiz, I told her that only she could make the decision herself as to go or not to go back home. The only thing she might wish to think about was the timing. If she decided to go back to Singapore after our new baby's birth, she would have to wait until next year. Otherwise, she probably had to plan the trip right now.

After a few days of soul searching, Olivia finally got rid of her agony. "I will follow San Sao's advice!" she told me in a firm voice. "I will go as soon as possible!" When I asked how she came to her decision, she replied, "In the last few days, I've given some thoughts to my shareholder status for the first time in my life. Regardless of the amount of the shares, that is a relation between a father and a daughter. How can I disavow the relationship between my father and me? Besides," Olivia raised her voice, "San Sao warned me about my future. As I see it, she was warning me about my children's future, too, so I've got to go!"

It was the middle of August 1961. Olivia submitted her application for an exit permit immediately. She also informed San Sao that she was following her advice to visit her in Singapore. At the time, famine was still running its course harshly in Mainland China. Communist policy towards overseas Chinese had become a little more lenient. Olivia was surprised that her application was approved within a week.

But once Olivia was approved to embark on her journey, a question came up right away. She had to decide how many and which of our children she would bring with her. And her decision would have a tremendous impact upon our children's future.

The Exit Permit Office only allowed an exit person to bring two children abroad. Olivia was approved to take Phillip and Jean. But we worried for David. He was nine and half years old at the time. Pretty soon, the "League of Communist Vanguards" would recruit him in school. After that, David's chance of going abroad would be very slim. Therefore, "to go or not to go with Mother" was extremely important for David at that juncture. We wished desperately that David could also get an exit permit.

I remember Olivia and I were hard put. We lost several nights of sleep dealing with the dilemma. At the last minute, we decided to take a risk. We prepared two sets of pictures. One had Olivia with Jean and Phillip. The other had David added. When the issuing date came, we replaced the original photo with the one having David added on. Luckily, the Public Security clerk did not check, so David was able to get the exit permit.

In order to go to Singapore, one had to go through Hong Kong. And to enter Hong Kong, one must first get to Guangzhou by train. On October the 18 of 1961, Olivia left Beijing with David, Phillip and Jean. I took leave from the office to accompany them on their way.

Father and Mother brought Pauline to see us off at the railway station. I believe their feelings were ambivalent. They surely were happy to see Olivia leaving with the three grandchildren for freedom, but they were also aware that they might never have a chance to see them again. At the same time, they could not be sure when Pauline would be able to unite with them. To take care of Pauline, they decided to move back to Bag Lane while keeping their rented room at Dafosi East Street just in case.

In Guangzhou, we went to Sister Hwang Lian's place first. Her husband Wan Changtai was then the chief engineer of the Guangzhou Power Plant, so they stayed in the western suburbs of the city. The next day, we went downtown to start Olivia's travel arrangements. Guangzhou was a worldly city because of its vicinity to Hong Kong. Walking on its streets, we felt like two boors coming to town. Suddenly, we became aware that we had lost our touch with the outside world for quite some time.

The first place we went for information was the China Travel Service. A clerk told Olivia that she needed a British visa to enter Hong Kong. Since she would never be able to get such a visa, she could only go to Hong Kong by smuggling. The China Travel Service was not in the smuggling business. Therefore, she might wish to go to a place called the Nanda Hotel to make those kind of arrangements.

When we got to the Nanda Hotel, however, we found it was a hotel only in name. Bustling with people, it actually handled secretive businesses. The agents at the front counter were very cool. Learning that Olivia intended to smuggle, they asked her to fill out a number of questionnaires. Most importantly, she had to provide them with her reference in Hong Kong.

At the time, Olivia had no Hong Kong reference. The agent instantly lost interest in her case. The Hong Kong reference was crucial, he emphasized, because his company had to collect fees before and after the smuggling operation from her reference.

The agents' attitude was rude. Olivia was disappointed and could not comply with their demand. Contemplating for a while, she pulled out her address book, borrowed a phone from a girl at the desk, and whispered to me, "I'm going to call Professor Chen."

I recalled at the moment that Olivia had planned to contact Professor Chen Xujing before. The reason she did not do it before leaving Beijing was because everything was in fluid. Now she needed Professor Chen's guidance and advice to proceed.

It happened like a miracle. When Olivia dialed Professor Chen Xujing's phone number, he was at the other end. Olivia talked to him for quite a while, smiling broadly before putting down the phone. She was very excited, holding my hand to leave the Nanda Hotel. As soon as we got outside, she told me that Professor Chen would meet us at the Overseas Chinese Mansion immediately.

The first time I had met Professor Chen Xujing was in 1956. He had come to see Olivia when he had been in Beijing for a conference. He was a renowned scholar of my father's age. I did not have the opportunity to be one of his students, but I had read many of his books. I could never forget that visit he paid us at home. The first thing he had done when he met Olivia was ask her to stretch out her hands. Then he had examined Olivia's palms to see whether there were warts or calluses. That meant he wanted to know how intensive had Olivia been engaged in manual labor. Only a loving father would do that to his beloved daughter.

When we met him in the lobby of the Overseas Chinese Mansion, Professor Chen Xujing appeared to be the same loving father. He first checked on Olivia's health and forthcoming maternity date. Without any delay, he booked two rooms for us in the Mansion, asking us to bring our children there with us. To facilitate Olivia's trip, he helped Olivia register with the Overseas Chinese Bureau of the Guangdong Province. Meanwhile, he made a number of phone calls to make sure that Olivia could get all the proper maternity assistance.

Professor Chen Xujing seemed to have a super-ability to run things smoothly, studiously and flawlessly. He invited us and our children for dinner at his home that very evening.

As president of Zhongshan University, Professor Chen Xujing had a car with a chauffer. David and Phillip were exhilarated to see a private sedan. They had only ridden in buses and vans before. Professor Chen Xujing was amused to watch the excited boys. "Kids, this is an old and small car." He patted their shoulders. "You haven't seen the real car yet. Wait until you meet your Uncle Kaitee!"

David and Phillip did not know they had an Uncle Kaitee. They probably could not make out what Professor Chen Xujing meant. But it reminded Olivia and me how deep his friendship with Kaitee was.

We were still under famine and Professor Chen Xujing had a big family to feed. Many of his relatives were counting on his support. The dinner that night must have cost him many rationing coupons. Olivia and I found it hard to fully express our appreciation.

As soon as we moved into the Overseas Chinese Mansion, Olivia sent a telegram to San Sao in Singapore, asking for help to get into Hong Kong. We were planning to relax for a few days, but Sister Hwang Lian came to visit us and brought us a bunch of mail from Beijing. In the mail, there was a letter from Singapore. Olivia read it and was astonished. She numbly passed it to me, and she signaled me to have a hard look.

The letter was written in longhand Chinese and bluntly told Olivia to stop planning to go back to Singapore. It asserted that the Singapore government would not let persons like her return. Neither would Hong Kong authority grant her an entry. Furthermore, the letter questioned why Olivia should wish to go back to Singapore after going to Communist China voluntarily.

The letter also argued that the family had welcomed back those members who had strayed into Mainland China without their knowing. But Olivia was different. She had gone back on purpose, so she should stay in Communist China.

I was also shocked after reading the letter. The longhand writing was flowery. Its language was rude, and its reasoning superficial. It did not look like it had been written by the man Olivia always praised, but at the end of the letter, the signature was "Kaitee." I did not know what to say, so I showed it to Olivia and asked her to have a second look.

"Brother Kaitee never wrote in Chinese!" Olivia responded quickly. After a while, she sounded as if she had just woken up from a sleep, and said, "Brother Kaitee never talked to people like this. This flowery scribe is not his style, even if he tries to write in Chinese!"

Olivia believed that it was a fake signature and that no secretary would dare to do it. She could not help thinking that someone in Singapore was trying to block her journey home. She felt lucky that the letter arrived in Beijing after she left. Otherwise, she might have hesitated to follow San Sao's advice and go home so quickly.

The letter caused Olivia some concern, but did little to dampen her determination. I was not comfortable with the tone of the letter and began to worry more about Olivia's safety. But Olivia told me that she was not afraid of that kind of bluffing. "Why should I be detracted by a letter?" she asked herself aloud, saying that she would definitely go as planned.

Olivia's maternity date was approaching. The staff of the Overseas Chinese Mansion wanted to be helpful, so they put Olivia on their priority list for people going to Hong Kong. They dispatched a travel agent to escort Olivia and the children to the border town of Shenzhen on October 25 of 1961. Since I had no special permit to go to the border areas and could not accompany Olivia, they requested me to stay in the hotel until she safely entered Hong Kong.

However, for three days, Olivia and the three kids were stuck in Shenzhen. They lined up with other travelers under the sun from morning to noon, but they were blocked at Luohu checkpoint. For reasons unknown, the British police simply refused to let them go across the border. They were frustrated and exhausted.

On the morning of October the 31, I suddenly learned that Olivia's maternity time had arrived and she had already been sent to the Shenzhen local hospital. The Bureau of Overseas Chinese checked with me to determine whether I wanted to join Olivia.

"Of course I would!" I was deeply stressed. "My children also need my care!"

But Shenzhen was at the border area under military control. One not only needed a special permit to go to the border area, but also a special taxi to get there. I filled out an application and requested a special taxi immediately. For the entire afternoon, it seemed like I was an ant crawling on a hot pan.

At last, a taxi pulled up at the front of the hotel after five o'clock. The driver brought me the permit to go to border area. With a leisurely smile, he told me that he was ready to take me to Shenzhen. I jumped in the taxi as if I were on a rescue mission.

13

Surprises in Shenzhen

The drive from Guangzhou to Shenzhen usually takes about an hour. However, before getting onto the highway, the taxi driver stopped many times to deliver and pick up packages. That might have been his standard practice, but the delay caused me anguish. Not until dusk were we truly on our way.

The sun was setting and the horizon was all painted in pink. We drove along the fantastic Pearl River Valley. The earth had become a spectacular array of colors. Birds soared in the sky before returning to their nests. Once in a while, we could even see the fishes bubbling in the creek along the valley.

The scenery gradually soothed my tension. Watching the birds flying against the sunset, two familiar lines of Wang Bo's poem suddenly flickered through my mind: "While the glow of sunset is flying with the lonely crow, the river shares its color with the sky in its flow."

It was amazing! Almost a thousand years ago, the Tang Dynasty poet Wang Bo seemed to have portrayed the breathtaking view for me! I put my worries aside and began to enjoy the sceneries.

It was the last day of October. In the north, the weather would be chilly. But it was still warm in the south. The Pearl River Valley was so fertile and a bountiful harvest was clearly in sight. It made the word "famine" absurd in this area.

The driver began to strike up a conversation with me. He tried to help me relax with some of his funny stories. He promised to send me directly to Shenzhen's hospital. After that, he would wheel me to the guesthouse to see my children. With a chuckle, he assured me that he would not leave me alone in this trip.

While we were talking, I felt the driver constantly slowing down the car. I became worried that it might delay our trip. The driver sensed my feeling, explaining that there were dogs around. "See the ones roaming toward us?" He applied his brakes quickly. "I can't risk running over them."

Indeed, I noticed that several dogs were crisscrossing the highway. The shining dots from their eyes reflected the car's headlights. I had seldom seen any dog ever since returning to the Mainland. "Why are there so many dogs here?" I asked the driver.

"Most dogs here belong to the army," the driver replied. "Local peasants also raise some dogs for sale. Hong Kong people are fond of dog meat!" He told me that Shenzhen was a fishing village north of Kowloon. Dog meat was one of its attractions. Hong Kong people liked to be served dog meat and bizarre fishes by the local restaurants.

Around nine o'clock, we finally got to the small Shenzhen hospital. Olivia was in the delivery room and her contractions had already begun. Surprised to see me at her side, she gripped me tightly as if she would not let me go again. But as soon as she was told that the baby might not come yet, her mind instantly switched to the children. She was worried about them in the guesthouse. She loosened her hold and beseeched me to go to take care of them.

The little town of Shenzhen was shrouded in darkness. The driver was right! There was no local transportation available at night in Shenzhen. I had to count on him the entire night.

When he brought me to the guesthouse, David, Phillip and Jean were all surprised and clung to me in tears like the abandoned kids. I consoled them and told them that everything would be fine from now on. I informed them that they would have a baby brother or sister pretty soon. Meanwhile, I had to go back to be with their mother in the hospital, but tomorrow morning we would all go together to see mother and the new baby.

I returned to Olivia's side that night around 11:30 p.m. She had just begun her hard labor, perspiring with pain. Seeing that I was nervous, the nurse advised me to leave the room for a while. I walked to the yard, looking at the dimly visible sky. To relax, I lit a cigarette, but before I could finish it, the clock struck midnight and a sonorous baby cry came through the open hallway door.

Midnight had just passed. Now it was November the first, the All Saints Day of 1961. I rushed immediately to Olivia's side. In her exhaustion, she told me with a smile that we had a son. We had agreed beforehand to give the name "Robert" to the baby boy.

Years later, Olivia often joked: "Bobby seemed to have made up his mind. He chose to come on the All Saints Day instead of Halloween. He got six 'ones' on his birthday! The month of November gave him two 'ones.' The first minute of the day, the first day of the month, and the year of '1961' brought him another four 'ones.' So he became a six 'ones' boy!"

Olivia stayed in the Shenzhen hospital for several more days. It was in walking distance from the guesthouse. Every day, David, Philip and Jean were so happy to go with me to visit their mother and their new baby brother. The family never seemed to have had such a chance to enjoy the country life and the wonders of nature.

Olivia received two visitors at the guesthouse after returning from the hospital. The first one was a servant sent by Mr. Han Shunguang, Kaitee's friend in Hong Kong. He brought Olivia delicacies and his master's business address and phone number.

Han Shunguang was then the honorary president of the Hainanese Association in Hong Kong. He owned an established export-import firm over there. He wanted Olivia to know that he was ready to welcome and assist her. Olivia was pleased to have received a solid reference in Hong Kong.

The second visitor, however, was a surprise. Olivia had never communicated with her sister-in-law Zheng Wenxiang before, so Zheng Wenxiang's sudden appearance in Shenzhen was totally unexpected. Zheng Wenxiang was the second wife of Olivia's brother Kaichong whose first wife was killed in a Japanese bombing in World War II. Kaichong and Zheng Wenxiang married after we had left the United States. But we had had a very brief acquaintance with her when we visited Kaichong in Indiana in 1950.

After ten years of separation, Olivia was happy to see a family member from Singapore again. In her weakness of maternity, she greeted Zheng Wenxiang and waited to hear the news her sister-in-law might bring her from home. But Zheng Wenxiang seemed to be in a rush. Without informing Olivia of her family's situation, she sat down in a business-like manner and straightforwardly questioned why Olivia harbored the idea of going home to Singapore.

Olivia was stunned and instantly fell into silence. She did not wish to tell the new sister-in-law sitting in front of her that she was answering the call of San Sao, another sister-in-law, to return home urgently. While Olivia kept her silence, Zheng Wenxiang seemed to turn to a different kind of urgency.

She told Olivia flatly that there was no way for Olivia to get back to Singapore. The Singapore government would never admit any person from Communist China. Neither would the Hong Kong police. They would not allow persons like Olivia to go across the border with her children.

Apparently, Zheng Wenxiang had learned from other sources that Olivia had had some previous difficulty going through the border check point at Lofu Bridge. She told Olivia not to risk her life with her kids by insisting to get through, and she warned Olivia that the British police would shoot them if they tried. She offered Olivia a wooden box of utility soap she had brought with her and strongly advised Olivia to go back to Beijing.

Throughout the whole meeting with Zheng Wenxiang, Olivia did not say a word up to that point. She only looked at the eyes of her sister-in-law. She seemed to have wavered little in her determination to go home. Thus, the whole room was covered by an awkward silence. I had not joined their conversation. We had only that one room at the guesthouse, so I could be only a silent onlooker from a corner.

In the silence, Zheng Wenxiang gradually sensed that Olivia would not take her suggestion. Changing to a more friendly tone, she began to confide to Olivia that she had been entrusted by her brothers to make sure Olivia had a safe journey home. Since Olivia was stuck in Shenzhen at the moment, she advised Olivia to think about going to Macao first, instead of trying to enter Hong Kong directly.

That was a drastic shift in attitude during Olivia's meeting with her sister-in-law. Having been let out of the hospital only two days before, Olivia was still very weak. But Zheng Wenxiang's proposal was a fresh idea to her, so she began to think.

Macao was then still a Portuguese colony located in the backwaters of the South China Sea. The tiny island was famous for its casinos and free access to visitors. No visa was needed for anyone to get into Macao.

After a long contemplation, Olivia agreed to change her route to avoid further difficulty in Shenzhen. Zheng Wenxiang became excited immediately, saying that her mother knew people in Macao and could help her rent a house there.

After Zheng Wenxiang left with some enthusiasm, I told Olivia that I was puzzled by the complexity of her family. But I congratulated her for her coolness, dignity and composure in her conversation with her sister-in-law.

"You know what?" Olivia answered. "At first I was confused by Zheng Wenxiang's insistence of my going back to Beijing. I thought she might have been worrying my home going would put a burden on my brothers. But I am a share holder of our family company, and I would never be a burden to anyone. Why should anyone worry about that?"

Wrapped in reflection, Olivia continued, "You know what? Today I had an epiphany…I might have found the author of that letter written in brother Kaitee's name!"

As soon as a decision had been made to change route, Olivia asked me to re-pack to go back to Guangzhou immediately. Now that her brother Kaitee had provided her with a Hong Kong connection, she was more confidant than before even if she had to detour through Macao.

On our train back to Guangzhou, we got a panoramic view of Shenzhen. It was a town surrounded by beautiful hilly farmland. No one could have guessed that Shenzhen would be a metro city forty years later. I did not have a chance to see the impressive landscape when I came at night, so I asked Olivia and the children to take a good look at the scenery. I reminded them to remember that this was the town where Robert was born.

Olivia and I decided on the train to name Robert "Li-shen" in Chinese. "Shen" represented "Shenzhen" to pay a tribute to Robert's birthplace.

Again, Professor Chen Xujing rendered us great help in Guangzhou for Olivia's trip to Macao. Zheng Wenxiang's mother did help in renting a place for Olivia and the children to live. At the same time, Professor Chen's friends assisted in arranging the children's schooling and Robert's care in Macao.

When Olivia left for Macao with the children, Robert was only eighteen days old. Before her departure, she and I had many heart-to-heart talks. The riddle in her family had not yet been cracked. The difficulties of returning to the free world began to loom higher. We both knew that the future was unpredictable and that Olivia might face a lot of other hardships.

I was unable to go with her. Olivia had to face all the hardships and dangers alone. I felt guilty for that, but I knew that I should not let a gloomy view hang over her head. I was also aware that Olivia might be sandwiched between two antagonistic worlds. She would be doomed if she remained in the Communist world, but she also might not be accepted by the free world. Even if she was accepted, she would have to restart her life.

In our intermittent discussions, Olivia told me that she was determined to raise our children in the free world. She assured me that she was not afraid of the possible difficulties. On the contrary, her worries would mostly be on Pauline, our parents and me from now on. I was deeply moved by her determination and courage. "Then, when worst comes to worst, please never turn back because of me!" I advised.

It was a chilly morning and the sky was overcast. I saw Olivia and the children off at a bus terminal. I had an awfully sad feeling that it might be our last farewell. We might never be able to reunite again. But I suppressed my feelings and tried to cheer everyone up. I still remember how Olivia sat at the back of the bus that morning. Robert was wrapped in a bundle in Olivia's lap. Meanwhile, Jean, Phillip and David were excited about their new trip.

After Olivia and the children left for Macao, I went to stay with my good friend Zhong Rexin for almost one week. He was teaching at Zhongshan University and had a small separate house on campus. His wife and son were in Hong Kong at the time, so his house became a temporary gathering place for his friends.

Staying on the campus of Zhongshan University, I was not only able to get close to Professor Chen Xujing, but also learn about Olivia's situation through the private phone connection with Macao. One evening after dinner, Professor Chen Xujing invited me to have tea at his residence.

Due to energy conservation, the campus was not fully lit. As we walked through a soccer field to his house, Professor Chen asked about my recent life. I mentioned a few heart-wrenching experiences, witnessing people advancing themselves at another's expenses. It was disgusting, I told him, to watch the opportunists climb up the political ladders.

"It's not uncommon these days," Professor Chen commented. "What you have seen were people climbing on each other's backs. I have people stepping on my nose to get ahead. You know, in the old society, money was the key. Now only political power counts." Listening to him in the semidarkness, I fell into silence. I had never expected that a scholar like him would speak out so frankly.

After the tea, Professor Chen Xujing led me into his study. It was a very small room occupied by a desk, two chairs, and a heavily loaded bookshelf, leaving little space to move around. His manuscripts were scattered on the desk, on the shelf and on the floor. Somehow, I was attracted to a pile in one corner.

"Oh, it's my draft on Xiongnu history," Professor Chen Xujing explained when I bent over to look at them. "You know, Xiongnu was a tribe of the Turkish people. They had great influence in Asian and European history. I started the book ten years ago, and now it is almost in its completion."

I was struck with awe by Professor Chen Xujing's energy and erudition. When I brought up a subject, he referred me right away to a historian. I told him that I knew little about this historian. He immediately pulled out a pen from his chest pocket. When he scribbled down the name of the historian and his major works, I noticed that his black fountain pen was bandaged all over. With courtesy, I commented, "You must have used your pen for a long time, Professor Chen. How old is it?"

"This one?" He held up his pen. "Oh. It's old. I bought it in 1925 for my thesis in Berlin. It has almost come apart now."

"Wow!" I exclaimed in surprise. "In 1925? That's the year I was born!"

"I see!" he laughed. "So it should go to you later."

Professor Chen Xujing wanted me to bring Zhong Rexin and Chen Dieyun for another evening tea the next day. They were my friends but also his faculty members. One taught English, and one was teaching and in charge of the university's agricultural research farm.

The next day, when I went with Zhong Rexin and Chen Dieyun, Professor Chen Xujing asked them about their living conditions as if he were their next-door neighbor. I never knew a university president could be so close to his faculty members.

At the tea party, Professor Chen Xujing once turned to Chen Dieyun. "May I ask a favor from you? Not for me, but for Professor Chen Yinke," he said with a smile. "You know, Professor Chen Yinke is blind and in poor health. He is now doing important research. I think he needs at least one carton of milk a day."

"Sure!" Chen Dieyun listened, and he jotted down Professor Chen Yinke's name. "He'll get the delivery, starting tomorrow."

A jewel scholar in Chinese history and literature, Professor Chen Yinke was world-renowned. He would probably never know how the president of the university had been trying to take care of him during the famine.

Before leaving that evening, I informed Professor Chen Xujing that I planned to visit my sister tomorrow. In a few days, I would go back to Beijing. He held my hand in contemplation. Then he told me that he would like to meet me one more time and invited me to his house the next evening.

It became my third visit to him. In retrospect, that was a critically important visit I made in my life. Professor Chen Xujing led me to sit by him out on his porch. He told me frankly that he anticipated Olivia would have lots of difficulty on her way home. Therefore, he thought that Olivia would soon need me badly.

"I know. I know it is extremely difficult for you to get exit permit," he said slowly at the end. "But I believe it's not entirely impossible." He paused and then emphasized. "Yes, I believe it's not entirely impossible! So you should be prepared. Try your best from now on."

I was overwhelmed by the affection he had shown me. Nobody in Communist China would dare to offer such an advice except perhaps between a father and a son. Olivia had taken Professor Chen Xujing as another of her fatherly brothers. Now Professor Chen Xujing had become my beneficent avuncular!

Under the Communist regime, my will for freedom had unconsciously been severely dulled. I remembered that during serious disillusions and depressions, sometimes I reminded Olivia that we were doomed. I told her that we were fortunate to build and preserve a family together. But I cautioned her that, like so many others, our days might be numbered, so we should enjoy every minute of life happily together.

That was the utmost pessimistic outlook. Now Professor Chen Xujing seemed to have ignited a new pilot light in my heart. My hope was rekindled.

Father and Mother were very happy when I returned to Beijing. They were anxious to know all the details of Olivia's trip, especially about Robert's situation in Shenzhen. Letters we sent them from Guangzhou and Shenzhen were hardly enough to provide all the information. Whenever I added an interesting episode in my oral report, they would exchange a heartfelt smile. They kept on patting Pauline, telling her how her mother, brothers and sister had arrived at a place she had not yet seen.

Dinnertime came. Before picking up his chopsticks, Father said solemnly, "Shingchi, we are blessed to have Kailan married into our family! The grandkids are now in a safer place. We must thank God for the blessings! Our ancestors must have done something good! Now we are harvesting the rewards! Let us all bow our heads in gratitude."

After dinner, though, Father and Mother somehow became tacit. Looking at me reticently, they seemed to ask me, "What's your plan? When will you bring Pauline to join Olivia? What do you intend to do from now on?" Those were questions absolutely beyond my ability to answer, so I maintained my awkward silence.

Grandmother brought Pauline to me from her lap. Pauline seemed to have grown a bit taller and was wearing a bigger coat. I looked at her coat more closely and found it was mended together with her sister's coat. Very quickly, Pauline fell asleep soundly in my lap.

Going back to the office, I found few people showing up to work because of the famine. However, there was a request sitting on my desk from the personnel office. I was asked to provide personal data on Zhong Rexin. It was unbelievable how swift and tight the surveillance was! Hardly a week had passed since I was with Zhong Rexin in Guangzhou. I would not be surprised if he were also requested to report something about me.

About the same time, a Beijing police officer also contacted me, demanding to know how many children Olivia had brought with her. My answer was, "Four."

The police officer countered, "She was supposed to bring only three. Why four?" I replied that we had five kids, and I was only able to take care of one. Since Olivia and the children had already gone, the issue was dropped.

The winter of 1961 felt extraordinarily cold in Beijing. Many employees of our Publishing House fell sick under famine. Editors were allowed to work at home, and only required to go to the office for meetings. Besides regular work, I immersed myself in letter writing and running back and forth to the post office. To dodge worries, I also resumed my visits to parks and museums as I had done in 1957.

The editorial departments of the Publishing House had never organized any party in the past. But on the Lunar New Year's Eve in early 1962, all editors were invited to a restaurant in Beihai Park. It was a gathering aimed at boosting spirits under the famine. Beihai was a scenic spot in Beijing, usually crowded with tourists. But it became a ghost park that winter. The lake was a huge sheet of ice. Walking alone toward the restaurant, I suddenly missed Olivia. We would have gone together that forlorn night if she were still here.

There was an open furnace set up by the restaurant for our party. Its flickering fire seemed to warm the partygoers' spirits. A small treat in famine was worth more than a feast in normal time. I met everyone in the editorial department except Wang Renshu, our president and editor-in-chief of the Publishing House. He had not been in his office since 1960. But nominally, he was still the chief. His absence brought me an uneasy feeling.

Was Wang Renshu sick or out of town? Strangely, nobody asked or talked about him. There was supposedly no political campaign under the famine. My guess was that he might have been put in some behind-the-scenes investigations if he were in political trouble. I tried to check with a few people who were usually close to him, but no one had an answer.

Wang Renshu was a talented literary critic and the author of many valuable books. He had been an old guard of the Chinese Communist Party. During World War II, he was in Southeast Asia. After the People's Republic of China came into being, he had served as the first Chinese ambassador to Indonesia. However, since early 1960, he had been attacked as a heretic for his views on "human nature" and "humanism."

According to the dogmatic doctrine of the Chinese Communists, there was no such thing as common "human nature." They maintained that since human beings had always been living in classed societies, their "nature" had been tinted by class differences. Therefore, the inquiry should focus on "human class nature" and not on "human common nature." Wang Renshu held that human beings did have some of their nature and feelings in common, even if that nature and those feelings might be tainted by class differences; and he believed in "humanism."

The first time I felt that Wang Renshu might be in trouble was when he put out a big poster to criticize himself in 1960. It was during in the Communist Party's "Rectification Campaign." Some Communists confessed that they had not strictly followed the line of the Party. Others regretted for their failures in remolding themselves to be the genuine "screws" of the revolution.

Curiously, Wang Renshu did not criticize himself along those lines. Neither did he reverse his views on "human nature" or "human feelings." Instead, he only felt sorry for himself because he never gone through any military battles since he had joined the Party in 1921. He lamented that he lacked military discipline.

Every Communist apparatchik had a sword hanging over his or her head. Sooner or later that sword might come down. I read Wang Renshu's poster several times, but I could not understand what he really meant. Before leaving for Guangzhou, I was told that the Ministry of Culture held a series of special conferences to attack "humanism" and Wang Renshu was targeted.

While pondering why Wang Renshu did not appear at the Lunar Year party, I was surprised to find that our deputy editor-in-chief Lou Shiyi came to my side. He was the party's host that night.

"How is Olivia?" He greeted me warmly. Before I could answer, he threw in a joke. "Actually, I'm asking you how you feel without Olivia."

Lou Shiyi was an established writer and was always amiable to people. I had not worked with him directly, but he was nice to me. I told him briefly about Olivia's trip to Macao. After that, he changed the subject abruptly. He asked me to write a book for the Publishing House, something to be included in the new "Little Book Series."

"Pick your own topic." He made his offer generously. "We can sign the contract as soon as you have a title." Seeing that I was hesitating, he added, "You know, the 'Little Book Series' is now very popular. It's Wu Han's idea."

I knew Wu Han was a celebrity. The "Little Book Series" had been a best seller. Favored by Mao Zedong, Wu Han was at the pinnacle of his fame at the time. It would be an opportunity to know and associate with him.

But I did not have the incentive. I restricted myself from creative writing in Communist China, although I had been interested in it since my teenage years. I was no fan of celebrities like Wu Han, so I never accepted Lou Shiyi's offer.

Who could have known that only four years later, Wu Han would become the first sacrifice on the altar of Mao Zedong's Cultural Revolution!

14

Anxieties in Different Cities

Thunder struck in Macao! Robert was ill and Olivia was in a panic. For more than a week, Robert's fever had been over a hundred degrees. The X-ray showed shadows in his lungs, which meant that he might have pulmonary tuberculosis. The doctors found it hard to treat a six-month-old baby in such a serious condition.

It was early May in 1962. Olivia expressed deep regret in her scribbled letter to us. She felt sorry for not having taken good care of Robert, and she was totally at a loss as to what to do. Father, Mother and I were all stunned in Beijing. Being a thousand miles away, we were also in panic for not being able to render any assistance.

Robert was staying in the Jingfu Hospital in Macao, a clinic affiliated with Mainland China. Olivia wanted to send his X-ray film to Beijing for consultation. That was a brilliant idea for medical diagnosis. But the important thing for me to do, I told myself again and again, was to be at Olivia's side right away.

I got up very early the next morning. The place for me to start my application for exit permit was my own working unit. Since Wang Renshu was no more the head of the Publishing House and his successor had not been announced, I did not know whom should I see. First, I tried the administrative office.

Famine was still holding the country hostage. People came in very late to work and scattered around listlessly. I waited for a long time before a woman showed up at the administrative office. When I asked to see the office chief, she told me casually that the chief had left. It was not the first time I felt that the Publishing House was in disarray.

In desperation, I went around to inquire about who was the interim head of our Publishing House. But nobody seemed to know or care. The last one I could think of was the head of the Printing Department. He was a Party member named Xu Juemin, the only administrative figure left.

I had no direct working relationship with Xue Juemin. When I ventured to his office, I was unsure if he would or could handle my application. I told him that it was urgent for me to go to Olivia to attend our sick baby. Surprisingly, he listened with sympathy. I showed him Olivia's letter, and he became even more sympathetic. At the end, against my expectation, he accepted my application, saying that he would submit it to the Ministry of Culture for approval. He cautioned me to be extra patient because it might take some time.

Thus, the first step was taken, and the first hurdle had been crossed. I felt somewhat relieved and wrote to Olivia that I would try as hard as I could to be at her side. I dared not mention my application because I did not want the uncertainty to cause her more worries.

In Communist China, applying for an exit permit was a risky business. The stakes were high and consequences were unpredictable. I knew that once I had stuck my neck out there would be no turning back. Like waiting for the verdict of a trial, I found it hard to maintain a peaceful and composed mind.

To avoid tension, I began to change my routines. Whenever I got a chance, I resumed the practice I had taken during my one-month vacation in 1956. Instead of staying home, I spent more time after work either at the teahouses, or in the parks and the museums. Sometimes, I even tried to bring Pauline to the zoo.

In 1962, the political situation in Mainland China was fluid. It portended for drastic changes. The famine was not totally over and the country was on the brink of collapse. One could sense through the media that the Communist top leadership was engaging in some kind of contentious debate.

More than a year ago, Mao Zedong persecuted Marshall Peng Dehuai, the Defense Minister, at the Leshan Conference. At the time, many top Communist leaders, such as Liu Shaoqi and Zhou Enlai, were sided with Mao Zedong. They lined up against Peng Dehuai for his opposition of the "Great Leap Forward Movement." Now many of the same top leaders seemed to have changed their minds and hearts.

For instance, Liu Shaoqi and his group switched their position. Unabashedly, they adopted many policies Peng Dehuai proposed in 1959. They wanted to stop Mao Zedong's demagogic and reckless adventures. Under Liu Shaoqi's auspices, they even convened a mega-sized meeting, calling it a "Conference of a Thousand Cadres," to redress the excess and damages caused by the "Great Leap Forward."

Similar to 1956, a kind of "false thaw" reappeared in Beijing. Views different from Mao Zedong's dictatorial doctrine could be heard in various places. At the teahouses, the scanty customers under the famine seemed to be interested in news and reports again.

In the fluid situation, however, Mao Zedong did not stand idle. When Liu Shaoqi and his group covertly challenged his policies, he allied himself quickly with Marshall Lin Biao, the man he appointed to replace Marshall Peng Dehuai. Mao Zedong always stuck to his tenet: "Political regimes grow out of the barrels of a gun."

Now gripping his tenet even tighter, Mao Zedong launched two political campaigns to confront Liu Shaoqi and the Party's civilian leadership. The first was a campaign for the whole country to emulate the military, elevating the military status. The second was a movement to promote a "personal cult" of Mao Zedong, making him not only the Chinese supreme leader, but also the top Marxist in the Communist camp.

Meanwhile, in order to cover up the strife within the Party and divert the public's attention from famine and other disasters, the Communists put more fuel in the long existing Taiwan Strait tension. Alleging that the Nationalists were planning to attack the Mainland from Taiwan, they mobilized the whole population against the possible invasion.

One morning in July, an impromptu meeting was called at the Publishing House. All employees were summoned to attend the mobilization meeting in the cafeteria. We were told that a Nationalist invasion was imminent. Thus, everyone should be watchful for suspicious persons or activities around.

Coincidentally, I sat with Xu Juemin at the same table at the mobilizing meeting. We would say hello to each other under normal circumstances, but this was a meeting under heightened tension. We avoided any eye contact throughout the meeting. I congratulated myself for submitting my application before the Taiwan Strait tension. It would be doubtful that Xu Juemin would dare to help if we were then under the "Taiwan Threat."

The sharp turn of events doused my plan with a bucket of cold water. I went home for lunch that day with an upset stomach. No one knew how long the "Taiwan Threat" would last. I lost my appetite altogether. Mother noticed my upset mood, and she wondered what had happened.

Just as I was trying to detract Mother's curiosity, a messenger from the street phone station came to fetch me to answer a phone call. Thank God! Professor Chen Xujing was in town. He told me he had just arrived in Beijing for a conference and wanted to invite me for lunch. I rushed to the Overseas Chinese Hotel where he was staying.

During the famine, Professor Chen Xujing had treated friends whenever he stayed in a hotel. I did not have a chance to inform him earlier about Olivia's crisis, nor could I get his advice before turning in my application for exit permit. After reporting to him what happened to Olivia and me, I also told him about the "Taiwan Strait Crisis" I had just heard about.

"Now everything becomes complicated!" I spoke out from my vexed mind. "I may not be able to join Olivia after all!"

"You just learned about the 'Taiwan Strait Crisis' this morning?" Professor Chen Xujing laughed. "Why can't you guys in the North keep abreast with what is happening! We learned of the coming crisis some time ago. Fujian is supposed to be on the frontline and some of my friends in Fujian contacted me two months ago. They plan to evacuate to Guangzhou should anything happen."

"What should I do now?" I was not interested in the possible war with Taiwan.

Professor Chen Xujing answered my question very slowly. "I didn't know Olivia was in crisis. You are right to plan to join her quickly. But now the situation is very complex." He paused before continuing. "At the moment, you may wish to withdraw your application for exit permit just for prudence sake. When the war fever is over, you can apply again." In the next breath, however, he emphasized: "This is only for safety. You have to decide for yourself."

I thanked Professor Chen Xujing for his advice. Before leaving, I told him that I would report to him about my decision soon. For the entire afternoon, with sunken heart and strained mind, I confined myself in my room. My heart insisted that I should go as quickly as possible under any circumstances. Likewise, my mind told me that I should stick to what I had planned to do since I had already stuck my neck out.

I laid out four reasons for myself to stick to my application. Firstly, Olivia and the children were in a real crisis. They needed me badly at their sides. Secondly, I had already handed in my application for exit permit. Political consequences would be the same even if I withdrew it now. Thirdly, my reason for leaving was because of the family emergency. When the emergency was resolved one way or the other, I would have no reason to apply for exit again. Lastly, who could predict that there would not be another war crisis when the current "Taiwan Threat" was gone? With the above reasons, I decided to stick to my application.

Olivia's sister Flora happened to drop by that afternoon. She was on her way to see Professor Chen Xujing too. Since I had straightened out my confusion, I thought she would be the best person to report my decision to Professor Chen Xuejing. I told her about all the reasons that led me to my decision. But, of course, I was not sure that she understood or agreed with my hair-splitting reasoning.

The "Taiwan Threat" lasted about half a year. The Nationalists did not attack the Mainland China from Taiwan. On the contrary, the Communists all of a sudden opened up the Guangdong border in the fall of 1962. An unprecedented exodus of Chinese refugees overwhelmed Hong Kong even with the British protests.

Amidst the Communist loosening of the border, my application for exit permit was approved before the end of August. I was jubilant and bought my train tickets that very afternoon. The next morning, Pauline and I were on our way to Guangzhou.

Father was ebullient when he saw that I had received the permit to exit. He hugged me tightly for a long time in his rented room at Dafosi East Street. He led me over to say goodbye to his friend. Then, we came back and sat together closely. I told him that as soon as Olivia and I settled down abroad, our top priority would be to get our next family reunion as soon as possible. Olivia and I would lie low until he and Mother joined us. I beseeched him to take good care of himself and Mother until we reunited.

Father listened intensively. His face lit up. After a brief reflection, however, he rose up slowly from his seat. "No, you two should not worry about us!" he said emphatically. "Your mother and I can take care of ourselves!" Walking back and forth in the room, he added, "You should not lie low either! No! You should strive forward! All of you! Strive forward!"

Alas! That was my father's final instruction to me.

Pauline and I left Beijing the next morning. Olivia's sister Flora came from the suburbs to see us off. She wanted to keep our parents company when Pauline and I departed. To my surprise, a friend named Sun Xiangning also showed up at our premises that early morning.

"Hi, it's nice to see you." I greeted him. "You have never been here before. Why drop in at this hour?"

"I have a meeting nearby," Sun Xiangning replied with a grin. "I thought it would be convenient for me to come and say goodbye." I reminded him that no meeting would ever take place at seven in the morning. He just laughed and looked at me.

Sun Xiangning was one of my college classmates, then working as a journalist at the same time. We did not know each other well at Wuhan

University. But when I came to work at the Ministry of Culture in 1951, I found him to be the secretary to Minister Shen Yanbing. Since then, we have known each other better, and we became close friends.

As secretary to the Minister of Culture, Sun Xiangning had best access to the literary, artistic and theatrical circles. He knew that I had been a fan of stage drama, opera, ballet and dance. Since he was handling the tickets of important shows for the big shots, he sometimes provided me with the opportunity to watch some important performances with leftover tickets. That helped me keep abreast with the performing arts.

I still remember that when watching the Soviet ballet *The Swan Lake* my ticket put me in the same wing with some high-ranking Communist leaders such as Zhou Enlai, Liu Shaoqi and Zhu De. While they sat in the front of the central row on the upper deck, my seat was at the front right row behind them. It was a vantage position to view their appearances and movements, their attitudes toward others, as well as the way they enjoyed various performances. Theatre was a venue in which the Communist politicians often revealed themselves slightly differently from their public images.

Pauline and I went to the same Overseas Chinese Mansion in Guangzhou where Olivia and I had stayed a year ago. Pauline was then six years old. She met her Auntie Hwang Liang and Uncle Wan Changtai for the first time. I got a chance to see my old friend Lian Rongzhu again. The last time we had met was in Beijing 1951. Since then he moved to Guangzhou, working as the chief accountant for a shipyard. We had a hearty reunion this time and parted in upbeat spirits.

One of the important things for me to do in Guangzhou was to thank Professor Chen Xujing for all his help and seek his advice before leaving the Mainland. Professor Chen Xuejing was very happy to see that I was on my way to join Olivia. He asked me specifically to set aside an afternoon for a private talk.

Like a loving uncle, he checked my itinerary in detail, and even wrote down some names of several reliable travel agencies for me. The most important advice he rendered to me was that I ought to stick to academic circles no matter how my career played out. To this day, his words remain my guidance, even though I did not fulfill all the goals I should have accomplished.

A riverboat took Pauline and me to Macao through the Pearl River. Olivia met us at a wharf along the seaport. I was still worrying about Robert's illness, so the first question I put to Olivia was, "How is Robert?"

To my surprise, Olivia answered with a big grin, "He is O.K. You'll see him soon."

The house Olivia rented was on a street called Huoyaoju Slant Alley. It was on top of a hill. Before meeting the children indoors, I saw Robert first outside the gate. There he was, leaning on the back of a girl servant. He was no more a little baby! Not knowing who I was, he offered me a toothless smile. I was surprised to find Robert as healthy as he was, so I turned immediately to Olivia, "What happened to Robert?"

Olivia smiled mischievously, as if she had kept a secret from me successfully. "I haven't gotten a chance to tell you," she explained in a cheerful voice. "The doctors totally changed their diagnosis on Robert. Since Robert's fever has gone, they found that what he had was an infection in his digestive system and not tuberculosis."

"What about the X-ray films?" I could not believe what I heard. "You told me the x-ray films showed that Robert has shadows in his lungs!"

"That was a false alarm!" Olivia began to tell me another story. "The hospital x-ray department made a grave mistake! They mixed up Robert's records with another boy's x-ray films. Thank God! It's all over now."

"I wish I had known it earlier!" I commented in ecstasy. "That's our blessing!"

"Maybe it's also God's will to let you come!" Olivia was moved with gratitude. "Maybe the hospital made the mistake to help us reunite!"

From the moment I stepped onto Macao's shore, I had returned to the free world. But strangely, I did not feel sure that I was truly on free soil. In the groceries and on the roadside vendors' stalls, there were plenty of food items for sale. But awkwardly, I still searched for rationing coupons when I made my payment. For a while, I even forgot how to put on my ties when I changed my apparel. There is still a picture in our album, showing me looking like a skeleton after the famine.

I was deeply moved as I found out about the hardships Olivia had gone through in the past year. She had sent David, Phillip and Jean to the nearby Yongyuan Middle School run by the Catholic Church. Now she enrolled Pauline there too. On top of all her daily chores, she had started tutoring at home to cope with her financial needs.

When we began to plan our future, Olivia confided to me that Macao was definitely not the place for us. Situated at the southern tip of Mainland China, it had no industry and other businesses except casinos. Therefore, there were almost no job opportunities. Besides, it was not really a safe place because both the Communists and the Nationalists had held onto their influences here.

October was a special month in Macao. Three national holidays days happened to come in the same month. October the first was for the People's Republic of China. October the tenth was for the Nationalist government in Taiwan. Then there was the Portuguese National Holiday also in October. After watching the celebrations put on by three different groups in the tiny colony, I felt relaxed and regained some perspectives to cope with our new environment.

Olivia and I decided to make an explorative trip to Hong Kong first. Under the sponsorship of Father Tian, the Yongyuan Middle School's principle, we both obtained a three-day visa to Hong Kong. To me, it was certainly an irony that, twelve years ago, we had no problem passing through Hong Kong on our way back to Mainland China. Now we could only go there by the guarantee of a clergyman and were not allowed to stay more than three days.

We did not know any of Hong Kong hotels except the Ascot House, a small British hotel in Happy Valley, so we booked a room there. There were only two persons we planned to visit. The first was Mr. Han Shunguang, Kaitee's friend, who sent his servant to Shenzhen to see Olivia a year ago. Because he offered to be our reference in Hong Kong, Olivia and I wished to find ways to enter Hong Kong through his assistance.

Han Shunguang's export-import firm was on Wenxian East Street, Hong Kong's old commercial center. He received us with great hospitality, instantly offering to hire me as his secretary to enable me to enter Hong Kong. But he cautioned me that it might not be successful because his firm was on Hong Kong immigration office's black list. He had tried to sponsor others, but ended in failure. Nevertheless, he assured Olivia and me that he was willing to be our guarantor if we chose to get into Hong Kong by other means.

The second person we went to visit was Pastor Meng Zhaoyi, a Seventh Day Adventist minister. He had been a friend to my grandfather. My uncle Paul in the United States had advised me to visit him as soon as I got to Hong Kong. Pastor Meng lived in Kowloon, across the Hong Kong proper.

Unfortunately, he was sick in bed when we arrived in his house adjacent to Hong Kong's old Qide Airport. The small airfield was bustling with flights. Now and then, an aircraft would take off or land. His cramped home was constantly shaken by the unstoppable noise.

Pastor Meng Zhaoyi knew I had voluntarily returned to the Mainland from the United States. Lying in bed, he seemed to be glad to see Olivia and me, but he greeted me right away with a question, "Do you know a Buddhist motto?" Before I asked the name of the motto, he recited it aloud: "A butcher can become a Buddha as soon as he lays down his cleaver!" Instantly I sensed he might have assumed that I was a Communist.

I never expected to get a lecture as serious as that. But I humbly replied that I had learned that particular Buddhist motto since childhood. I told him that I had never been a "butcher" or a Communist. In fact, I had just fled from Communist China because I did not want to be cleaved by the butcher.

At the moment, I was unsure Pastor Meng would believe what I said, but he appeared to take my words at their face value. Before we left, he insisted on having our hotel's name and room number. He told me that someone would go to see me tomorrow. That was a sour experience. I got the taste of being sandwiched in between two worlds.

Pastor Meng Zhaoyi was a man of his word. The next morning, we indeed had a visitor at the Ascot House. The visitor was the principal of Seventh Day Adventist Middle School. He introduced himself as Lu Qingda, saying Pastor Meng wanted him to come to see us. Although we had never met before, he offered to hire Olivia and me immediately to teach in his school in Happy Valley.

He proposed that each of us would get a monthly salary of H.K $500 plus free board and room. Since I had a M.A. degree from the United States, I could get H.K. $200 more a month. He also told us that he knew we were presently in Macao. Should we accept his offer, he would immediately apply for us to come to Hong Kong officially.

For Olivia and I, the offer was a delightful surprise. We had no jobs at the time, and badly needed some income. The offer sounded attractive because it would enable us to enter Hong Kong through the school's sponsorship. But we found it hard to accept any offer right away. First of all, Olivia was still planning to go back to Singapore. We could not commit ourselves to work in Hong Kong permanently. Besides, the proposed salaries could hardly meet the needs of a big family.

When we thanked Lu Qingda and declined his offer, Olivia and I thought he might not be happy. But he did not show any sign of disappointment. Instead, he continued to chat with us amiably. He informed us that Pastor Meng Zhaoyi had already set up an appointment for us to meet an American Adventist elder tomorrow at the Seventh Day Adventist Church's headquarters in Qingshuiwan.

I became quite confused and asked Lu Qingda why I should meet an American elder I did not know. "This American elder says he had heard about you in the United States." Lu Qingda replied. "You know, he might help you tremendously." Nevertheless, I still hesitated, arguing that Qingshuiwan was too far away, and that my visa only allowed me to stay in Hong Kong another day.

Lu Qingda laughed at my argument. "Everything has already been arranged by Pastor Meng Zhaoyi," He finally told me what had been going on without my knowledge. "You won't be going to Qingshuwan alone. Pastor Meng's son will meet you at the Jianshazui Harbor at ten o'clock tomorrow morning. He'll accompany you all the way to Qingshuiwan and bring you back by taxi. What are you worrying about? Everything will be fine!" I bet Lu Qingda had never seen such a stubborn and numb refugee like me.

Pastor Meng Zhaoyi might have tried his best to help me. I appreciated his benign assistance, but I was not interested in working for his church. At the time, Olivia and I still had things to check out in Hong Kong before our visas expired after tomorrow. Yet, we also found it hard to turn down Pastor Meng Zhaoyi's arrangement, so we told Lu Qingda that we would try to meet Pastor Meng's son tomorrow, but we were not sure that we could go to Qingshuiwan.

Jianshazui Harbor was on the Kowloon side of Hong Kong Territory. We had to catch the ferry to Kowloon. Curiously, on our way to the ferry next morning, I was attracted to a tall building nearby. It was the Chartered Bank, one of the oldest established banks in England. Somehow, I just could not take my eyes away from it. As if mesmerized, a scene from Charles Dickens' *A Tale of Two Cities* suddenly popped up in my mind.

It was during the violent French Revolution. An old English bank clerk was rushing to Paris to meet a client, a French aristocrat in jail. His mission was to assist his client in jail, rescuing him if possible from the turbulent upheaval.

That scene was so vivid in my vision. I slowed down my pace absentmindedly. I could not help reflecting the current situation. We were now in the upheavals and turbulences similar to the violent French Revolution. Here was the Chartered Bank, one of the old banks from England. Could it perform a similar function in another historical upheaval in another revolution?

I stopped to tell Olivia that I decided not to waste time in Qingshuiwan. I pointed to the Chartered Bank, and suggested that we open an account there. Olivia raised her head, stared at the Chartered Bank for a while, and nodded in agreement. She had been tired of those little local banks in Macao and Hong Kong, so she had more reasons to shift to a bigger bank.

Since we had decided not to go to Qingshuiwan, we discussed our options in front the Chartered Bank. Swiftly, we arrived at two conclusions. First, we would not rely on anyone to get us into Hong Kong. Smuggling was the only way left for us. Second, we would not be brainwashed by any other political or religious ideology.

Thus, when we got to the Jianshazui Harbor and met Pastor Meng Zhaoyi's son, we thanked his father's arrangement, but we informed him that we decided not go to Qingshuwan. Afterward, we spent a good deal of time at the Chartered Bank. Thanks to God, the account we opened there that day not only assisted us later during our stay in Hong Kong, but also enabled us to support and rescue our kin in Mainland China for almost thirty years.

Ever since she had come to Macao, Olivia had been receiving some support from brother Kaitee. The remittances, however, often came miserably late to meet her needs. It had to go through Zheng Wenxiang's family in Hong Kong. And the transactions of some local banks were awfully slow. In the meantime, the house rented by Zheng Wenxiang was on the hilltop. Its rent was exceptional high, eating off a big chunk off Olivia's monthly budget. That was why Olivia had to work as a tutor right after getting into Macao.

When we returned to Macao from Hong Kong, one thing we never expected to see was a man sitting at our front door. He was our landlord waiting to collect rent. Our payment was a week behind. He demanded to have cash right away. Since we did not have the amount in hand, we could only ask for another postponement in embarrassment.

The landlord went away grudgingly that day. He returned a few days later. Finding that we were still short of cash, he threatened to evict us openly. It was humiliating! The encounter almost foiled our plans of going to Hong Kong.

Thank God again! Before being evicted, we were unexpectedly rescued at the last minute by an elderly lady. This time, the rescuer was the principal of the Caigao Middle School. She was also a returned student from the United States. She knew Olivia through some of her students.

She came to ask Olivia to consider an offer from a church. A nursing home owned by the church had been emptied for demolition. For the time being, she said that Olivia and her family were welcome to use the nursing home without charge.

The principal from the Caigao Middle School was gentle, elegant and polite. Olivia accepted the offer with thanks. We were curious how the principal of a middle school knew about our distress. After all, Macao was a small city. News and gossip traveled quickly within its bounds. Probably, some of the students Olivia tutored spread the news of our pending eviction. It was a regret that we could not give thanks to those who helped.

The rescue provided us with a temporary shelter. The empty nursing home was nice but full of termites. We were very lucky. The crumbling stairways did not collapse before our whole family left for Hong Kong.

15

Refugee Life in Motion

A man came to pick me up before sunset in Macao. After leaving the old nursing home, he drove adroitly around the town. He kept on zigzagging as if to prevent me from knowing his route.

Finally, he stopped in front of a big house by the seaside. A middle-aged woman answered the door. He called her Seventh Aunt Zhou. After he left, the woman led me to a worshiping chamber through a hallway. She signaled me to sit down at one corner and proceeded to her own rituals.

The worshiping chamber was a hodgepodge of gods, selected from Buddhism, Taoism and some other Chinese folk religions. On the shrine, the statues of Buddha and Guanyin were sitting side by side with the Taoist Eight Celestials. The legendary hero, the red-faced Guangong, was there too, standing gallantly right below and alongside the Immortals.

The room was filled with incense. With burning joss sticks in her hands, Seventh Aunt Zhou knelt down before the shrine and began her prayers. I could not make out what she was praying. But I guessed they might have something to do with our smuggling. From the way the driver dealt with her, I believed she must have been one of the ringleaders.

A man emerged and brought me outside after Seventh Aunt Zhou finished her ritual. The sky was darkening. He walked me to a nearby pier where a dilapidated wooden boat was tied. From the dim light of the dusk, I noticed that a big motor engine was installed to the wooden boat. Instantly, I realized that that was the boat to take us to Hong Kong that night.

There were about twenty people at the waterfront. When boarding time arrived, two sailors lined us up and oversaw us going underneath the deck. "Squeeze!" They kept on pushing all the passengers. "Squeeze down farther!" Obviously, every inch in the boat belly meant profit to them. They did not stop pushing until the passengers were packed like sardines in a can. Then, they covered the top opening with a heavy plank.

In Cantonese, smuggling was dubbed "wad xie" ("packed snakes"). That was a good description for smuggling. People were jammed in the smuggling boats like snakes in cages. But my experience told me that there might be a slight difference between snakes and human beings. Whereas snakes could wriggle among each other in a cage, people could hardly move their limbs packed tightly in the pitch darkness.

Accidents in smuggling were seldom known to the public. People knew the danger of unseaworthy boats in smuggling, but they ignored it. The exorbitant fees for smuggling often put people in indentured servitude or other hazards. But that had not discouraged the determined ones. For political or economic reasons, they braced up to change their fate through smuggling.

The tortures in Chinese Communist prisons and labor camps could never stop people from smuggling either. When people decided to smuggle, they were putting their lives on the line to make a choice between two evils: either live under the tyrannical rule or risk their lives for a better future.

That was why smuggling had been going on as long as human history and why smuggling was still a hot business in various parts of the contemporary world.

In the 1960s, sailing from Macao to Hong Kong usually took two hours. Our smuggling boat traveled much longer. It stopped several times on its way. The sailors kept on asking us to keep quiet down below. It might be a signal that we were entering Hong Kong waters. We could hear someone climbing onboard when the engine shut off. As soon as they left, the engine started again. Most likely, they were the ones collecting the tolls.

Finally, we arrived in Hong Kong before dawn. Once out of the "snake cage," many of us could hardly move our limbs at first. Up on the deck, the dim daylight showed that we were at a congested waterfront. Around us, there were so many sampans and motorboats. We were glad that we had entered Hong Kong at last.

"Don't be too happy! We've only gotten into Little Hong Kong, not Hong Kong proper. The smuggling journey has not finished yet!" someone cautioned. Indeed, a new crew came aboard. We were led to a big nearby sampan to have sodas and breakfast.

Under the lamplights, the smuggling passengers had a chance to see each other for the first time. I followed others to find a seat, but I was tailed by a fellow passenger. He kept on pointing to my jacket and mumbling something.

I did not know Cantonese at the time, so I could not make out what the man meant. Finally, he poked at my shoulder. I turned my head and found that my jacket was soiled on the back. Someone must have vomited onto my coat during the "wad xie." The man volunteered to help. He helped me wipe off the hardened stuff. I really wanted to express my appreciation. Since I could not do it orally through Cantonese, I relied heavily on my body language.

My soiled suit happened to be my only Sunday dress at the moment. It was from Macao. Consumer prices in Macao were only half of those in Hong Kong at the time. Olivia insisted I buy it for a new image in Hong Kong. Someone almost foiled her good intention and plan.

The sky turned overcast outside when we went ashore to get into Hong Kong proper. A woman guide asked me to follow her with several other passengers. She wanted us to keep some distance from one another to avoid suspicion. There was a bus stop at the top of the hill. We went uphill toward it like a ragtag squad.

I was worn out by the overnight smuggling. As soon as we reached the hilltop, however, I saw a newspaper stand on the roadside. That suddenly lifted up my spirits. I stopped right away, picking up a copy of the daily paper, and paying the vendor with a coin from my pocket.

But before I could finish scanning the headlines, the vendor called me, "Sir, this is a Macao coin!" He spoke Mandarin Chinese, apparently knowing that I was not a Cantonese. "We don't use it here." I did not have Hong Kong coins yet so I apologetically handed back the newspaper.

It was probably a couple minutes delay. However, it caused lots of trouble. While I was talking to the newspaper vendor, a bus had already pulled up at the bus stop. The woman guide waved desperately, asking me to run up, but the bus driver would not wait. Stepping on the gas, he let the bus rumble ahead.

So I was left alone at the hill stop. Waiting in line for the next bus, I learned from the other passengers that we had to go across the mountain to get to Hong Kong proper. After the coin accident, I prepared the Hong Kong paper money for my bus fare beforehand.

Mr. Han Shunguang was very happy to see me. He wondered why I was not escorted by a smuggling handler. I told my story in Little Hong Kong. He laughed and suggested that I go for some rest. "Don't bother with the smuggler!" He wanted me to feel at home. "When they come to collect money, I'll deal with them myself."

Han Shunguang's export-import firm was housed in a traditional Chinese business center. The ceilings of the house were exceedingly high. Using only the entire ground floor as his business office, Han Shunguang had added a small room in between the ceiling and the floor. He offered for me to stay in that attic room.

I badly needed a nap. When I went to the room, I found it was tiny but nice. A bed, a small desk and a chair met my basic needs. The only thing I had to watch out for was that I might bump my head whenever I stood straight because the ceiling of the room was very low. However, the attic room had its advantages. I could overhear what was going on below while enjoying a kind of privacy.

As predicted, two smugglers soon came to collect the fee for my smuggling. Han Shunguang argued with them in his office. From the attic room, I heard him questioning them where I was. Then he reprimanded them for leaving me alone in Little Hong Kong. After the smugglers asked for an excuse, Han Shunguang reluctantly paid them the balance of the smuggling money without tip. The two smugglers seemed more than happy, thanking him profusely.

After staying at the attic room one day, I found I was blessed to have such a perfect footing in Hong Kong. Han Shunguang offered me the use of his office phone any time to get in touch with local people. Located in the old Hong Kong business center, his office was convenient to get to many places I had to go.

For instance, the post office happened to be around the corner. Not far away, was Dexing Harbor, where daily ferryboats from Macao anchored. A few ferryboat busboys later became the loyal messengers between Olivia and me. In addition, there were so many eateries around that I did not have to worry about my meals every day.

I bet very few refugees had such a good place to start. I had always been grateful for the luck bestowed on me. At the time, I desperately needed a job. But my top priority was to bring Olivia and the children over quickly.

Hong Kong had long been a seaport of refugees. "Smuggling" was not a degrading term there. As mentioned, several months before, there was a huge exodus from Mainland China. After smuggling into Hong Kong myself, I could see a lot of those Chinese Mainlanders walking on the streets, working in factories or at construction sites or other places. They had come ahead of me, but we were all newcomers and new refugees.

Some Hong Kong residents, the older generations of refugees, might have been uncomfortable to see the newcomers. But sooner or later they would accept those latecomers as fellow Hong Kongees. That was the secret to Hong Kong's success; all the newcomers would soon transform themselves into a powerful economic force. In the latter part of the twentieth century, they helped Hong Kong to launch its miraculous economic takeoff in the world.

The Hong Kong authorities under the British government did not seem to welcome the new arrivals at first. The sudden mass exodus of the refugees might have scared them in the summer of 1962. After receiving aide from the United Nations and the United States, however, they began to adopt a more lenient policy toward the refugees.

The new policy was that whoever got into Hong Kong would be granted residency, if they were not caught during their smuggling journey. Meanwhile, many churches, civic and philanthropic organizations had cooperated with the Hong Kong authorities. Their combined operations made Hong Kong a heaven of refugees for a number of years.

I had personally witnessed many of those humanitarian operations. At the same time, I had also seen a lot of new businesses sprout up to cater the refugees' needs. For example, a number of business firms were set up for finding jobs for the refugees. Around the Hong Kong Immigration office, vendors had photo stands to assist the refugees to apply for their resident I.D. cards.

I went to such a photo stand before going into the immigration office. The vender took a quick look at me and shook his head. "No, sir! You won't get your resident card! You look like a man working in an office." He quickly took off his jacket and handed it to me. "Put on my jacket!" He also asked me to take off my tie. "You know, they don't like people with an education."

I could do nothing but comply. After changing my jacket, I stood humbly in front of his camera, but that was still not enough. The vendor thought that I looked too bookish. Like a movie director, he came toward me and ruffled up my hair. "Now you look like a real farmhand!" He finally clicked his camera.

I told Han Shunguang about my funny experience at the roadside photo stand. He laughed with amusement. After a second thought, however, he cautioned, "Don't take the guy seriously! Those street vendors are trying to make a quick buck." To make sure that I could get my resident card, he added, "Let me get help from a friend. Two hundred dollars will do. He knows someone in the immigration office."

With the photo of a farmhand, plus an inside connection, I felt more than confident that I would get my resident card smoothly. When the day came for me to pick up my I.D., I sauntered into the immigration office and found it extremely crowded. A large sign was posted at the entrance, directing the Cantonese applicants to one line and other applicants to another.

I followed the non-Cantonese line. One officer happened to walk by. He looked at me closely and nodded with a knowing smile. I immediately felt that Han Shunguang's arrangement was at work. But all of a sudden, I heard that my name was being called from far away.

Opposite to the entrance, there was a roll of long tables in the big hall. I edged through the crowd, and I saw an English officer waving at me. When I got to his table, he smiled and asked me to go with him to an office room. The English officer was not in police uniform. He invited me to have a seat and told me politely that he only would like to chat with me.

I was surprised to be singled out of all the applicants for resident cards. But the English officer did not mention my application at all. His interest was only on Mainland China's situation, especially those political campaigns. I maintained my standing as a farm worker, but he just laughed away my excuses. Then, he told me he was interested in knowing more about the "Anti-Rightist Campaign." I replied that I was not a "Rightist" in 1957.

The unscheduled "chat" lasted at least half an hour. At that point, I reminded the English officer that I had come for my I.D. card. He apologetically stood up and told an aide to issue it to me. Meanwhile, he still tried to make an appointment with me. But I declined, saying that as a refugee I had a lot of work to do. The English officer had no right to delay me, so we finally said goodbye.

At Han Shunguang's place, I met two friends who rendered me great assistance. One was Lu Huashen. Another was Cao Lianjie. Both of them were my elders by at least ten years.

Lu Huashen had been the librarian at both Lingnan and Zhongshan Universities. Professor Chen Xujing introduced Olivia to Lu Huashen's wife in Macao. Now when Lu Huashen himself came to Hong Kong, Professor Chen Xujing asked him to contact me. We became good friends in no time.

Lu Huashen and I were both out of work when we first came to Hong Kong, so we kept each other company for quite a while. He came to see me every day at Han Shunguang's place. At that juncture, Olivia and the children were ready to come over. I was looking for a place to live and a school for the children.

Lu Huashen was a Cantonese and knew Hong Kong well. He helped me quickly on both accounts. First, through one of his acquaintances, I rented a room in a boarded up house in Kowloon. Second, through his recommendation, Lingnan Middle School admitted all of our children.

Once the preliminary preparations were made, Olivia arranged to have the four older children come to Hong Kong in two groups. Since they were too young to smuggle, they came as the fake family members of certain Hong Kong legal residents. By putting their pictures on those legal residents' traveling papers, they got a free passage to Hong Kong. Of course, as if in smuggling, each of our children had to pay the smuggling fee.

David and Phillip came from Macao with a couple first. I picked them up at Dexing Harbor. I still remember how happy they were when they saw me. After paying the fees to the couple that brought them over, I took David and Phillip to lunch. "Daddy, Mommy sewed up our pockets!" Both of them pointed to their shirts. "Mommy said there is money in it," Phillip whispered.

After lunch, I told David and Phillip that we still did not have a place to stay. We had already rented a room, but we could not move in until we prepaid the rent. However, they had been admitted to a boarding school, so I would send them to the school that very afternoon.

Phillip had had some experience in a live-in kindergarten. But David had never attended a boarding school. At first, they were reluctant. But they understood that we had no choice, so with their luggage in hand, we climbed up the Happy Valley hills by bus. They entered Lingnan School that very afternoon.

Jean and Pauline came over with a woman, pretending to be her daughters. I also met them at Dexing Harbor. They were only six and seven years old, but they seemed to understand well the hazard of their journey. They hugged me tightly with tears when I took them over from the woman.

With the money Olivia had sewed in David and Phillip's pockets, I had just gotten the keys to the room on Austin Road, so I brought Jean and Pauline straight to our rented room. Like the old nursing home in Macao, it was also in a building already boarded up for demolition. The difference was that we only had one room in the entire locked up building.

Jean and Pauline had also been enrolled into Lingnan, but the school did not have boarding facilities for little girls. Therefore, I had to start a new schedule. I would first bring them from Kowloon to Hong Kong by ferry, and then, by bus to Lingnan School at the hilltop of Happy Valley every weekday morning. In the afternoon, we would take the same route reversed.

I vividly remember that when I went to pick up Jean and Pauline I usually stayed with David and Phillip for a while. We would sit together to check what their needs were and resolve any problems that might have come up. Looking back, it is hard to imagine how I was able to maintain such a tight schedule. Maybe it should be attributed to the only pair of shoes I wore at the time. They were worn down to their soles.

Under the tight schedule, the only time left for me to do something was between ten in the morning to two in the afternoon. My anxiety was more on the family's future than the heavy duties at hand. Thanks to Cao Lianjie and Hong Shenghua, the two elder friends, who appeared at that very juncture and led me to some translating and writing works in those compressed hours.

I did not know Cao Lianjie before. He was a schoolmate of my uncles and sisters. Learning from Pastor Meng Zhaoyi that I was in Hong Kong, he paid a surprise visit to me at Han Shunguang's place, brought me to lunch and offered to help me when we got acquainted.

He used his own experience to encourage me to brace through the difficulties in refugee's life. He told me that he had been a preacher of Seventh Day Adventist church many years before. After the Communists took over the Mainland, he was forced to put aside his religion and work at a savings and loans bank. He and his wife escaped to Hong Kong ten years ago, and they had encountered many hardships. He tried to resume his work as a preacher, but the church rejected him, demanding he re-baptize before taking up any church work.

"Isn't that insulting?" He laughed. "I bet you'll receive your share of different kind of insults. But don't ever lose your confidence. We can make it!" He said that he was better off in Hong Kong now, and he was waiting for his visa to join his wife in the United States.

Cao Lianjie continued to visit me even after I moved to Austin Road. One night, he dropped in to bring a special message. He told me that one of his classmates, Hong Shenghua, was anxious to meet me after learning that I was in Hong Kong.

"Hong Shenghua is now in Hong Kong?" I was surprised to hear.

"He is now the head of VOA here. You know him?" Cao Lianjie asked.

"I knew him in New York. We were kind of neighbors. We lived on the 122 Street and Broadway. They lived at 123 Street and Amsterdam. His wife also studied in Columbia. Both of them attended my wedding in 1950," I told him in a breath.

"No wonder Hong Shenghua wants to meet you so badly," Cao Lianjie commented with a smile. "Here is his phone number and address."

The world seemed such a small place sometimes. Hong Shenghua and I would never imagine that we would be meeting in Hong Kong someday. When I went to see him, he still talked about our wedding in New York City.

He was curious about our life in Mainland China. I told him that both Olivia and I had been working as editors and translators in a publishing house in Beijing. We were glad that we had survived through all the political turmoil.

"Did you say you had been working as an editor and translator? And, in a publishing house?" Hong Shenghua instantly became excited. Without another word, he brought me to his friend Li Rutong, then the editor at the United States Information Services.

Li Rutong was also from Columbia University. After we were introduced, he immediately wheeled his office chair to a bookshelf. Pulling out a book from the shelf, he handed it to Hong Shenghua, and he said to me with a smile, "That's your translation. I've read it."

Thus, skipping all the normal procedures, I became one of their regular translators and writers right on the spot. With God's blessing, I was able to earn something to support my family and myself. The books I translated were primarily classical and contemporary works in the social sciences. Sometimes, I was also asked to handle materials less familiar to me, such as music and architecture. But most importantly, my long hibernated yearning for creative writing was revived.

The ferryboat busboys between Macao and Hong Kong proved to be very helpful to us. They brought back and forth not only our mail, but also our manuscripts. I usually did the rough drafts in long hand, and Olivia edited and copied them onto manuscript sheets. It had been our teamwork procedure ever since we had married even under dire circumstances.

Olivia was scheduled to smuggle in early February of 1963. The date was set on the Lunar New Year's Eve. To exempt Robert from smuggling, she had arranged Robert's nanny Ah Sheng to have a three-day visa to bring Robert to Hong Kong beforehand. During the Lunar Year holiday, David and Phillip were home from school. All seven of us, including old nanny Ah Sheng were jammed in the forlorn rented room.

There was no furniture except two bed planks. Neither was there a kitchen in the boarded building. We had to pick up our meals, food and drinks from the grocery store or have items brought to us from nearby eateries. Nevertheless, we prepared a few delicacies to celebrate the spring festival that evening.

According to the smuggling schedule, Olivia was supposed to arrive on Lunar New Year's Eve. It was a secret I had kept from the children and nanny Ah Sheng. In the room, only I waited anxiously and nervously for Olivia to walk in at any minute. The clock ticked away the time. I could not help constantly going outside to check the gate to make sure that Olivia was able to locate our boarded up building, but the neighborhood was extremely quiet. All families seemed to be celebrating the new season at home.

Midnight passed. The Lunar New Year Day had dawned. There was still no knock on the door and Olivia still did not appear. While the children slept soundly, I became more edgy in my vigil. When nanny Ah Sheng got up to put things in order, I walked out drowsily to a grocery to prepare our breakfast.

As usual, a deck of newspapers was piled on the floor of the store. As a habit, I cast a quick glance at the day's headlines. I was shocked instantly when I saw a picture showing the smuggling passengers lining up in detention on the front page. The newspaper reported how the Hong Kong police had caught a boat last night.

I bought a copy of the new daily, and rushed back with a day's meal for all of us. I examined the picture carefully, praying Olivia was not in it. All the detained passengers were facing at the camera. Only a well-dressed beautiful lady had her head turned away. "That's Olivia!" I cried out in my heart. "I don't recognize the coat, but that's her! She was dodging the camera!"

A crisis had struck us again. After arranging a few things for the children, I dashed to the police headquarters in Zhonghuan. A police officer checked and confirmed that a smuggling boat had been caught last night. However, he told me that all the passengers were being held at Zhizhu Detainee Center.

Zhonghuan was in the center of Hong Kong, but Zhizhu was far away. I had to take the trolley to get there. I bought a loaf of bread before riding on the trolley. I stuck a note inside the bread. In case I was not allowed to see Olivia, I wanted to send her the loaf of the bread to let her know that we were all fine.

But when I got to Zhizhu, a guard announced coldly that all detainees from last night's raid had already been deported back to Macao. That was another hard blow! I returned to Austin Road like a drowned man. The children did not know what had happened and still greeted me with cheerful faces. I felt even more helpless for not daring to tell them the crisis. I told them I needed a rest after running some errands. Actually, I was worrying about the setbacks that lay ahead.

Nanny Ah Sheng's visa to Hong Kong would expire the next day. Without her, it would be extremely difficult, if not impossible, for me to take care of all five kids. I thought I should try to get an extension for her visa the next morning to enable her to stay on with us.

Therefore, I accompanied Ah Sheng to the Hong Kong immigration office. Like a lamb who had ventured straight into the mouth of a wolf, Ah

Sheng was immediately detained in the Hong Kong immigration office. A female officer announced that her visa expired on that day, so she would immediately be sent back to Macao.

So my worries became true. More setbacks were indeed awaiting us. Paradoxically, I got my first lesson about being a stupid, law-abiding resident in Hong Kong. One could stay in Hong Kong illegally but was not allowed to apply legally. There was no channel for petition or appeal.

But the milk had already been spilled. I could do nothing but summon all my energy to take over the honorable duties of Olivia and Ah Sheng. Thanks to Robert, Pauline, Jean, Phillip and David! They were most conscious and helpful during the crisis. At the time, Robert had just started to learn to walk. I still remember vividly how he ventured his first step toward me while I was writing my first chapter of *The Waves and the Sand* on a bed plank.

Our crisis was somewhat relieved within a week. A Christian family we knew in Macao volunteered to help at that critical juncture. Pang Quan, the head of the family, had a business in Macao. His wife, a registered nurse, was working in Hong Kong, so they traveled constantly between Hong Kong and Macao.

Pang Quan first helped by bringing Robert and Phillip to Olivia in Macao. Then, he took Phillip back to Hong Kong for school. At the same time, he assisted Olivia in her second smuggling attempt.

16

Scratching Out a Living
on a Scribe

On an early morning in May 1963, Olivia safely arrived in Hong Kong. Her last failure to enter Hong Kong was caused by a dispute among smuggling ringleaders. To avoid exposure, the Pangs invited Olivia and Robert to their home before embarking the second time. Robert could not go for smuggling. The Pangs brought him to Hong Kong by ferryboat the same day when Olivia arrived.

I went to Dexing Harbor to meet Robert and the Pangs that evening. For some reasons unknown, the harbor was lighted and decorated. "Are these decorations for Robert's home coming?" I joked in a happy mood.

I was not sure how Robert would feel after staying one night alone with the Pangs. But Robert seemed to be all right with the Pangs. He did not cry at all when he was brought out of the gateway by Pang Quan. As soon as he saw me, he smiled broadly and jumped into my arms. He was excited to see the colorful lights. Pointing to the decorations, he kept on mumbling something and forgot the Pangs altogether.

Our family was finally reunited at Austin Road! A lot of tears were shed. Mother was the pillar in our family. After all the setbacks, we now gained some security. The children found their moorings. We each seemed to have received an adrenaline shot.

Olivia took up her tasks immediately. She said we should not continue to stay in the unfurnished room in a boarded up building, so we decided that we should move from Kowloon to Hong Kong proper right away. At the same time, Olivia also encouraged me to concentrate on my work from now on. She assured me that we would be happy in our life as long as we faced the difficulty bravely.

Hong Kong was just about to take off economically at that juncture. Soon it was going to be one of the world's financial centers. A housing boom was the harbinger of the unprecedented development. New apartment buildings were shooting up all over the port city like mushrooms. Within a week, we leased a small apartment unit in North Point's Southern Mansion.

North Point was then a newly developed area. Rent was cheap and within our affordability. We were very happy to have our first rented premises in Hong Kong. Now David and Phillip did not have to be at boarding school anymore. They went to school with their sisters by a car pool. Jean and Pauline also did not have to babysit Robert so much. And, Robert was most happy to have Mommy alone at his side.

Olivia seemed to have gotten her badly needed vacation too! She had been under continual stress since 1961. As she relaxed, she also changed her apparel to the conventional housewife's costume. That was new to me, and it seemed to give me more incentive to work hard.

Of all of us in the family, I considered myself to be the luckiest. I believed that I had reaped the largest benefit from our family reunion because it rendered me opportunities to concentrate on my work. That was why I was able to translate half a dozen books in 1963 alone. Among them, there were a few titles from the Harvard series on American society. In addition, I continued to write my full-length novel, *The Waves and the Sand*, and it was almost done.

The Waves and the Sand was a story about two young lovers in Communist China. Both of them came from "bourgeois" families in the previous Nationalist regime. The hero's father was an industrialist and his lover, the heroine, was the daughter of his erstwhile college president. They met and fell passionately in love while they worked together in a university in Beijing.

Attracted by the Communist cause, the hero had given up his college education during World War II and gone to Yanan, the Mega town of the Chinese Communists. He would have been quite successful in his cadre career had he unconscionably climbed up the ladder provided by the Communists. But he had a strong conscience, and his conscience had constantly bothered him, especially when he was participating in and witnessing the inhuman operations during Communist campaigns.

Therefore, the hero was perplexed, confused and disillusioned. After falling in love with the heroine, he gained his peace of mind for a short while. However, during the "Ming Fang Movement," his conscience made him speak out openly at a meeting. He admitted with contrition that in a few political campaigns, he personally treated people as if they were not human beings. The confession made him an Anti-Party "Rightist," so he was exiled to a labor camp and kept there until his death.

On the contrary, the heroine was younger, and had no interest or experience in politics. Her father, a university president, was a victim under the Communist regime. Therefore, politics was something she had been trying to avoid. But her love with the hero dragged her into the same pit of persecution. The young couple had not yet been officially married. However, a baby boy was born when the hero was far way in labor camp. Whether the unmarried mother and the fatherless child could survive were still unknown when the story drew to its end.

The Chinese Communists rarely admitted their mistakes and crimes. To them, the "repentance" the hero made was a "crime." But it was extremely doubtful that the Chinese people could ever be able to regain their conscience without certain genuine "repentance." And, to shake off the yoke the Communists had put on them, they absolutely needed to regain their conscience.

The Waves and the Sand was probably the first novel to describe the importance and the difficulty of rekindling conscience in Communist China. It was probably also one of the first Chinese novels to portray the Communist "Anti-Rightist" and the "Great Leap Forward" campaigns, as well as the Great Famine in the late 1950s and early 1960s.

While writing the novel, Olivia had helped me from the very beginning. At the time, we were separated between Macao and Hong Kong. After we reunited, the pace of my writing quickened. But there was no Chinese typewriter at the time, and word processors or computers were not yet invented. Therefore, Olivia could only use carbon paper to make copies of my manuscript. It was not easy to imagine how hard she had to press to copy them with four carbon papers underneath.

There was an episode when *The Waves and the Sand* went to print that almost made me give up its publication. I did not know the publisher was related to the Nationalists. Without notifying me or asking my permission, he arbitrarily changed the geographical name "Beijing" to "Beiping" in my novel. I was shocked when I read the galley proof. It told me that I had been drawn into a ridiculous but serious conflict between the Nationalists and the Communists.

For many years and in many dynasties, Beijing had been the capital of China. In the 1920s, when the Nationalist came to power, they moved the capital to Nanjing, and changed the name of the abandoned capital to

Beiping. However, after the Communists conquered the country in 1949, they renamed it back to Beijing from Beiping when they made the traditional city their capital.

But the retreated Nationalists refused to accept the change made by the Communists in their bitterness of defeat. They continued to insist that Beijing should be called Beiping and made it a loyalty test of the speaker's political identity. Thus, they branded the person who used the term of Beijing for the Chinese capital as a Communist or a Communist sympathizer. For them, a semantic dispute became a life-and-death political struggle.

The Nationalists still had strong clout in Hong Kong at the time. They controlled many media, including the firm that contracted to publish my novel. I protested to my publisher for his arbitrary change, and I demanded he follow my manuscript strictly.

In the beginning, the publisher tried to dodge the issue. He explained that he had not changed a word of my manuscript except a minor geographical name. I told him that it would be ludicrous for a novel on current China to call Beijing as Beiping. The readers would be confused.

Then the publisher became adamant. While he agreed to adapt Beiping to Beijing, he insisted I add an explanatory note. I flatly refused, telling him I would rather void the contract than to add such a note. A deadlock unavoidably ensued.

The wrangling lasted almost a full week. I was lucky, because I was counting on translation, not on creative writing, for my living. When I finally prepared to return the first installment of my royalty, the publisher gave in. I was even given extra deluxe copies as souvenirs when the book was published.

I used a number of pen names in Hong Kong. The author's name for *The Waves and the Sand* was "Jiang Wen." Many people have only known me by it since the 1960s. My other pennames included "Qin Xiu Ming," "Wei Liang" and "Jiang Hao." I shall put all my writings under the penname of "Jiang Wen" if republished in the future.

In addition to *The Waves and the Sand*, I had also written a novelette entitled *Old Man Tang*, as well as a number of articles and a play in 1963 and 1964. After leaving Communist China, I began to find Hong Kong a free place to reactivate my mind and my pen. The seaport seemed to have become my second native town.

As soon as we settled down in Hong Kong, we communicated more often with Father and Mother. Our financial support to them also became more substantial. In 1964, Mother had a cholesterol surgery. She reunited with all of my three sisters when they went to Beijing to take care of her. Father was so happy that he dubbed Mother and her three daughters as the "Four Golden Flowers."

Our rented apartment at the Southern Mansion was poorly built. Only three months after its completion, its structural defects began to be unveiled. Leaking pipes and cracking walls appeared everywhere. In the meantime, since it was a building for low-income people, security also became a problem. Hong Kong was then in a severe shortage of drinking water. Therefore our problems multiplied.

On top of all these daily headaches, a horrible thing happened one day. A Taiwan "most wanted" murderer, Li Zaifa, was caught on the second floor of the Mansion. All the residents were terrified. For a few days, some locked themselves in their own apartments. Olivia and I began to wonder whether we should move to another place.

It was in June of 1963 when Olivia's sister-in-law, Zheng Wenxiang, unexpectedly came to Hong Kong to visit us again. Olivia was unprepared but happy to see her after Shenzhen. She also wanted to pay hospitality to her sister-in-law but was unable to do so because she had not been notified beforehand. However, dressed in the attire of a Hong Kong housewife, she walked with her sister-in-law around the apartment building. Zheng Wenxiang must have had a bad impression of the condition of the Southern Mansion and had reported her findings to Olivia's brothers in Singapore.

Not long after, Olivia received a notice from her family's company in Singapore, saying that the company had bought an apartment in Happy Valley, Hong Kong. The note also informed Olivia that her brother Kaitee wished that she would use the premises as long as she and her family were in Hong Kong. It was a surprise and a timely relief for us to find a place to stay away from the Southern Mansion.

Following the notice, Olivia went happily to pick up the keys for her family's company's Happy Valley apartment. But when she got to the place mentioned in the notice, she found it was a lawyer's office. Before she could get the keys, a clerk demanded that she sign a deck of legal papers. Olivia was confused. She did not have the time and the necessary knowledge to go through those legal documents before signing them, so she gave back the papers to the clerk and declined to accept the apartment keys from an unknown lawyer.

Olivia was stubborn. Her reasoning was that since the apartment belonged to her family company, it should not be any Hong Kong lawyer's business.

Therefore, not until a month later, after signing a two-line receipt to her own family's company, did we move into the apartment in Happy Valley.

Unfortunately, I began to encounter some health problems at that juncture. My left middle ear had undergone a surgery in Beijing in 1950. Due to negligence, the infection flared up again without my notice in August 1963.

My youngest uncle's, Joseph's, wife was from the Philippines. Her nephew, a Philippine navy officer, was passing through Hong Kong that month. It was a pleasure for me to host a relative in Hong Kong, so I accompanied the navy officer for a whole day in the port city, sightseeing, shopping and having dinner in the evening.

Seldom had I allowed myself to spend a full day outdoors like that, so that was a kind of break for me too. But to my surprise, I vomited and had diarrhea that night. At first, I thought it was that the rich dinner did me in. However, soon I began to have vertigo and had to be sent to an emergency room of a hospital.

After examining me, a doctor found out that my vertigo and vomiting were not caused by the food, but by a severe infection in my left middle ear. He gave me some antibiotics for temporary relief, but he told me to go to an ENT specialist for surgery. Sadly, however, I was unable to follow his advice at the time. First, I could not afford to have a surgery at the moment. Second, we were in the midst of moving to Happy Valley from North Point.

Happy Valley was in a nice and quiet area and Lingnan Middle School was on the top of its back hill. The apartment building we moved in was called the Baode Mansion, not far from Hong Kong's famous horse racing tracks. Now the children were even closer to their school. I also found it was more conducive to my work.

Olivia had tried to remodel the apartment for our needs because it was small like many Hong Kong apartments. To provide me with a little study, she used her architectural talent. Finally, through partition, she succeeded in creating a tiny room for me, enough to squeeze in a small desk and a skinny person. "It's smaller than Professor Chen Xujing's study!" I joked to myself, but I was exceedingly satisfied.

Christmas of 1963 is still a sweet memory in my mind. The children organized a family party in the little apartment in Baode Mansion. They put together a Christmas show, and everyone had a role in it. I still remember how it ended. Before the curtain dropped, a girl (played by Pauline) led a little boy (Robert) to the center of the stage. They started to sing a Christmas song. All of us joined in the singing to celebrate our reunion in Hong Kong.

The year of 1964 was as busy and fruitful as 1963. Despite my occasional vertigo, I continued to translate and write books. Besides the publication of *The Waves and the Sand*, my novelette *Old Man Tang* also appeared in four installments in a popular monthly magazine called *World Today*.

Olivia had met some friends from Singapore in Hong Kong. One of them was Huang Mingzhu, who had been in Beijing with us in the 1950s. Being the apple of her parents' eye and tired of living under Communist control, Huang Mingzhu went back to Singapore in 1960, but things had changed at home since she left.

Now her family business was being run by her two brothers and not her parents. And her brothers and the in-laws did not care for her. Therefore, Huang Mingzhu found herself miserable in Singapore. Besides, she missed her husband and worried about her older son, so she finally decided to go back to the Mainland.

Huang Mingzhu and Olivia had both attended Nanyang Girl's Middle School in Singapore when they were young. Her husband happened to have once been our colleague at the Literature Publishing House. When Olivia was stuck in Macao, she volunteered to help by visiting Olivia's brother Kaitee in Singapore. She felt that she and Olivia were on the same boat in many ways, so on her way back to the Mainland, she wanted to have a heart-to-heart talk with us in Hong Kong.

Olivia and I invited Huang Mingzhu for a farewell dinner. She confided to us that she was forced to go back to Communist China. All her frustrations, hardships and dilemmas sounded familiar to us. Her experience was emblematic. She and her husband were doomed in the Communist world, yet the free world would not accept them back.

I sadly recalled the discussions Olivia and I had before she left for the Mainland. We had been fortunate to have gotten assistance at critical junctures. Our fortitude might have helped a little in bracing through the obstacles, but it seemed that Fate had always been the ultimate arbitrator.

Huang Mingzhu went back to Mainland China in 1964. Two years later, the horrible "Cultural Revolution" erupted. There was no way to find out about her situation thereafter. We could only pray and hope that she and her family survived the turmoil.

In our busy lives in Hong Kong, Lu Huashen and I had kept in constant touch. We were both unemployed when we got there. As refugees, we shared many feelings, thoughts and hardships. He brought me a big piece of good news about himself in late 1963. He finally had been appointed to be the librarian of Xinya College, a post he had expected and waited for a whole year.

He was elated to be able to work again in his own field. Xinya was one of the three colleges that would soon become components of a new Hong Kong Chinese University. Knowing that I was also interested in teaching, Lu Huashen urged me to seek a teaching post there. In his enthusiastic efforts, he even introduced me to a number of faculty members he knew in various colleges.

In May of 1964, through all the new acquaintances, I got to know a retired American professor named Halleck Rose. He was then the chairman of an American Academic Society in Hong Kong. At the same time, he also worked at the International Rescue Committee, an organization aimed at rescuing refugees around the world.

Dr. Halleck Rose learned that Olivia and I were students returned from the United States. After getting acquainted, he was curious why we did not apply for immigration to the United States. In our first chats, he asked why Olivia and I were satisfied remaining in Hong Kong as refugees.

I told him that I had two uncles in the United States. According to U.S immigration law, uncles were not qualified to sponsor nephews. That was why I never harbored any idea of going back to the United States.

Furthermore, I mentioned that from the end of the Qing Dynasty to the recent exodus, generations of Chinese refugees were waiting in Hong Kong to be immigrated somewhere. The U.S. Consulate in Hong Kong had been overwhelmed with applications. My chance of immigration would be close to nil even if I tried.

Dr. Halleck Rose listened to my explanation without any comment. Before parting, however, he wanted me to bring Olivia to see him as soon as possible. When Olivia and I were in his office, he found out quickly that Olivia's sister Helen was living in Nebraska. With a quick smile, he told us that Nebraska happened to be his home state. He advised Olivia to apply for immigration immediately while contacting her sister for the sponsorship.

At that meeting, Dr. Rose reminded me that refugee life was precarious. He told me frankly that to get a permanent teaching post in Hong Kong might be even more difficult than immigration. When he heard of the Beijing-and-Beiping controversy I had had with my publisher, he cautioned me further that Hong Kong was a complicated place for a refugee like me.

Olivia sent a letter right away to her sister Helen asking for her sponsorship. Helen responded enthusiastically at first, but she suddenly withdrew her sponsorship later with no reason given. Olivia was stunned by the flip-flop, so we went to see Dr. Rose again.

In embarrassment, Olivia informed Dr. Rose what had happened. We thought the lack of sponsorship might forfeit Olivia's application. But Dr. Rose did not seem to be bothered by the zigzag. He fell back in his chair with laughter. "Your experience is not unique, Mrs. Hwang!" he consoled Olivia. "People sometimes have difficulties rescuing their kin. This is one thing I have learned after working at the International Rescue Committee."

Then, Dr. Rose bent over his desk, digging into Olivia's application. After a while, he suddenly lifted up his head and stared at Olivia: "Ha! Ha! I didn't know that you were born in Malaya. In your case, you won't have any problem! You can apply for yourself without sponsorship. Maybe you'll get your visa quicker than many others!"

Olivia and I could not believe what we heard. Dr. Rose explained to us that there had been a recent ruling in the U.S. immigration law. All Chinese applicants could now use the quota of the country of their birth rather than China.

"As far as I know, the Malayan quota is now wide open." Dr. Rose smiled radiantly. "Olivia, go get your birth certificate quickly! You may be on your way to the States within two months if everything goes smoothly."

It was July of 1964 and Olivia and I were ebullient. A flickering light seemed to have appeared at the end of our dark tunnel. We began to think of how to get Olivia's birth certificate as quickly as possible.

However, Olivia had been born almost forty years ago in Segamat, Malaya. In order to apply for her birth certificate, she had to go back to Malaya. It was doubtful that the Malaysian government would grant her a visa. Besides, collecting all the data needed for her birth certificate application seemed impossible to her. We were at a loss how to start.

But thank God! As if in another miracle, someone knocked on our door one day. The visitor was Robin Woon, the husband of Olivia's beloved niece Ailin. We had never met him before. He had just come from Malaya and brought Olivia a gift from Ailin. What was the gift? Olivia's birth certificate! For heaven's sake, we could not believe it.

Olivia's niece Ailin had been a lawyer in Singapore and Malaya. She knew that Olivia needed her birth certificate to go back to Singapore. Ever since Olivia came out of Mainland China, she had been working hard on Olivia's birth certificate.

For a person like Olivia, she needed affidavits from old relatives to testify to her birth. It took Ailin many months to gather all the necessary data, and she went through the lengthy legal tangles to obtain Olivia's birth certificate. She and Robin might never realize what an amazing and timely assistance they had rendered to Olivia.

Dr. Rose's estimation was right. Olivia handed in her birth certificate in August of 1964. She and the children received their visas the next month. Even though I had to stay behind, the future of our family seemed to have gotten a new opening. Since another chapter of our lives had begun, we had to plan ahead.

At that juncture, Olivia and I entered a financial crunch. She and the children were ready to go, but we were short of the fee to get across the Pacific Ocean. Fortunately, the International Rescue Committee offered us a loan of $1,527.50 to cover Olivia's sea voyage. In the provisory note we signed, we arranged to pay back the loan in thirty installments, $63.65 each month.

Meanwhile, we reported Olivia's pending immigration to Beijing and Singapore. Father and Mother had never dreamed that Olivia and the kids would be going to the United States so soon. In his jubilation, Father wrote us almost daily.

Brother Kaitee was also elated. He insisted that Olivia immediately bring her family back to Singapore for a reunion before embarking to the United States. He not only issued air tickets for us to fly to Singapore, but he also arranged to pay Olivia's first class fares for the American Presidential Lines.

Hong Kong was hit by a hurricane that week. Ferocious winds and rains were lashing our windows. Olivia and I were at a loss as what to do. We knew that we were in a financial crunch, and that brother Kaitee had been extremely generous. But since we had already gotten a loan for Olivia's ocean journey, we both decided not to burden brother Kaitee, so we wrote to thank him, but we declined his kind offer for the ocean liner fee.

As for the invited trip to Singapore, Olivia was hesitant because she had to embark to the United States in two weeks, and there were still lots of unknowns back in Singapore. At the same time, I did not wish Olivia's forthcoming voyage to have any complications, so we also returned the issued air tickets to the airline.

To our surprise, our declinations made brother Kaitee terribly upset. From Singapore, Olivia's other brother Kaiteng cabled her, urging her to follow brother Kaitee's request. He said that he too wished to meet all of us. He reminded Olivia that she had to say goodbye to the elders in both Singapore and Malaya.

Olivia had been taking brother Kaitee as her father-like brother. The last thing she wanted to do was to hurt his feelings, so in early October of 1964, we put aside all our plans, packed up at the last minute, and flew to Singapore.

It was Olivia's first trip home after our marriage. She and the children had immigration papers to the United States so they were exempted from getting visas to enter Singapore. I had neither immigration papers nor visas. But thanks to the Singapore government, I was also admitted courteously to the place where Olivia was born.

17

An Impromptu Trip to Singapore

To a certain extent, going back to Singapore was surreal to Olivia in 1964. She had never expected that it would happen so easily after being blocked so many times in the past. It was also unplanned because she was just about to go to the United States. I could sense that her feelings were mixed when we boarded the plane.

We scheduled our trip to Singapore in between the seventh and fourteenth of October of 1964. The *S.S. President Wilson* was going to sail to United States on the October eighteenth from Hong Kong. Thus, Olivia would only have three days to pack for the journey after returning from Singapore. Both the ocean journey and the Singapore trip had their unknown elements. We could not help worrying.

I had no idea whom I would meet in Singapore. But Olivia was very anxious to see her "mother-like" San Sao and her "father-like" brother Kaitee. She would also like to meet Ailin and Sister Qing Xiang to thank them for their assistance. Last but not least, she wanted to see Brother Kaiteng, who had left for Switzerland when she was little.

Olivia did not expect to be treated as a guest, but when we arrived in Singapore, her brothers Kaitee and Kaiteng welcomed us at the airport. Then we were sent to a Malayan hostel near Kaitee's house. After that, several Quek elders dropped in to greet Olivia, including Olivia's stepmother He Liying

According to Chinese custom, a returned daughter would usually stay with family members. Hostels or hotels were reserved for guests. The accommodation we received seemed to imply that we had been recognized as both family members and guests. Kaitee and Kaiteng were very courteous. They seemed to have everything well planned and carried out in low key.

The next morning, Kaiteng accompanied us to visit the family elders. The Queks had settled in the Malay Peninsular for at least three generations. Now their descendants had scattered over many towns and villages. Their hard work had transformed some jungles into plantations, farmlands or factories. Yet it was very impressive to notice that they very strictly retained many of the Chinese traditions.

For instance, they still valued highly the filial duty and the family ties. While those values were weakened or brushed away in Mainland China, many Chinese families in Southeast Asia still held them high. They found those values were compatible with the modernity they enjoyed.

Similarly, the Chinese language appeared to be quite alive in some Malayan multi-lingual communities. On our trip, I met a young engineer in a plantation by chance. His mastery of the Chinese language might dwarf some engineers in Mainland China.

Malaya was rich in natural resources. It also had a good road system. We stopped on the first day at a town called Segamat and stayed there overnight in a guesthouse. Olivia kept looking, before nightfall, at an old cottage alongside a running creek. It appeared to still be in good shape. After a while, Olivia said that she was sure she had lived there when she was little.

Our next stops in Malaya were Baruo and Malacca. Kaiteng led us to visit San Sao there. Olivia got her first chance to embrace San Sao heartily, thanking San Sao for calling her to come home. San Sao was very happy to see Olivia, immediately taking us to pay a visit to the tomb of her late husband, Olivia's late cousin Kaikee. Olivia wished to see her niece Ailin, San Sao's daughter, but she was told that Ailin lived in another town. The current trip was arranged to visit only the elders.

The next elder we visited was Bo Mu, the wife of Olivia's late uncle Juchuan. I had heard stories about Bo Mu and San Sao from Olivia before. They were close to Olivia's mother before she died in 1929. Bo Mu had a beautiful garden house. She showed us a big dining room that could feast at least fifty people.

While walking around, Olivia told me about her uncle, Juchuan. Gallant and generous, Uncle Juchuan was a renowned community leader. Joining the conversation, Bo Mu recalled that when her husband was alive, her house had always been full of guests, and cooking had never stopped in her kitchen. She had to buy groceries in bulk quantity to feed the family members and guests. For friends, it was well known that food and shelter were always available at Juchuan's residence.

We could visualize the glorious days of the house. At the time of our visit, there were still a number of live-in guests. They helped entertain us and told us many stories about themselves. After a rich lunch, Bo Mu told us that she would join us two days later. She had already arranged to go with us to see her son in Fuyong, a Malayan city quite far away.

That afternoon, we also visited Olivia's fourth auntie, Si Wu. She was the midwife of Olivia's birth in Segamat. Olivia had not seen her many years. Si Wu looked old and fragile. Olivia felt that her chance to meet Si Wu again was slim. Therefore, she hugged and kissed this auntie of hers again and again.

Olivia's parents were buried in different places in Malaya. Brother Kaiteng led us first to the tombs of Olivia's late father and her first mother. Nearby was the burial site of Olivia's uncle, Quek Juchuan. We visited their tombs one by one with respect, praying them to rest well in heavens.

Finally, we were brought to the tomb of Olivia's own mother in Baruo. Built on top of a beautiful mound, and at the center of her father's favorite plantation, the tomb was surrounded by a circle of well-trimmed trees. As soon as we climbed up the mound, Olivia knelt down in front of her mother's tomb.

At the moment, a young relative tugged at my sleeves. He whispered to remind me that I was not required to follow the traditional Chinese ritual. But without a second thought, I followed Olivia and knelt down at her side. The relative might have been surprised to see us using the superstition to express our love in grief.

Olivia's father Quek Shin, my late father-in-law, had been one of the most successful Chinese entrepreneurs in Malaya and Singapore. What we saw in Baruo, several thousands of acres of palm oil plantation, was part of his enterprise. He owned thousands more acres of rubber plantations in other parts of Malaya. To manage his business in faraway locations, he had had to rely on aircraft. In fact, at the peak of his career, he counted on a small personal aircraft in the 1930s.

As Olivia remembered, the most valued asset of her father was probably his pricey coconut plantation in Zhangyi, Singapore. When Singapore became independent, the government bought it through legislation. Now it was the world known Zhangyi International Airport in Singapore.

However, what set Olivia's father apart from his peers in his time was probably not the vast plantations he owned, but the factories he built to produce palm oil and other products. He purposely chose the Chinese character "Shin" as his given name. In Chinese, "Shin" meant "new" and "innovative." Apparently, he had tried hard to "renew" himself and his enterprise. World War II interrupted and wiped out many of his operations and many of his dreams were shattered by the annihilation.

As soon as we arrived in Singapore, brother Kaitee told Olivia that her father had left two personal items for her. One was a handwritten copy of the Chinese Nationalist Constitution of 1946. The other was Olivia's birth certificate her father had obtained in 1952.

The handwritten Chinese Nationalist Constitution brought back Olivia's memory of the Shanghai days. Her father was then a delegate to the Chinese National Congress. Each delegate was given a copy of the handwritten Constitution as a souvenir. Olivia's birth certificate was issued to her father by the Malayan government after her father went to Joho to take oath in 1952.

Olivia could not figure out why her father had also made a special trip to Joho to take oath and get a birth certificate for her. Was he planning to bring Olivia back sometime? It had all become bygone episodes. Olivia could not help thinking how nice it would have been if she could have gotten her birth certificate earlier. Lots of anxieties might have been saved when she applied for her U. S. immigrant visa.

Now her father had gone and brother Kaitee had become the head of her family. Although he looked much older, he was still the same brother she knew. His good nature had not changed. Always making people feel at ease, he remained a self-effacing person, generous to others but parsimonious to himself.

From Malaya, we returned to Singapore for one day rest. Kaitee invited us to his home for lunch and dinner. Before going, I thought his residence would be similar to Bo Mu's. When we got there, we found he and his father lived on Lloyd Road, in two old, adjacent rented townhouses.

Lloyd Road was in a secluded area, close to the Governor's Mansion. It still retained some glories of the past. But the neighborhood was old and seemed to be lacking of modern amenities. The fact that Olivia's father and her eldest brother chose to live there said a lot about their parsimonious lifestyle.

For more than half a century, the headquarters of their family company, the Quek Shin & Sons, had been located on No.1 Prince Street. That was in the heart of Singapore's old financial center. It also told a lot of Olivia's father and brother Kaitee's managerial style.

Kaitee and his wife Pan Xinghun had four sons and one daughter. While their oldest son Yuanchao and daughter Yuanyuan (Anna) were not in very good health, their second son Yuanhong had been working for the family company, helping to manage the plantations. When we visited them, their other two sons, Yuansam (Sam) and Yuanhua (Warren), were still in their teens.

At Kaitee's house, Olivia was surprised to find that her stepmother He Liying lived next door. She had not been able to see her stepmother for years. But I happened to have had a chance to meet her once in Hong Kong right after I had smuggled there before the end of 1962, so I was not completely a stranger-stepson-in-law to He Liying. She courteously invited me over to her house after lunch.

Walking to her cabinet, she took out an artifact from it. "Look. This is a gift your father sent to us." She showed me a carved statue. "Sister Qing Xiang brought it back from the Mainland several years ago. I still did not get a chance to send your father a thank-you note."

I scanned the carved statue, and I recalled vaguely that Father did wish to send some gift to the Quek family. That was during the famine when Sister Qing Xiang went to see Olivia. I was moved by Father's act under those dire circumstances. "Would you please send my thanks to your father?" He Liying was standing next to me. I nodded and thanked her courtesy before I left.

Olivia had told me many things about her brother Kaiteng. But this was the first time I got a chance to meet him in person in Singapore. Two things might have helped us in our acquaintance. One was our shared interest in books. The other was the need to cope with our poor health.

Kaiteng had had tuberculosis since childhood. At the time, the most advanced treatment for tuberculosis was through surgery. Therefore, his elder brother Kaitee accompanied him to Switzerland for such a treatment. Coincidentally, World War II broke out after his surgery. Therefore, he was confined in a sanatorium in the Alps for recovery.

He was certainly fortunate to be able to stay in peaceful Switzerland while the world plunged into annihilation. But in a sick bed, his isolation in the Alpine might also have taken a toll in his youthful years. Olivia had shown me some of Kaiteng's letters and photos she kept since 1946. They showed how strongly Kaiteng had stayed attached to his kin in his loneliness on the snowy Swiss mountains.

This time, we learned that Kaiteng had finally come home to Singapore in the early 1950s. His father and brothers all welcomed him with great love and expectation, but sickness seemed to have deprived him from specializing in a particular field. He had a wide range of knowledge, but he was not particularly interested in business. Thus, he took on only minor duties in his family company.

In the meantime, being a bachelor too long, Kaiteng seemed to have also lost his resolution of walking onto the marriage altar, so he chose only to live with his companion, Agnes Liang, throughout his life. Agnes Liang was a divorcee, and much older than Kaiteng. They had been pen friends before meeting each other. They led a secluded life in Singapore for almost forty years.

While traveling in Singapore and Malaya, Kaiteng and I found quite a few subjects we were both interested in, so the trip was not boring for us while Olivia got more than an earful at every stop on our way. Gradually, she learned what had actually happened while she had been away for all these years.

Piece by piece, from the fragmented information, a picture seemed to have appeared in Olivia's mind. First, her father fell into illness in the Japanese War Camp. He was fortunate to have his fourth wife He Liying at his side to take care of him, but his health had never fully recovered afterward.

Second, her stepmother He Liying had given birth to two children, a girl and a boy. His father was happy to have another son Kaizhen at his senior age, and he seemed to love him more than all the other sons. To show his love to his youngest son, Olivia's father bestowed his most important assets, such as the Zhanyi Plantation to Kaizhen even before Kaizhen became an adult.

Unfortunately, Olivia was told that a terrible tragedy happened. Kaizhen was then still a teenager in school. One day, while running across a small street, he was struck by a truck and died on the scene. That was an unbelievable tragedy. Olivia had never had a chance to see her youngest stepbrother, yet she was sure that the truck had not only struck down Kaizhen, but also given his father a heavy blow. At the time, his father was approaching his late sixties. Emotionally, the loss of a beloved son was unrecoverable. Financially, he had to pay a huge inheritance tax to claim back the properties he bestowed to his youngest son.

Usually, domestic conflicts were unavoidable in big families, especially the wealthy ones. Family companies often lost their vitality when many hands were on the same driving wheel. Olivia's family company did not seem to have escaped the fate. When everyone in the family wanted their voices to be heard, the pressure cooker of the family might have to burst to release some of its heat.

After learning of the family stories during our impromptu trip to Singapore, Olivia could not help to lament, "Poor Kaitee! He has been the vault of our family's pressure cooker. It's amazing that he has not been totally worn out!"

Olivia seemed to have a special sympathy for her brother Kaitee. She told me that familial obedience was of cardinal importance in a traditional Chinese family. Kaitee, as the eldest son, had always followed his father's direction when his father was alive. His stepmother and he were almost the same age. He had to accommodate everyone. In the family's internal strife, he often became the first victim in the crossfire.

Olivia's sympathy for brother Kaitee often reminded me of a famous novel named *Family*, written by the prominent Chinese modern writer Pa Jin. In the novel, Pa Jin portrayed an eldest son in a traditional Chinese family in modern times. Pulled by traditional and modern forces at the same time, the hero not only suffered in the conflicts between different generations, but he also became a victim of the family's internal strife.

Compared to the hero in Pa Jin's novel, Olivia and I found Kaitee might have gone through even more difficulties. For instance, after the Communist takeover of Mainland China, he had to move his paper factory from Chongqing to Taiwan, and then had it folded up. Not long afterward, he was sent by his father to Brazil to explore business opportunities, but his mission had not been successful before he was summoned home.

"Sometimes a business empire is hard to build," as one saying goes, "but it might be even harder to maintain." In her impromptu trip home, Olivia witnessed how hard Kaitee had been trying to maintain his father's little business empire, the Quek Shin and Sons.

Following Bo Mu's plan, we went with her to visit Olivia's cousin Kaidong in Fuyong. It was our fourth day in Singapore and Malaya. Two cars brought us over there on a bright morning. Kaidong was a member of the Malayan parliament, so one car had an "MP" tag on its front.

Kaidong had a big house with a vast lawn and a botanical garden. When we got there, his children had already started a sports game. He was playing with the kids. David, Phillip, Jean, Pauline and Robert jumped in after some hesitation.

I found that Kaidong and I needed no introduction to each other. He had been in Mainland China during World War II and had attended college there. Now he was a Malayan politician, but his interests seemed to lie more in sports than in politics. He told me that he had always volunteered to lead Malayan sport teams for international tournaments. We had enough common experiences to chat, so he met me afterward whenever he dropped by Hong Kong.

Olivia had countless things to chat about with her kin. I could not join any of their conversations because I could not understand either Cantonese or Hainanese dialects. To relieve me from my boredom, therefore, she advised me to enjoy the fabulous Hainanese cuisine cooked by Bo Mu and Sister Qing Xiang.

I had never had the famous Hainanese chicken rice before. It was indeed fabulous! After a taste from that day, I never missed a chance to have it again, either in Olivia's family or a restaurant in Singapore.

Bo Mu was not only a superb cook with many cuisine recipes, but she was also a diligent collector of secret prescriptions of medicine. When she heard that Phillip and I had asthma, she immediately gave Olivia a prescription, telling her how to use grapefruit and some herbal medicine to cure us.

Sister Qing Xiang had been in Beijing. Olivia thanked her for informing San Sao of the dire situation under famine in Mainland China. Sister Qing Xiang was always tacit. She seemed to be attached to Olivia. Twenty more years later, after Bo Mu passed away, she had once planned to visit us in the United States. Sadly, that plan never materialized.

Time flew fast. On the fifth day of our visit, Kaitee and Kaiteng wanted to break the ice between Olivia and her brother Kaichong since they had not yet gotten a chance to communicate directly with each other after Olivia had come out from Mainland China. They planned and brought us to pay Kaichong a visit.

Weather in Singapore was always warmer in the afternoon. Kaichong lived in a beautiful separate garden house previously used by his father. When we got there, Zheng Wenxiang received us courteously, but Kaichong was taking his shower. That was a particularly humid day. With no air conditioning and all the windows closed, the living room was unbearably stuffy. After waiting quite a while, Kaitee said humorously that everyone needed a shower, but why had Kaichong chose to take his shower at that hour?

Olivia finally decided to bring the children out for fresh air. After returning to our hostel, she was upset for her brother Kaichong's refusal to see us. To me, Kaichong seemed to have become another person, totally changed from the brother-in-law I knew in 1950. I could not figure out what had happened to him in the last fourteen years.

Ever since the Halicrafter radio had brought us trouble in Communist China, I had harbored a hope that someday I could tell Kaichong the whole story in person. I wanted to thank him for providing me with the chance, through his gift, to understand the Communist system in depth. Now it all seemed in vain.

Why had Kaichong suddenly become so absentminded? Why did he appear to have lost interest and feelings for the people and things around him? It became an unfathomable myth for Olivia and me in Hong Kong and Singapore.

After we settled down in the United States, we gradually learned from people who had similar frustrations that Kaichong might have suffered from amnesia. But we were not medical doctors. Nobody could be sure what caused Kaichong's sufferings. All we could do was show our love and feelings to him.

Beginning in the 1970s, Olivia and I had visited Kaichong in his hotel or other places when he came to the East Coast of the United States. We were most happy when his wife Zheng Wenxiang and his son Sam and daughter-in-law, accompanied him to visit us before the turn of the century. I still remember that Kaichong and I found that we both were ice cream lovers. Instead of using wine, therefore, we toasted to each other with ice cream for the happy days we had had in 1950.

Our impromptu trip to Singapore finally came to its end. On the eve of our flight back to Hong Kong, Kaitee and his wife came to our hostel to say goodbye. We spent almost an hour together.

Olivia and I thanked Kaitee from the bottom of our hearts for the trust and assistance he had rendered us all these years.

Kaitee always had an everlasting tacit smile around his lips. Like Olivia, I found in him a father-like brother.

18

Hong Kong
and the United States

Transpacific passenger transportation still somewhat relied on ships in the 1960s. Jet flights had not yet totally replaced ocean liners, so ordinary immigrants in the Far East still counted on those ships to bring their belongings to their new countries. On October 18 of 1964, Olivia and the children boarded the *S.S. President Wilson* sailing for San Francisco.

October the 18 is a memorable day in our family. Three years ago, on October the 18 of 1961, Olivia and the children had left Beijing. Five years later, on October the 18 of 1966, my father passed away under the horrible Cultural Revolution. On the same date of October the 18 of 1984, we had his urn brought over to the United States and buried at the Gate of Heaven Cemetery in Maryland.

Bringing five kids aging from two to twelve across the Pacific Ocean was not an easy task. Olivia herself was prone to seasickness. Sometimes she had to be confined in bed. Therefore, David, Phillip, Jean and Pauline had to take care of themselves. In addition, they also had to keep an eye on their little brother Robert. For safety's sake, Olivia had prepared a long leash for some one to hold onto Robert. With that leash around his chest and shoulders, Robert could toddle on the open deck.

It was hard for me to say goodbye to Olivia and the children. Olivia was going to face a new environment once again herself. She had to cope with the challenges of immigration. This time, what would be separating us was the vast Pacific Ocean.

Strangely, Robert was very much attached to me that day when I saw him off. He would not let me go when I was supposed to leave the ship. I had to make an excuse to detract him. I told him that I was going to buy him some of his favorite steamed roasted pork bun "chashoubau." Since then, "chashoubau" was a reminder of our family's ocean voyage of 1964.

On that day, Frank Wong came with me to see Olivia and the children off. He was one of our old friends since 1949 and had helped to arrange our wedding ceremony at the China Institute in New York City. When he and his wife, Zeng Meixia, also returned to Mainland China, we had seen one another in Beijing sometimes, but we totally lost contact after he was branded as a "Rightist" and sent to a labor camp after 1958.

I found Frank in Hong Kong only two days before Olivia's ocean journey. The story of how I located him was very interesting. It all started from a letter we received from Father after we returned to Hong Kong from Singapore. In the letter, Father slipped in a note, telling me that Frank's wife, Zeng Meixia, wanted me to know Frank's Hong Kong address.

Frank Wong was in Hong Kong! Olivia and I were pleasantly surprised. There were only three more days before Olivia would leave for San Francisco, but we still decided to find him right away. I followed the given address on the note and arrived at a two-story house. An old man answered the door with an unfriendly manner. He knew I was not Cantonese, so he sent me away by shaking his head at the name I wrote down on a slip.

I was disappointed, but not frustrated. I reasoned that it might be possible that the name of the street was right but the house number wrong. Therefore, I tried to check the neighboring houses. Frank Wong was called Huang Honghui in Chinese. Yet, he also used Huang Yuchuan as his designated name sometimes. I added his designated name in my list of inquiry. But some neighbors even closed their doors on me without bothering to shake their heads. There seemed no way that I could locate Frank!

However, just as I planned to leave, a boy popped up on the scene. He walked over to the house on my address note. His appearance seemed to have a striking resemblance to that of Frank's. I ran instantly to stop him from entering the door. The boy was stunned and turned to stare at me. The more I looked at him, the more I was convinced that he must be related to Frank. At first, he tried to evade my questions. But after my continual cajolery and pleading, he finally gave me a smile, and let me into the house.

"Uncle! Someone is here to see you!" he began to call aloud toward upstairs. "Uncle, Uncle! Here is someone to see you." Since there was no response, he raised his voice to its highest pitch.

Believe it or not, just like the Arabic robber's secret words had cracked a stone door in *The Thousand and One Nights*, the boy's screaming made the sliding attic door miraculously open. A man stuck his head out gingerly from behind. It was Frank! As soon as he saw me, Frank rushed down and hugged me like crazy.

"Why do you lock yourself up in the attic?" I put my first question to him. Frank told me that he was still living in fear. He had returned to Hong Kong just a week ago. His mother, brother and sister were all in Hong Kong, and he chose to stay with his sister. The little boy was his nephew.

I remember that it took me some time to shake off my fear after I left Communist China. Nightmares still came back to haunt me once for a while so I fully understood Frank's feelings. Frank was much older than me, and he had started his career much earlier. In the 1940s, for instance, when I was still in school, he had already been an editor and reporter for the popular Chinese magazine *Shiyuchao* (*Time and Tide*). He was also a photographer and reporter for the *Renminhuabao* (*People's Pictorial Monthly*).

After we met, Frank came to visit me almost daily. My novel, *The Waves and the Sand,* had just come off the press. He read it and loved it. He told me that it was unbelievable that my novel could have portrayed scenes he had witnessed at the labor camp and dealt with many issues he also wished to raise.

Frank and I had not seen each other for eight full years. During that period, he had been exiled to Beidahuang, a ruthless labor camp in the Northeast. He was further fascinated by my novel's description of that labor camp because it had depicted vividly many scenarios he personally had encountered. Thus he had immediately felt a connection with the characters in the novel.

After Olivia left for the United States, I stayed in Baode Mansion alone. My middle ear infection and vertigo unfortunately got worse. I was then contracted to translate Alex Tocqueville's *Democracy in America*. Frank was a true Hong Kongee and happened to have many local connections. He helped me find someone to take care of my daily chores, so that I was able to work on my translation even when I was not feeling too well.

It took eighteen days for Olivia and the children to get to San Francisco. My uncle Paul had always been in Los Angeles. He had been a medical doctor there since 1950. When Olivia and I went back to Mainland China that year, we visited him and spent two days with him in Los Angeles.

Now Uncle Paul invited Olivia and the children for a stopover at his home. He arranged to have a friend meet them in San Francisco and bring them to Los Angeles. He and his wife, Auntie Thelma, were then living in Whittier. They accommodated and entertained the children very nicely.

While hosting Olivia, Uncle Paul suggested to Olivia that she might wish to stay on the West Coast. He even offered Olivia a job at his clinic. But Olivia was more familiar with the East Coast, and she also had a special attachment to the Maryland suburbs where she and I had spent our honeymoon. Besides, the International Rescue Committee had provided Olivia with assistance in New York City and Washington, D.C. With those options in hand, Olivia thought it was too early for her to decide where to settle down, so she thanked Uncle Paul, but followed the original itinerary to the East Coast.

Uncle Joseph was then in Maryland. He had attended our wedding in New York City in 1950. His wife had come to the United States later from the Philippines. Now they had two daughters, both older than our children. Maryland schools impressed Olivia as soon as she arrived at Uncle Joseph's home, so she decided not to proceed to Washington, D.C. or New York City, and she immediately enrolled the children into nearby elementary and middle schools.

That was a wise decision. Yet, it carried with it some problems. The arrival of a family of six to a small family of four made the house overcrowded. It unavoidably put burdens not only on the hosts, but also on the guests. David was in the same class in school with his "little aunt." He became the first one to get the brunt. Upset by many things, he demanded to go back and stay with me in Hong Kong.

As an immigrant mother of five, Olivia was then concentrating on getting a job. Yet, the children had their frustrations as well. She could do nothing to satisfy David except accepting his request. I consented to her decision from Hong Kong, and we began to prepare for David's return right away.

David had become a U.S. resident after his immigration. I thought at first that there should be no problem for his coming back to Hong Kong temporarily. But when I went to apply for his reentry, the Hong Kong immigration office told me that since David was a minor, he needed a guarantor in addition to his own father for reentry. It was a kind of emergency. Thanks to May Song! She delightfully volunteered to be David's guarantor. Therefore, I was ready for David any minute.

However, things took a sharp turn. While I was waiting for David's return, Olivia made another decision. Instead of sending David back to Hong Kong or renting an apartment to ease the tension, she decisively purchased a house of our own.

Maryland housing was booming at that juncture. A medium-size detached house was worth about $30,000 with a down payment of $2,500. Of course, Olivia did not have the money for down payment in hand. No matter how she juggled, the $2,500 simply could not come out from her pocketbook. Finally, she ventured to show to the builder her shareholder certificate in her family company. Surprisingly, the builder was impressed and offered her a second mortgage right away.

Succeeding in purchasing a new house, Olivia moved immediately with the children into 13009 Flint Rock Drive, Beltsville, Maryland. The children were all exhilarated to have our first home. Naturally, David did not have to come back to Hong Kong anymore. The family seemed to be relieved in its first phase of immigration.

That was January of 1965, and the weather in Washington, D.C. was particularly cold. After moving into our new house, Olivia began a new routine. Every weekday morning, she would walk Phillip, Jean and Pauline to the nearby Calverton Elementary School, then drive David to High Point High, and drop Robert off at the day-care center. After the children were in the right places, she would take up two important tasks. First, she wanted to find a way to speed up my immigration. Second, she was going to look for a job for herself.

At the time, Olivia only had a small Volkswagen. She braced herself up one day, and she drove to downtown Washington with Phillip and Robert under heavy snow. She went to Capitol Hill to visit Senator Brewster to appeal for my immigration.

Senator Brewster was sympathetic to her appeal. He promptly introduced a private bill to facilitate my immigration. The private bill was numbered S. 925, requiring the administration of the Immigration and Nationality to have my immigration charged "to the quota for Malaysia." So Olivia accomplished her first task and I was assured to an earlier immigration.

About the same time, Olivia was hired as a typist by the Central Library of the University of Maryland. She worked there almost six months until a brand new library school was established. Deciding to go to school again, she applied and was admitted to the new library school's first-year class.

All these were bold moves. It took strong will, guts and hard work. A year later, after my arrival in the United States, she finally succeeded in receiving her MLS degree. Instantly, she changed her status from a typist to a professional librarian.

Starting to work as a reference librarian at the university's engineering library, she was then promoted to be a science cataloger at the central McKeldin Library. Two years later, she advanced to managerial positions: first as the head of receiving, and then the assistant head of the acquisitions department. Altogether, she worked in the University of Maryland school system for more than six years.

While Olivia was struggling as a new immigrant in the United States, I was fighting my illness alone in Hong Kong. As my middle ear infection and vertigo became more serious, a surgery was unavoidable, although I was still not yet fully prepared financially.

May Song was always sympathetic to friends in need. She immediately introduced me to a female doctor named Dr. Lu. Doctor Lu referred me to Dr. George Tsai, a famous Hong Kong ENT surgeon. To get a free surgery, Dr. Tsai referred me to the Donghua Hospital, a local philanthropic medical center for the poor.

I still remember that it was an overcast morning. Frank Wong accompanied me to the hospital. I dropped off a letter on my way to inform Olivia that I was going for a surgery. I asked her not to worry because Frank was with me, and I promised to keep her informed.

Unfortunately, not long after the surgery, my middle ear infection reoccurred. Dr. Tsai found out that the infected area had to be cleaned again. But I could not be treated at the philanthropic center again. Since Dr. Tsai could only see me at his private clinic, I had to pay as a regular patient. Again, I was lucky to have Frank at my side when I fainted after the second surgery that very evening.

It was around March of 1965. Even though I had to go to the hospital and the doctor's office frequently, I tried to work as hard as I could. Meanwhile, the publication of *The Waves and the Sand* seemed to have led me to many new acquaintances.

Among them were two literary figures I admired. One was May Song's husband, Song Qi (Stephen Song), an established literary critic. The other was the famous novelist Xu Yu.

Song Qi invited me to dinner at his home. I was surprised to find that he was not in very good health. He had a private hospital bed installed in one of his rooms. His knowledge of literature and art was very broad and deep. Therefore, it was fascinating to talk and listen to him. He told me he was impressed by the originality and creativity of *The Waves and The Sand,* and encouraged me to write more.

During that visit, I learned that Song Qi and his family had come to Hong Kong from Shanghai after 1949. The Song family was very rich. It was said that they had once owned an entire street in Shanghai, but the interests of his father and himself were mainly on drama and literature.

Song Qi's father, Song Chunqiao, was well known in early twentieth century China. He had brought and promoted modern stage shows in China.

Like his father, Song Qi seemed to have little interest in wealth. He was a magnet to many outstanding literary figures, such as Fu Lei in Shanghai and Zhang Ailing abroad.

Before I left, Song Qi gave me a copy of Zhang Ailing's short stories. He told me that he knew Zhang Ailing well and liked her works. Forty years later, when Zhang Ailing passed away in San Francisco, it was reported that she had named Song Qi as the guardian of her belongings after her death.

Zhang Ailing had immigrated to the United States in the early 1960s. I had arrived in Hong Kong shortly after she left. Should she have been in Hong Kong in 1965, I would probably have been able to meet her through May Song and Song Qi. In 1966, I was told that she liked *The Waves and the Sand* and expressed interest in translating it into English. It was a pity that her plan did not materialize.

May Song was a gentle and elegant lady. Her assistance to Olivia and me was enormous. It was she who told me that I had vertigo. It was she who introduced me to doctors for my surgery. It was she too who helped Olivia to prepare for her immigration. Up to now, many of Olivia's clothes and other belongings still bear her fingerprints. As mentioned, when David wished to come back to Hong Kong from Maryland, it was also May Song who volunteered to be his guarantor.

Another person I met through my publication was Xu Yu. I had read his fascinating novelettes when I was young. He brought me a dozen of his works as gifts, and congratulated me for writing *The Waves and the Sand.*

I had asked him about his experience in writing fiction. He reflected and said that he often made "tempo" an important ingredient in his work. He also mentioned that he seldom wrote a story from beginning to end. Instead, he had a habit of writing portion by portion, and pieced them together afterward to make a cohesive story. It was a pity that we lost contact with each other later.

Olivia's cousin Kaidong came to Hong Kong several times in 1965. He often stayed at the old Hilton Hotel on Garden Road. When he came to Happy Valley to visit me, he was fond of telling the Quek family stories. He told me how the Quek ancestors migrated from Fenyang County of Shanxi Province in the north to Hainan Island at the southern tip of China.

Why did the Queks immigrate farther south, from Hainan Island to Malaya? Kaidong repeated to me that episode several times. It was because the small branch of the Hainan Quek family was very poor. One Lunar New Year's Eve, when they got together to celebrate, there was only one pound of meat for all of them. Thus, the young and strong steeled their hearts. His grandfather ventured out to the sea first. Then, his father and his uncle followed. Now one can find many Queks all over Malaya and Singapore.

When I met Kaidong the first time in Malaya, I only found that he was more interested in sports than in politics. Getting to know him better in Hong Kong, I realized that he was not interested in politics at all, be it local, national, or international. In Hong Kong, he seemed to have spent a lot of time learning how to live a metropolitan life.

There were snobbish people in Hong Kong. They considered Singapore and Malaya less developed areas, so they were accustomed to taking advantage of friends from Southeast Asia. A group of Nationalist exiles seemed particularly stuck to Kaidong. They wanted to do business in Malaya or draw Kaidong to Hong Kong to join them.

Kaidong was not a countryside boor. He knew he had been encircled. Yet he did not fence off the flattering and sometimes even appeared to enjoy it. He had introduced to me a few of those exiled Nationalists. Among them, there was a man named Lee with a funny credential, seeking to get into the Malayan textbook market.

One early morning, Kaidong invited me to have breakfast at the Hilton Hotel. He was still in bed when I got there. Someone knocked on the door. Kaidong got up slowly. A woman's voice was heard when the door was opened, "Wow, Mr. Quek, still not up yet? You're really lazy!"

Kaidong introduced her to me as a local movie star. The woman walked in with a leisurely gait. "Remember last night at dinner? Mr. Lee kept reminding me to come early this morning." While talking to Kaidong, she was also looking for the vanity table in the corner. Viewing herself in a mirror, she continued, "Mr. Lee said you are a busy guy! You wanted someone to go shopping with you."

Kaidong was changing his pajamas and did not reply. The woman continued in sweet voice, "You know, Mr. Lee is a nasty guy! He called me so early this morning. I was taking my shower. He was afraid that I might be late! See, my hair is still wet." She stepped forward, taking Kaidong's hand to touch her hair. Kaidong evaded and tried to put on his suit. I took the chance to make an excuse and leave.

Four years later, we heard that Kaidong had left Malaya. He moved to Hong Kong, and set up a shoe factory over there. In his prime years, he had been energetic and enterprising. He should have had a very successful life, but tragic news reached us in the United States not long after. Kaidong had passed away due to a nose cancer. I was shocked and saddened by the tragedy. It was such a loss to his family and all the people who knew and loved him!

Hong Kong got a debacle in 1965. First, the housing boom busted. A few developers jumped out of the skyscraper windows. Second, some banks failed due to their speculations on real estates. Many depositors suffered miserably.

I was not affected by the turmoil, because the Chartered Bank was solid and intact. My concern was chiefly Olivia and the children. Letters between us were voluminous. Ever since the private bill for my immigration was introduced in the U.S. Senate, I was waiting anxiously to go to America.

Yes, America seemed to be more relevant to me now. I had read and translated many books on America in the past. As I translated Tocqueville's *Democracy in America*, the book provided me with a new perspective on America.

Tocqueville's *Democracy in America* was a classic study of American political culture. Published in France in 1835, it had been translated into many languages, but not into Chinese. As a pioneer in political sociology, Tocqueville had also been an outstanding political forecaster. For instance, his insight led him to predict that America and Russia would become two political giants. It was amazing to find that his prediction had come true in the late twentieth century.

The Vietnam War was escalating in 1965. Area studies became a hot commodity in research. Funded by various foundations and institutions, many American scholars flocked to Hong Kong and other major cities in the Far East. A friend introduced me to Dr. Yu Deji, a Chinese professor teaching journalism at Columbia University.

At the time, it was not a small feat for a Chinese scholar to teach journalism in the United States. When we met at a coffee shop, we talked about many things in general. Casually, Yu Deji mentioned that he had graduated from Jinling University and had had a close classmate named Yang Shuxun in Mainland China. Since he was in Hong Kong, he was anxious find out the real situation of his good friend Yang Shuxun.

"Did you say you know Yang Shuxun?" I could not believe my ears. "He is a close friend of mine too! When I was in Columbia in 1950, he was at the teachers college. Actually, he and I were editors of the *Journal for Chinese Students in America* in New York City."

Yu Deji jumped from his seat in excitement. He told me he and Yang Shuxun were in the same class and had both majored in English. During

World War II, they had run a tutoring school to make a living together. He was eager to know more about Yang Shuxun's current situation. I informed him that, as far as I knew, Yang Shuxun was teaching English in Beijing. Now he was a professor at the Foreign Language Institute. The last time I had seen him, Yang Shuxun was married to a medical doctor.

Ever since finding out that we had a mutual friend, Yu Deji seemed to have taken me as one of his friends. He strongly urged me to resume my studies at Columbia after learning about the interruption of my graduate work. For that reason, he introduced me to A. Doak Barnett, another Columbia professor who happened to be in Hong Kong.

At the time, A. Doak Barnett was one of the top China specialists in the United States. His major work on China had just come out in 1965. After we met for lunch, he agreed to be my advisor and promised to take care of my readmission and scholarship at Columbia University. Since I was going back to Columbia, Barnett also introduced me to Michael Oksenberg who had just graduated from there.

Michael Oksenberg had an interesting background. He told me that he was from Belgium, but his ancestors were American Loyalists. After their defeat in the Independence War in the 1770s, many American Loyalists had fled to Belgium. Now after almost two hundred years, as a descendant of the Loyalists, he returned to the United States.

Twelve years later, Michael Oksenberg became a security council member in the Carter administration. In the 1970s, he participated in the normalization of relations between Communist China and the United States. He was also active in teaching and doing research work on China in the ensuing years.

In Hong Kong, Frank Wong was working at the Union Research Center, while I was finishing up my translation of the volume one of *Democracy in America*. We continued to get together quite often. One weekend in July, we met at a friend's party. When we were alone, he confided to me that he had made a hard decision to separate with his wife Zeng Meixia.

I was very surprised to hear of Frank's decision even though I knew his relations with his wife had not been so good. The seriousness of Frank's tone made me uneasy. I told him that divorce was a serious personal matter and that only the persons involved could make decisions for themselves, but his wife and children were still in Communist China at the moment. It might be better to rescue them out first and decide the matter later.

Then, Frank fell into a depressed mood, saying he had written lots of letters to rescue his wife but all in vain. He told me that he could not see eye-to-eye with Zeng Meixia on many things. That was why he wanted to quit now. I was at a loss as to how to help. However, before parting, I made an offer to Frank to draft letters for him henceforth to rescue Zeng Meixia and her children.

Thank God! Zeng Meixia and her children got their exit permits in less than two months. They arrived in Hong Kong in October of 1965. With good connections, Frank put their children in school, and he found Zeng Meixia a language teaching post right away.

Zeng Meixia knew Olivia and me well. She had played the role of an old lady in my play *Nostalgia in Turbulence*. In Mainland China, she visited my parents frequently after I left, so I was anxious to check with her on my parents' situation, especially my father's health.

Zeng Meixia told me that when she got her exit permit, she went to see my parents immediately. Both of them were happy and excited for her. She saw that my father was extremely weak at the time. She confided to me in a low voice that while she was talking to my parents, my father had never stopped coughing. During her one-hour visit to them, she noticed that my mother had helped remove at least three cups of my father's mucus.

My heart sunk when I listened to Zeng Meixia's description. Father had never mentioned his coughing and illness to us. He wrote more and more letters, not only to Olivia and me, but also to his grandchildren, as if he were in good health. Not long ago, he even sent David a long letter after David started to learn German. Enthusiastically, he described how he began to learn German himself half a century ago. He encouraged David to study hard. Those invaluable letters are still in our family collection. It was extremely sad to find out that Father had written those letters under miserable conditions.

Olivia and I had been planning to rescue my parents since 1963. Professor Chen Xujing had given us valuable advice in our efforts, suggesting that we move our parents first from Beijing to the south. Weather in Guangzhou would be good for their health. We were thinking about renting an apartment unit in the new Overseas Chinese community in Guangzhou for them.

But alas! Before we could do anything, however, the deadly "Cultural Revolution" erupted and raged all over Mainland China. My parents became the first victims. They were brutalized and sent back to their hometown Omei, thousands of miles away from Beijing. My father took his own life on October 18, 1966.

Toward the end of 1965, a new U.S. immigration law was enacted. I happened to be the first one in Hong Kong designated to immigrate to the

United States after the new law came into effect. A number of media wanted to interview me for the occasion, but I was too anxious to go, so I declined any publicity.

On the morning of December 5, 1965, I left Hong Kong on a Pan Am flight. A splendid sunset on the same day was awaiting me in San Francisco.

Postscript

Life is not something that can be rehearsed or repeated. Once it has happened, it has happened. Whatever mistakes, failures or successes one made cannot be altered.

Olivia and I have been married for fifty-five years. We have gone back and forth between the East and West many times. There are different worlds within this world of ours. In this memoir, I wished to record what we have encountered and/or witnessed in various cultures and under different political regimes.

A memoir can be quite personal if it deals only with the author's own family and life. It can be broader if it seeks to portray the places, the times, and the cultures that the author has lived in. I believe my memoir might have fallen somewhere in between, not purely personal, nor an exclusive portrayal of my time.

It would be my great pleasure if it could serve not only the members of Olivia's and my family, but also all the readers who might find it worth reading.

Olivia and I have spent half of our lives in the East and half in the West. It was said that the "West could never meet the East." I think it might be true as an abstract concept, but the East and West have crisscrossed in our lives several times. Therefore, we seem to have an obligation to record how Eastern and the Western cultures converging in our lives.

Since I have spent about forty years in China and forty in the United States, my memoir will be divided into two volumes. *In and Out of China* is the first, depicting how Olivia and I went back to China under the Communist regime. The second volume *Melting Pot and Salad Bar* will portray how we immigrated to a land of opportunity to be melted and/or put into the "Salad Bar."

I conceived the idea of writing this memoir in 1998, but was distracted by many things. It was not until 2003 when my granddaughter, Serina Hwang

Jensen, came to me for one of her school projects that I rekindled my interest in writing my memoir.

As soon as Serina learned of my wish, she offered to be my assistant. With the encouragement and support of her mother, Pauline, she has been very helpful in my project since then.

Thus, a three-generation venture began. From Danville, California, to Long Island, New York, from Wilmington, Delaware, to Columbia, Maryland—an immigrant family was linked together by my project.

It is difficult to express my gratitude fully to those who have aided in the process. Among them, Olivia has been, of course, the most helpful. She keeps always our correspondences and records neatly. The guest signature book of our wedding, for instance, is still intact. A copy of the provisory note for her ocean fare is also still in our file. Without Olivia's documentation, participation and collaboration, I doubt that my recollection could be resurrected easily.

My manuscript was submitted to PublishAmerica. Ms. Jeni Watterson, the Acquisition Editor, and Mr. Michele Omran, the Acquisitions Supervisor, accepted it quickly. Then Ms. Sarah Becker and Ms. Sandra Baker rendered editorial assistance. The other Author Support Teams were helpful too. To all of them, I owe sincere thanks.

Now that *In and Out of China* is going to print, I have to continue to work diligently on *Melting Pot and Salad Bar*, the second volume of my memoir.